2183

CW00322470

Is the Red F
Flying?
The Political Economy of
the Soviet Union

Albert Szymanski

To my parents, Al and Verna, and sister Judy.

Zed Press, 57 Caledonian Road, London N1 9DN

Is the Red Flag Flying? was first published
by Zed Press, 57 Caledonian Road, London
N1 9DN in June 1979.

Copyright © Albert Szymanski

ISBN Hb 0 905762 35 5
     Pb 0 905762 36 3

Printed by Redwood Burn Ltd.,
Trowbridge and Esher
Typeset by Lyn Caldwell
Designed by Mayblin/Shaw

Other Books by Albert Szymanski

The Capitalist State and the Politics of Class (Boston:
Winthrop Publishing Co., 1977)
*Class, Consciousness, and Contradictions: An Introduction
to Sociology* (Jointly with Ted Goertzel) (New York: Van
Nostrand, 1978)

Contents

Acknowledgements

Any intellectual work is a collective product. An author such as myself merely manifests the various intellectual currents and social forces of his time. The chief social force leading me to write this book was the debate in the American 'new communist movement' which had grown up out of the ashes of the Students for Democratic Society (S.D.S.) in the early 1970s. The generation of American radicals formed in the movements of the 1960s were very much attracted to the Vietnamese, Cuban and Chinese revolutions. We were attracted to the first two because of their heroic resistance to the imperialism of our own country and to the latter because it seemed, during the years of the 'Great Proletarian Cultural Revolution', to be building a form of socialism true to the Communist ideal (and thus qualitatively different from what we thought was the Soviet betrayal of socialist ideals). Accepting the anti-Soviet notions current amongst all those who grew up in the U.S. in the 1950s, it was natural for us to accept the analysis offered of the Soviet Union by the Chinese. Although the Chinese began calling the Soviet Union capitalist as early as 1967 it was not until around 1972-73 that those remnants of S.D.S. which had taken a Marxist-Leninist path began seriously to discuss and digest their analysis. In 1974 two influential works appeared: *Red Papers No. 7: How Capitalism has been Restored in the Soviet Union*, published by the Revolutionary Union (now the Revolutionary Communist Party), and Martin Nicolaus's *Restoration of Capitalism in the U.S.S.R.*, sponsored at the time by the October League (now the Communist Party [Marxist-Leninist]). They sparked off considerable discussion within the new American Marxist-Leninist left and led to many groups and individuals accepting the thesis of these two works.

At the time I was in a politically independent collective within which many individual members were tending to accept the Chinese thesis. Under pressure of the debates within this group, in turn a reflection of the larger discussion in the U.S. left in 1973-74, I began to investigate the question of the class nature of the Soviet Union, both in order to resolve it in my own mind and to contribute to the discussion. Thus, more than anything else, it is the Anna Louise Strong Collective, the broader U.S. left (especially the Revolutionary Union and Martin Nicolaus) and finally the Communist Party of China which must be acknowledged as the primary stimuli for undertaking

1

this work.

I owe a great deal to Jerry Lembcke, also a member of the Collective at the time we began our discussion of the Chinese thesis. Jerry and I simultaneously undertook the study of Soviet society for the same reasons reaching essentially the same conclusion. In the course of our separate investigations we provided each other with considerable assistance. This work consequently owes more to Jerry than to any other individual.

I must also thank those who taught me social science, above all Juan Linz and Terry Hopkins. Without the effort they invested in me this work would not have been.

My friends during the period in which this work took shape are partially responsible for it, having provided both emotional support and intellectual stimulation. I especially would like to thank Bert Knorr, Sue Jacobs, Peter Dreier, Harry Humphries, Gail Lemberger and Madeleine MacDonald.

My parents Al and Verna as well as my sister Judy have given me consistent support on all levels. In a very real sense I owe most to them.

As always the research librarians at the University of Oregon, my typist Doris Boylan, copy editor Miranda Davies, and all those who did the physical work of typesetting, printing and distributing the book must be thanked for the essential contributions they have made.

Those Soviet sociologists of the last decade or so who have produced empirical studies of their society and also the less hysterical Western Sovietologists who have produced reasonably objective empirical studies of aspects of the Soviet Union must also be thanked for providing most of the data on which this study has been based. Special thanks must be given to Murray Yanowich, Paul Gregory and Robert Stuart, Robert Osborn, David Parkin, O.I. Shkaraton, T.H. Rigby and H. Gordon Skilling. Also, to those who read earlier drafts of either the entire manuscript or particular chapters submitted as articles to various U.S. left journals, namely the reviewers for the *Review of Radical Political Economics* (for chapter three), *Social Science Quarterly* (for chapter four), *Science and Society* (for chapter five) and *The Berkeley Journal of Sociology* (for chapter six). Roger van Zwanenberg and Robert Molteno of Zed Press must be especially thanked for their helpful comments which have made the manuscript considerably stronger.

My intellectual debt to Paul Sweezy (in spite of our complete disagreement on this issue) and to the *Monthly Review* tradition of which he has been the principal representative, is considerable, as is the debt of our entire generation of radical scholars. Sweezy must be especially thanked because of the debates which were published in *Monthly Review* in the late 1960s and early 1970s around the question of the Soviet Union. Although I eventually came to reject both the positions of Bettelheim and of Sweezy in their famous debate, the issues they raised clearly had a major impact on the outcome of my investigation.

Finally I wish to acknowledge the Soviet people and the Communist Party of the Soviet Union who for too long have had to bear the double burden of being the world's first socialist country (with all the pain and hardship world capitalism has made incumbent on that role) and the criticism and attacks of other progressive forces around the world (not just the Chinese and their supporters) who, holding too high an ideal about what can be accomplished in the short run and having an insufficient understanding of social forces and historical possibilities, have added to the difficulties faced by the Soviets. Had it not been for the considerable, however imperfect, Soviet achievements in building a socialist society and the world-wide controversies this effort has provoked, it is quite obvious that this work would not exist.

Albert Szymanski
December 1978

1. Introduction

Since the October Revolution of 1917 there has been considerable debate among both socialists and enemies of socialism on the class nature of the Soviet Union. This debate waxes and wanes over time in good measure as a function of the international policies of the Soviet Union and its enemies. The last few years have seen a great revival of interest in the question among sympathizers of the People's Republic of China, which since 1967 has claimed that capitalism has been restored in the Soviet Union. Many of the issues and arguments raised by various branches of the Trotskyist movement in the 1930s and 1940s are once again being discussed in response to this debate. On the other hand defenders of the Soviet Union continue to claim that the country is socialist.[1]

The Nature of the Soviet Union: A Crucial Question

Since 1967 the Communist Party of China has been arguing that capitalism has been re-established in the Soviet Union.[2] Segments of the radical left around the world have echoed the Chinese claim. In the United States the most important groups which have attempted to defend the Chinese thesis have been the Revolutionary Communist Party (formerly the Revolutionary Union), the Communist Party (Marxist-Leninist) (formerly the October League), and the journal *Monthly Review* which has published numerous articles since 1967 by Paul Sweezy, Charles Bettelheim and others who defend the Chinese thesis.

The Chinese have argued: 'This "new stage in the development of the Soviet society on the way to communism" so much advertised by the Soviet leading group is nothing but total and complete restoration of capitalism.'[3] Chairman Mao has added that the newly restored capitalism in the Soviet Union is further a capitalism of the 'fascist type'. 'The Soviet Union today is under the dictatorship of the bourgeoisie, a dictatorship of the big bourgeoisie, a dictatorship of the German fascist type, a dictatorship of the Hitler type.'[4]

The Revolutionary Communist Party, one of the two principal claimants to 'Maoist' orthodoxy in the U.S., follows suit by arguing:

This [state capitalist] economy, now fairly well established, although still in the process of evolution, is not based on serving the needs of the broad masses of the Soviet working people. It is in no respect controlled by them. It is an economy based on the principle of the exploitation of man by man; on the extraction of surplus value from the workers by a new ruling class of state monopoly capitalists.[5]

For some time the October League endorsed Martin Nicolaus's (one of its former leaders) booklet *The Restoration of Capitalism in the U.S.S.R.,* which argued:

[The Soviet leadership] erected an out-and-out capitalist economic structure of a state monopoly capitalist type. It is today a consolidated economic system that conforms in all essential features to the classical analysis of imperialism given by Lenin.[6]

In many ways the Chinese analysis of the Soviet Union is unfortunate because it has led some progressive forces around the world to oppose revolutionary movements in Latin America and Africa because of their acceptance of assistance from the Soviet Union. The Chinese analysis has also spread division and demoralization among Marxist forces. The facts of the matter would seem to speak so clearly against the claim that there has been a significant increase in the role of capitalist forces in the Soviet economy in the last 25 years. Nevertheless, because of the great prestige of the Chinese Revolution and the considerable accomplishment in building socialism achieved by the Chinese Communist Party, it is necessary to treat the Chinese claims with respect. It is therefore necessary for those of us who disagree with these claims to attempt conscientiously to refute their arguments.

The question of the class nature of the Soviet Union is by no means an academic one, fit mainly for university seminars and the like. As the arguments and policies of the Chinese have made clear, one's analysis of the nature of the Soviet Union affects how one relates to this most powerful socialist country in the world, a country which is also the world's most rapidly growing economic and military power. Whether one accepts its leadership, or works closely with it freely accepting the aid it offers, or merely forms a guarded alliance with it, or in contrast holds it at arms length or even develops hostile relations to it, depends on what one sees as the results of such a relationship. What do the Soviets want? Do they offer aid and advice only to become new masters? Are they really interested in revolutionary change and national independence? Are they reliable allies? These are questions which face the entire world revolutionary and progressive movement. They are especially acute for the revolutionary and anti-imperialist movements of the Third World. Is the course of the Cuban revolution which accepts Soviet leadership valid for other countries? Is the course followed by the M.P.L.A., Vietnam and the Ethiopian Dergue, all of which accept the support of the Soviets, correct? Should, in turn, the Chinese leadership be trusted? These questions and many more are rooted in one's analysis of the Soviet Union. It is thus imperative for revolutionaries throughout the world to do a careful and scientific analysis of the class nature of Soviet society in order to have a firm theoretical base on which to build revolutionary strategies. And these strategies, given the growing Soviet role in the Third World, necessitate taking a position on Soviet leadership and assistance. No serious revolutionaries can avoid taking these decisions.

A serious problem in attempting objectively to determine the class nature of the Soviet Union is the obvious political implications of such an analysis. Few if any issues since 1917 have been of greater political consequence than this one. In almost all cases one's adherence to one or other view of the nature of the Soviet social formation is determined by one's prior ideological commitments. It is no accident that ideological commitments largely determine positions on the Soviet Union, for much is at stake. As the first country in the world to make a revolution which proclaimed itself the instrument of the working class, and as the most powerful country in the world today which makes the claim of being socialist (i.e. a society in which the working class rules), all those with a stake one way or the other in the question of the viability of socialism must take a position on its nature. On the one hand, many feel that to make a socialist revolution (particularly in the West) we must demonstrate both the viability and superiority of the socialist way of life by pointing to a concrete example which has endured for over 60 years and which has made continuous progress towards the communist goal in spite of incredible odds. Other socialists, in contrast, feel that the interests of a socialist revolution can best be served by distancing themselves as far as possible from the Soviet Union because of its public image (again particularly in the West) of being a 'Stalinist dictatorship', a 'State Capitalism' or a 'Bureaucratic Collectivism'. Of course, all anti-communists must discredit the Soviet claim to be a country where the working class rules, in order to discredit the very idea that socialism is possible. Capitalist apologists who argue that in spite of its problems capitalism is the system which best serves the Western and Third World working class have to show that, even when the working class makes a revolution, a new elite inevitably arises to oppress the workers, i.e. that 'it is not worth the bother to change the government'.

Assumptions and Motivations Underlying This Book

The reader may wish to know where I have come from. As a third generation American of Polish-Italian ancestry I grew up in a small New England factory town in the 1950s, which was a period of intense anti-communism both within my family and within American society at large. My early interest in history and science fiction, as well as a strong residue of Catholicism, led me in the late 1950s to identify with socialism as an abstract principle (an identification achieved solely through reading since I never met a socialist until my sophomore year in college), and also in the early 1960s to identify with the growing civil rights and peace movements in the U.S.A. I became a student activist, joining the Students for Democratic Society in 1961. As the S.D.S. and the American student movement moved left during the 1960s I moved with it. I began to call myself a Marxist in 1964, and after a thorough reading of the classics of Marxism-Leninism, a Leninist in 1966. As a graduate student of sociology at Columbia University from 1964 to 1970, I became involved in the student rebellion of 1968. This experience and its aftermath had a considerable impact on my consciousness.

Like most members of S.D.S. in the late 1960s, I came to see Vietnam, Cuba and China as the three revolutionary beacons of the world, and to regard the model of 'the old left', the Soviet Union, with considerable scepticism. As I came to a Marxist consciousness my conception of the Soviet Union changed but little over what it had been before I was a socialist. I regarded it as some kind of 'Stalinist', or at least heavily bureaucratic society, little better than American capitalism, although — it had to be conceded — a society which often played a progressive role in the world. Our identification with China became especially strong during the Cultural Revolution which highlighted the differences between the Soviet and Chinese models of socialism. We in the New Left enthusiastically endorsed the Chinese development of what seemed like decentralized, participatory and non-authoritarian socialism. This led us to have great respect for the Chinese leadership, especially Mao Tse-tung. It was quite natural for us, therefore, to accept what the Chinese were saying about the Soviet Union, not only because of our respect for them, but because it fitted in so well with what most Americans brought up in the 1950s had been so thoroughly conditioned to believe about the U.S.S.R. It was easy to become a revolutionary on the basis of identification with China if one did not have to re-evaluate and reject all that one had been taught about the 'evils of communism' in the Soviet Union. The Chinese were, we believed, qualitatively different from the Soviets. All we had been taught about 'Stalinism', bureaucracy, terror, lack of freedom etc. as the correlates of communism, were in fact correlates only of Soviet communism and not of 'real' communism as typified by the Chinese. It was a tempting analysis, and accepted by most of us.

Nevertheless, although the Chinese had been calling the Soviet Union capitalist since 1967, few of us took them literally at that time. We had not yet come mechanically to accept everything the Chinese (or Albanian) leadership said as literal truth. It was not until the early 1970s, 1973 being the pivotal year, that the Marxist-Leninist remnants of the New Left seriously confronted the actual Chinese position that capitalism had literally been restored in the Soviet Union. While the major 'Maoist' groups, including the Revolutionary Union (now the Revolutionary Communist Party) and the October League (now the Communist Party [Marxist-Leninist]) dutifully adopted the Chinese position, many more independent American Marxist sympathizers of China, including myself, baulked.

Feeling something was basically wrong with the Chinese analysis, now actively promoted by the leading 'Maoist' groups in the U.S., but not feeling that the Soviet Union was socialist, I began to study carefully the question of its nature in order to figure out to my own satisfaction what kind of a society it was.

When I began my study I was inclined to believe that the Soviet Union was neither capitalist nor socialist, but a unique 'third thing' somewhat along the lines of the Bureaucratic Collectivism described by Max Schachtman (albeit a bit more humane and progressive than he suggested). I was thus quite surprised to find through my reading of mostly pro-capitalist and anti-Soviet, but more or less scholarly sources, that the Soviet Union was a far different type of society than I had imagined.

Summary of This Book

The literature on the class nature of the Soviet Union is difficult to digest and evaluate because of considerable divergencies in terminology and frames of reference among the various writers who have addressed the question. Not only does academic Anglo-Saxon Sovietology differ more or less completely in terminology and frame of reference from Marxism, but within the Marxist tradition itself there is considerable disagreement about the uses of terms and the criteria to be applied in categorizing social formations. In the next chapter I try to untangle what is meant by 'capitalism' and 'socialism', and I develop a classificatory schema of the main types of society by setting out reasonable criteria of what a socialist society can be expected to look like. Concepts like ownership, control and class are carefully scrutinized, as are the various possible mechanisms of popular control, in an attempt to develop the conceptual tools prerequisite to an empirical investigation of the question.

The third chapter examines recent studies by Western economists on the role of commodity, capital and labour markets in the Soviet Union. The role of the state plan, profits, the law of value, investment, inflation, unemployment and economic cycles are all examined, as are the Lieberman-Kosygin Reforms. Whether there are any tendencies for the rate of profit to fall (or rate of surplus to rise) is also evaluated. The chapter concludes that the Soviet Union is not dominated by the laws of markets, as is the case under capitalism.

Chapter Four examines recent empirical research by both Soviet and Western social scientists on different aspects of social stratification in the Soviet Union. It addresses the question of whether or not social classes, similar to those in the West, exist. Data are carefully examined on income inequality and its trends, the role of the 'social wage', conditions of labour among the various groups, the attitudes of different strata, patterns of friendship and inter-marriage, inter-generational carryovers in status, and access to education. I conclude that, although there are important differences in status and income between groups in the Soviet Union, these differences are substantially less than in the West, show no tendency to increase, and are not sufficient to categorize the different status groups as consolidated social classes. However, two distinctive social groups, the technical and professional intelligentsia *and* the working class, can be distinguished with the former having somewhat more prerogatives than the socialist ideal would seem to justify.

The conventional wisdom of many Western radicals as well as of the Western establishment which tells us that the Soviet Union is not a democratic society is challenged in Chapter Five. I examine recently available empirical data on political processes in the Soviet Union, including on public debates, political participation, support for the regime, the role and composition of the Communist Party and patterns of social mobility amongst top decision makers. The theory of the 'relative autonomy of the state' is also applied to the Soviet Union. The conclusion is that democratic processes, albeit somewhat distorted, are very real in the Soviet Union. Also, the locus of political power lies more with the highly skilled workers, experts, scientists, engineers and technicians of various kinds than with either an elite of bureaucrats and managers, or with the manual section of the working class.

Chapters Six, Seven, Eight and Nine try to resolve the question of whether the U.S.S.R. is essentially 'social imperialist', or 'hegemonic', or 'proletarian internationalist' (i.e. benevolent and progressive) in its foreign relations. The term 'social imperialism' used by China against the Soviet Union is defined and aggregate economic relations between the Soviet Union and Eastern Europe, and the Soviet Union and the Third World, are carefully examined for evidence of such a phenomenon. The Soviet foreign trade organizations are analysed, as is the composition of, trends in, and terms of trade between the Soviets and other countries. Soviet economic and military assistance to both Eastern Europe and the Third World are examined. The Council of Mutual Economic Assistance is also looked at for evidence of Soviet dominance and Soviet gain. Joint economic enterprises participated in by the Soviet Union and other countries, and the trends in such institutions, are studied. The effect of close economic relations with the Soviet Union on the rate of growth and industrialization of Eastern Europe is discussed. The motives and strength of the Soviet military are also examined, as are specific Soviet involvements in the affairs of various Eastern European and Third World countries. Here I focus on the Soviet role in those countries where the Chinese and their supporters have most often directed their accusations: Czechoslovakia, India, Bangladesh, Cambodia, Cuba, Angola, Ethiopia and China (before 1961).

My overall conclusion is that the Soviet Union cannot be considered a 'social imperialist' country, although there are elements of hegemonism in its for the most part progressive foreign economic and political relations. Although the Soviet Union sometimes pressures other countries to conform to its concepts of socialist development, it can in no reasonable sense be accused of 'social imperialism', a concept which implies aiding the forces of political reaction and holding back the growth of socialism in order to pursue self-serving economic and military gains for the Soviet Union (or, more particularly, for some ruling class within the Soviet Union).

The last chapter looks at the Soviet Union in retrospect, attempting to account for how it has become what it is. It summarizes the arguments of the earlier chapters to reach a conclusion on the class nature of Soviet society and makes a projection about the future development of the Soviet Union. The questions of 'Stalin' and the development of Soviet hegemonism in the world communist movement are treated at some length. I conclude that the Soviet Union is a socialist society, albeit a technocratic state socialism in which a new petty bourgeoisie of scientists, economists, technicians and other professionals play a disproportionate role in comparison with the manual working class. The U.S.S.R. is then a society in which a coalition of this new technical petty bourgeoisie rules together with the manual working class. In the final section of the chapter I suggest that the smooth progress over the last generation towards more and more equality and greater and greater popular participation might be halted by the resistance of the technical intelligentsia, and a cultural revolution of the Chinese type consequently occur in which the working class may finally subordinate this stratum.

A Note on Sources

The empirical investigation in this book tries to stay as close to the facts generally accepted by Anglo-Saxon sovietologists as possible. Except for some unofficial sociological studies produced by Soviet sociologists, I rely mostly on information and data accepted by these authors as valid. Because of the strong political commitments in the various statements produced by China, Albania and their supporters on the one side, and by the Soviet Union and its supporters on the other, such polemics — however useful they might otherwise be — are mostly ignored in this analysis. To do otherwise would open my argument to the criticism that my sources were so biased as to make my case unconvincing to all those who are not already convinced of the correctness of my conclusion. A basic principle of scientific historiography is that evidence gathered in favour of a hypothesis, from those observers whose bias is obviously unsympathetic to it, is far more reliable than that from those who are sympathetic. This is because those hostile to a hypothesis can always be expected to bend reality a bit in order to support their prejudices; thus if a bent reality still supports a conclusion opposite to what the author wants us to believe, then the quality of the evidence is likely to be pretty good. A basic, and for the most part unquestioned, premise of Western sovietology is that the productive classes are not in power in the Soviet Union (i.e. that it is not socialist by the classical definition) and that there is considerably more freedom, democracy, public debate, activity by trade unions, etc. in the West than in the Soviet Union. Another popular, but not completely universal, position among sovietologists is that there is a convergence between the Soviet Union and the U.S. Since, therefore, the bias of sovietologists is to convince their readers that socialism is not a reality in the Soviet Union, that authentic democracy and freedom do not exist there, that market forces are playing an increasing role and that the country is coming more and more to look like the U.S., evidence found to the contrary in their writings is likely to be valid.

I have also to a lesser degree used unofficial studies done by Soviet sociologists now available in the West. Soviet leaders have considerable interest in knowing more about Soviet social structure and the attitudes of the Soviet people, just as the leaders of the U.S. have in knowing about theirs. Such information is a prerequisite on which to base policies. Since both countries need the scientific information-gathering techniques of modern sociology, this discipline has developed in both. Just as we trust information gathered by Western social scientists for their leaders, we must also generally trust that gathered by Soviet social scientists for the same reason. Decision makers , cannot afford to base their decisions on fabrication or unreliable information; they need true facts if their decisions are to be the right ones. Such data generally needs only to be reconceptualized to fit the questions asked by critical researchers.[7]

Recently the empirical literature available on the Soviet Union has also expanded because of the increasing need of the dominant interests in the U.S. to understand the U.S.S.R. better. This need has been met by such organs of the capitalist class as the Ford Foundation, Rockefeller Foundation and U.S. State Department which fund much of U.S. research on Soviet society. This book is thus obviously indebted to such institutions which have so generously (of course unwittingly) provided support!

References

1.   For two of the most developed arguments in defence of the Chinese position that capitalism has been restored in the Soviet Union, see Martin Nicolaus, *Restoration of Capitalism in the U.S.S.R.*, (Chicago: Liberator Press, 1975); and the Revolutionary Union, *How Capitalism has been restored in the Soviet Union and What this means for the World Struggle*, (Chicago: The Revolutionary Union, 1974).
      For what is probably the best statement of the same argument within the Trotskyist tradition see Tony Cliff: *State Capitalism in Russia*, (London: Pluto Press, 1974). An important statement in defence of the thesis that the Soviet Union is capitalist is contained in the essays by Paul Sweezy and Charles Bettelheim, *On the Transition to Socialism*, (New York: Monthly Review, 1971).
      For some of the better statements of Trotsky's position that the Soviet Union is a 'deformed worker's state' see Leon Trotsky, *The Revolution Betrayed*, (New York: Pioneer Publishers, 1945); Ernest Mandel, *Marxist Economic Theory*, (New York: Monthly Review Press, 1968), Ch. 15; and Isaac Deutscher, *The Unfinished Revolution*, (New York: Oxford, 1967).
      Another branch of Trotskyism, represented by the International Socialists in the U.S.A., defends the thesis that both the Soviet Union and the People's Republic of China are 'bureaucratic collectivist'. For the classical statement of this position see Max Schachtman, *The*

Bureaucratic Revolution, (New York: The Donald Press, 1962). Related to this position are the arguments of Karl Wittfogel in his *Oriental Despotism,* (New Haven: Yale University Press,1957); and James Burnham in his *The Managerial Revolution,* (Bloomington, Indiana: Indiana University Press, 1966). This latter school argues that the Soviet Union is a social formation that is neither capitalist nor socialist, but rather a 'third thing'.
For defence of the position that the Soviet Union is now a socialist society, see any of a number of recent publications by the Soviets themselves. For example, M. Perfilyev, *Soviet Democracy and Bourgeois Sovietology,* (Moscow: Progress Publishers, n.d.); Progress Publishers, *The Soviet Form of Popular Government,* (Moscow: Progress Publishers, 1972); Progress Publishers, *The Soviet Union Today,* (Moscow: Progress Publishers, 1975); G. Shahnazarov, *Socialist Democracy,* (Moscow: Progress Publishers, 1974).

2.   For statements of the official Chinese position see: *How the Soviet Revisionists Carry Out All-Round Restoration of Capitalism in the U.S.S.R.,* (Peking: Foreign Languages Press, 1968); Yenan Books, (ed.), *Social Imperialism: Reprints from Peking Review,* (Berkeley, California: Yenan Books, n.d.); Yenan Books, (ed.), *Social Imperialism: The Soviet Union Today,* (Berkeley, California: Yenan Books, 1977) (reprints from the Peking Review).

3.   Hsinhua, 29 October 1967, reprinted in *How the Soviet Revisionists Carry Out All-Round Restoration, op. cit.,* p.7.

4.   Peking Review, 30 January 1976. Reprinted in *Social Imperialism: The Soviet Union Today, op. cit.,* p.1.

5.   Revolutionary Union, *op. cit.,* p.34.

6.   Martin Nicolaus, *op. cit.,* p.5. I have laid out a systematic critique of the arguments of Martin Nicolaus and the Revolutionary Communist Party (formerly the Revolutionary Union) in a review essay of *Restorat of Capitalism in the U.S.S.R.* and *Red Papers 7: How Capitalism has been Restored in the Soviet Union and What this Means for the World Struggle.* See *Science and Society,* 41:3, Fall 1977.

7.   For a good discussion of the validity of statistics collected by ruling class agencies, see the North American Congress on Latin America, *NACLA Research Methodology Guide,* (New York, 1970).

2. What is a Socialist Society?

In this chapter I will try to clarify the basic terms relevant to a discussion of the nature of the Soviet Union. Before we can scientifically analyse whether the Soviet Union is capitalist, socialist or some other form of society, we must agree on how the terms we use are to be employed, since much of the disagreement on this question stems either from misunderstandings about the meaning of words or from the inconsistent application of terms. Thus, the specification of our terms in this chapter is an essential preliminary step before undertaking the empirical investigation which is tackled in the following chapters.

Criteria for Categorizing Social Formations

The Marxist tradition distinguishes relations of production, mode of production and social formation. The terms — capitalist, feudal, slave and socialist — can be applied to each of these three concepts. *Relations of production* refer to the way in which the producing and controlling classes relate to one another in the production process. *Mode of production* refers to the mode or way in which production takes place. This concept includes the relations of production as well as the techniques of production. Automated production, the factory system, agriculture, horticulture, hunting and gathering, as fundamental forms of the productive forces or techniques of production, are a part of the mode of production. We can thus refer to industrial capitalism, agrarian capitalism, industrial slavery, agricultural feudalism etc. as modes of production. While there is a historical coincidence between capitalist relations of production and industrial technique, and between slave and feudal relations of production and agricultural technique, there is no necessary association of these techniques with these relations of production. Industrial slavery as well as agricultural capitalism have existed as important modes of production though perhaps never as the dominant mode of production. There is, however, an economic reason why feudal and slave relations of production become associated with agricultural production while capitalist relations become associated with industrial technology; this reason has to do with maximizing the rate of exploitation. The term *social formation* refers to the aggregate of modes of production that make up a given economy. It is quite possible for slave labour to exist alongside free labour and serfdom, as well as simple commodity production (as was clearly the case in the South of the U.S.A. before 1865, for example). But normally one set of productive relations is dominant in any given social formation. This dominant set of relations of production determines the fundamental logic of that social formation as a whole.

A social formation can therefore be defined in terms of its dominant relations of production. This need not mean the relations of production in which the largest number of producers are involved, nor the set of productive relations that produce the greatest amount of surplus value (not necessarily the same thing). The dominant relations of production, rather, are those relations whose basic logic structures the form and movement of the whole social formation. Thus, for example, the U.S. was a capitalist social formation in 1860 despite there being more slaves, freeholding farmers and artisans than there were industrial workers. The very existence of slavery in the U.S. was a product of industrial capitalism's need for raw materials, while the prevalence of freehold production was likewise conditioned by the rapidly growing food and raw material needs of the capitalist industries and their workers. It is likewise possible to have a socialist society in which the majority of the producing classes are not working in collectively owned and controlled enterprises, provided that the logic of such enterprises structures the rest of the economy.

The *mode of production* must be kept analytically distinct from the *mode of distribution*. Major modes of distribution include: (a) communal distribution according to need; (b) redistributive networks from producers to a chief and then back to the producers; (c) market or barter distribution of commodities according to income or wealth, with production units being self-sufficient; and (d) socialist distribution according to work.

Marxists have traditionally categorized societies in terms of those relations of production dominant in a social formation. Often categorization is based on the dominant mode of production, but this is defined primarily in terms of the relations of production within that mode. I will categorize societies by their dominant relations of production.

I see six fundamentally different types of relations of production (of course there are intermediate and mixed cases): (a) collective production, where all adults are producers, there is no exploiting class and labour is done in common; (b) household production, where all adults are producers, there is no exploiting class, but labour is done by individual families controlling their own means of production; (c) slavery, where the bodies of the producing class are the property of the exploiting class, and disposable by them at will; (d) serfdom, where the producing class is tied to the means of production (typically the land), but cannot be bought and sold, and in addition has rights in its own labour and in some of the means of production; (e) peasantry, where the producing class is not tied to the land, maintains rights to the land, but is exploited through rents and taxes by the exploiting class; (f) capitalism, where the producing class is free to sell its labour power to any one who will buy it, the producing class not having any significant rights in the means of production.

We thus have four basic types of class society (or social formations) and two basic types of non-class society. All forms of class society have two major classes, one which owns and controls the means of production, but does not do most of the actual production, and another which does not own or control the means of production, but works for those that do in such a manner that allows the owning/controlling class to appropriate the surplus labour of the productive class for disposal by the dominant class.

There seem to be two basic variants of non-class society: household and collective production. In *household production,* each family is an economic unit (Marx's simple commodity production, his Germanic mode of production, and the earliest phase of his Ancient Mode of Production). *Collective production* in turn can be divided into five sub-types according to the level of technology, the role of the state and the division of labour. First there is primitive communism, as described by Engels in his *Origins of Private Property, the Family and the State,* which in turn is divided into 'savagery' or hunting and gathering society, and 'barbarism' or horticultural society. Then there is post-capitalist society which can be divided into socialism (where a state and division of labour persist) and communism (where they do not). Socialism can be divided into two basic types according to the location of initiative in overall strategic decision making and in the locus of day-to-day operational decision making. In *state socialism* ownership and fundamental control is collective, but initiative and operational decision making is concentrated in the hands of state officials. In *decentralized socialism* on the other hand, ownership and control is in the hands of the collective producers who maintain the initiative, and make the day-to-day operational decisions.

The four basic forms of class society — slavery, serfdom, peasantry and capitalism — can in turn be divided by the dominant form of ownership and control of productive property within each. The key difference here is whether or not ownership and control is in the hands primarily of private individuals or of the state bureaucracy. While important in determining the overall logic of the social formation, the form of ownership and control is not as important as the basic relations of production. We thus have eight basic forms of class society: (1) *state slavery* (as existed in the Ancient Greek City states; (2) *private slavery* (as was prevalent in the Caribbean area from the 17th to 19th centuries); (3) *state serfdom,* a major form in pre-emancipation Russia; (4) *manorial feudalism,* the dominant social form in Western Europe during the middle ages; (5) *state peasantry,* the dominant form in the Near East and South Asia from the beginning of class society until the 19th century; (6) *landlord peasantry,* which was the dominant form in Europe between the elimination of serfdom and the rise of capitalism and also in most of the Third World in the 20th century; (7) *market capitalism* (in both its competitive and monopoly forms), which has been predominant in the European world since the mid 19th century; and (8)*state capitalism,* where the state

15

A Categorization of Social Formations in terms of their Basic Relations of Production

Relations of Production	Degree of Centralization of Basic Initiatives and Day-to-Day Decision Making	
	Centralized (Collective Control)	Decentralized (Family Control)
'Primitive' Societies		
'Primitive' Classless Societies: Absence of exploiting class. All producers essentially equal. Techniques of production primitive. Societies small.	*'Primitive' Communism* ('Slavonic Mode of Production') (a) Savagery (Hunting and Gathering) (b) Barbarism (Horticulture)	*Household Production:* Simple Commodity Production, the 'German Mode of Production', the early phase of the 'Ancient Mode of Production'. The household is the basic unit of production and distribution. There may or may not be markets.
Class Societies	**Control in the Hands of the State**	**Control in the Hands of Private Individuals**
Slavery: The bodies of the producing class are property of exploiting class. The producing class has no rights in means of production.	*State Slavery:* e.g. Ancient Greek City States.	*Private Slavery:* e.g. the Caribbean region in the 17th-19th centuries. Predominance of markets including markets in human beings.
Feudalism (1) Serfdom: The producing class tied to the land but cannot be bought and sold. It maintains some rights in means of production.	*State Serfdom:* e.g. A major form in Russia prior to emancipation.	*Manorial Feudalism:* The dominant form during the middle ages in Western Europe and perhaps in pre-19th century Japan. Production for use. Manors largely self-sufficient economic and political units.
Feudalism (2) Peasantry: The producing class is free (not tied to the land) but is exploited through rents and taxes while maintaining rights to means of production.	*State Peasantry:* The 'Oriental Mode of Production'. The dominant form in the Near East and South Asia until the 19th century.	*Landlord Peasantry:* The dominant form in pre-20th century China, 19th and 20th century Latin America, South Asia, pre-capitalist Europe, and 20th century Arab World.

market Capitalism. Predominant form in late 19th and 20th century Europe, Japan, North America. Predominance of private ownership and laws of markets.
a) *Competitive Capitalism:* Predominance of small competitive firms.
b) *Monopoly Capitalism:* Predominance of a few corporations in each market. Distortion of many laws of competitive markets.

State Capitalism. The state owns and controls the means of production and employs wage labour in exploitation of the producing class that controls the state. Laws of markets do not generally operate.

but has no rights in means of production. Must sell its labour power to exploiting class which has all rights in the means of production.

Advanced Classless Societies

-*Socialism:* The producing class(es) own and control means of production and the state. Division of labour exists but there is no exploiting class which dominates and benefits from the exploitation of the labour power of the producers. Advanced industrial techniques of production. Societies are large.

State Socialism: Basic initiatives and day-to-day control with state officials. This form of socialism has a 'power elite' which is fundamentally under the control of the producing class. There are delimited commodity markets.
a) *Charismatic Socialism:* e.g. Cuba 1961-1975. Predominant role of leaders.
b) *Bureaucratic Socialism:* Predominant role of bureaucracy (deformed in favour of elite strata).
c) *State Market Socialism:* Predominant role of markets with day-to-day decision making by managers rather than producers.
d) *Technocratic Socialism:* Leading role of experts, scientists, etc., who do not especially gain at expense of producers.

Decentralized Socialism: Basic initiatives and day-to-day operational control in hands of the producers.
a) *Decentralized Market Socialism:* Yugoslavia (predominant role of markets with decision making by producers' collectives).
b) *Communal Socialism:* e.g. China during the Cultural Revolution. Predominant role of collective decision making without reliance on markets.

Advanced Communism: No state, no division of labour, no markets. Basic initiatives and day-to-day operational control are in hands of the producers who own and control all the means of production and operate them and share the product of their labour collectively on the principle of 'from each according to their ability, to each according to their needs'.

owns and controls the means of production and so replaces the operation of the laws of the market by central planning. While clear examples of partial state capitalism exist wherever there is considerable state ownership of the means of production, whether or not any countries of the world today can be categorized as fundamentally state capitalist is in good part the subject of this investigation.

In market capitalism another major distinction is between monopoly and competitive capitalism according to the scope given to the operation of commodity markets. In *competitive capitalism* there are no significant restraints on free commodity markets, while under *monopoly capitalism* a handful of giant corporations are able in good part to set major commodity prices at levels above their value, either through collusion or by sympathetic state regulation. The establishment of monopoly pricing results in the modification of many of the laws of competitive markets, such as the form, frequency and character of economic cycles, the falling rate of profit, the long-term movement of prices, etc., but monopoly pricing does not alter the fundamental character of a market economy being determined by forces beyond the control of the owning class. Thus both competitive and monopoly capitalism differ in a fundamental respect from state capitalism where the laws of markets have been contained by the existence of state planning in both production and distribution.

Capitalism

The classical Marxist definition of capitalism in terms of the exploitation of the labouring class by the class that owns and controls the means of production through labour markets (i.e. labour power is a commodity) is clear. But among contemporary radicals there is no consensus about the precise definition of capitalism. Consequently, when the issue is raised of whether or not capitalism has been restored in the Soviet Union, some participants in the debate mean something very different from others.

Authors associated with the journal *Monthly Review,* in particular Paul Sweezy and Gunder Frank, as well as those associated with the 'World Systems Theory', notably Immanuel Wallerstein, define capitalism in terms of the hegemony of markets *in general,* not in terms of the existence specifically of wage labour markets (i.e. where labour power is a commodity). Sweezy took this position in his classical debate with Maurice Dobb over the transition from feudalism to capitalism. Gunder Frank did likewise in his influential book *Capitalism and Underdevelopment in Latin America,* as did Immanuel Wallerstein in his *The Modern World System.*[1] Paul Sweezy, in his argument that capitalism has been restored in the U.S.S.R. defines capitalism as:

... control of enterprises in the enterprises themselves, coordination
through the market, and reliance on material incentives — these three
factors, taken together, make inevitable a strong tendency toward an
economic order which, whatever one may choose to call it, functions
more and more like capitalism.
If enterprises are run by small groups with a view to maximizing profits
through production of commodities for the market, you have the
essential production and class relations of capitalism.[2]

Martin Nicolaus, in his booklet which argues that capitalism has been
restored in the U.S.S.R., likewise defines capitalism in terms of the existence
of markets in general, and not in terms of the exploitation of the labouring
class through labour markets:

[The power to fire workers] implies that labor power is a commodity to
be bought and sold like any other; or, to put it the other way around,
wherever labor power has the character of a commodity, there the owner
of the means of production has the right to throw the workers out onto
the street.
The necessary mate and companion to this right is the owner's right to
sell (or buy) means of production also like any other commodity, e.g., by
shutting down unprofitable divisions, discontinuing one type of production
in favor of another, etc...
It is precisely the exercise of these two powers, ... that convert the
owner of the means of production into a capitalist and convert a society's
relations of production into relations of a capitalist character.[3]

The traditional Marxist definition of capitalism, on the other hand, was
upheld by both Maurice Dobb and Charles Bettelheim in their debates with
Sweezy. Similarly, Ernesto Laclau systematically criticized Andre Gunder
Frank, and Robert Brenner, Alex Dupuy and Paul Fitzgerald have likewise
criticized Immanuel Wallerstein, for defining capitalism in terms of the
hegemony of market forces generally.[4] In this book the term 'capitalism' is
employed strictly in the classical Marxist sense.
The *sole* defining characteristic, therefore, of whether a social formation
is capitalist is whether wage labour is the primary form by which the
producing population is exploited by the owning and controlling class. The
existence and role of commodity and capital markets, and their laws, is thus
not a defining characteristic of capitalism. A society can be capitalist and *not*
be determined by any other aspect of the laws of the market except the laws
of the labour market. State capitalism then is *not* necessarily subject to the
law of value, under-consumption, inflation, equalization of the rate of profit,
a falling rate of profit or any other laws which are a product of the operation
of *capital* and *commodity* markets. These and all other related laws of market
capitalism (whether monopoly or competitive) stem from the logic of capital
and commodity markets, and need not apply to every society where wage
labour is a commodity. Consequently, to demonstrate that a society is

capitalist, it is necessary only to show two things: (1) that an exploiting class exists, which appropriates the surplus labour of the producing population and disposes of it according to its own interests; and (2) that the predominant mode of exploitation is through wage labour. While the first is the defining characteristic of all forms of class society, the second is the specific characteristic of all forms of capitalist society.

A demonstration that the laws of commodity and capital markets structure the social formation, shows only that such a society is a *market* society of which there are at least five basic types, only *one* of which is capitalist: (1) simple commodity production with exchange; (2) private slavery (where human bodies are commodities as well as everything else); (3) landlord peasantry with commodity production; (4) market capitalism; and (5) market socialism (where although the producing classes own and control the means of production, the laws of the market nevertheless operate). Failure to distinguish between market economies of various types and capitalism is a source of much confusion in the debate about whether or not the Soviet Union is capitalist. It is essential to understand that market societies need *not* be capitalist, and capitalist societies need *not* necessarily be governed by capital and commodity markets. It should be noted, however, that it is probably the case that all forms of market societies *tend* to evolve towards market capitalism.

Ownership, Control and Day-to-Day Operation

Usage of the terms 'ownership', 'control' and 'operation' must be made clear. Control means the power to decide how physical resources will be used and expanded, what is to be produced, and how labour is to be allocated. It includes the ability to see that decisions are implemented, even against the will of others. Ownership means legitimate control, i.e. control that is recognized and accepted by the exploited class. Ownership also implies that the dominant class can dispose of what they control in any manner they like, including selling it to others and passing it on to their children after their deaths. It follows that a group may have full power to control property throughout their lifetimes, but not have power to transfer it to others either through sale or inheritance (i.e. they do not have ownership rights). Or a set of individuals may have full power to control property, but only for a limited time. While there may be a tendency for control to transform itself into ownership over time, the two concepts must be kept distinct. The most important concept in defining social formations is control, not ownership. Thus a society must be considered capitalist if a group of people control the means of production, whether or not they have a legitimate right to them, and whether or not they have the power to dispose of property as they wish. The defining characteristic of a capitalist society is only that an exploiting group appropriates the surplus labour of the producing class through wage labour and disposes of it in its own interest.

'Operation' refers to the day-to-day running of the means of production. It is possible that a group that does not control the means of production may exercise day-to-day decision making power. For example, the stock-holders of a major corporation may own it, a financial interest group based in a major bank may control basic decisions such as investments and overall production and distribution plans, but managers may exercise the day-to-day operational decision making. Much of the literature, therefore, on which of these groups control corporations is relevant to a discussion of the class nature of the Soviet Union.

The differences between control and ownership can perhaps be illustrated with the examples of the military and the Catholic Church. The top prelates of the Church, as well as military commanders in an army dictatorship, have fairly fundamental control over their institutions as well as day-to-day operational decision making powers. But they do not have the power to alienate their control or to pass it on to their descendants. Attempts to do so would most probably be met by massive resistance on the part of both the hierarchy and rank and file of these institutions, so strong are the prohibitions against such actions. In other words their (delimited) control is considered to be fully legitimate – e.g. the Pope's rule is law. But full ownership rights including the right to alienate his position in favour of another of his choosing and the right to pass it on to relatives is denied, both *de facto* and *de jure*. It could be argued that, although top military officers and prelates cannot pass their posts on to their children or nephews, nevertheless *collectively* (not individually) they do have ownership rights in the armed forces or Church because their children or nephews are more likely to go to military academies or religious training schools and become officers and prelates in turn, than are the children of the common people. This would be the case if there was a significantly higher probability of top officials being the children of other top officials than being the children of members of other social groups. Thus a notion of collective, as opposed to individual, ownership and control by a class must be entertained as a real possibility. Consequently it is not sufficient to demonstrate that officials cannot alienate posts or property to specific other individuals, to demonstrate that they do not have full control or even ownership *as a class* over the means of production. To demonstrate the existence of control without ownership, it must be shown that most top state officials did not achieve their position because of their ancestors' similar status.

These distinctions between ownership, control and operation are very important in defining exactly what we mean by socialism. Socialism and communism are those types of society where the means of production are owned and controlled by the producing classes, and where production is done collectively rather than in households. The distinction between socialism and communism lies in the mode of distribution (respectively, according to work and according to need), the existence or otherwise of a state, and the existence or otherwise of a division of labour between manual and mental work. The difference between socialism and communism does not lie in the basic character of the relations of production. In both cases the producing classes co-operate among themselves to produce, and exploitation does not exist. But socialism may or may not involve the collective operation of the means of production. The immediate producers may or may not make the day-to-day production decisions. As long as they authentically determine the fundamental decisions — such as the nature of the product, the basic structure of the production process, the fundamental distribution of the product, etc. — the society is socialist. For example, it is certainly as conceivable for the working class, as for the capitalist class, to hire managers to direct the day-to-day operation of a factory while fundamental control remains in the hands of those that hired them. It is as possible for there to be a socialist society where the immediate producers do not exercise day-to-day control, as it is possible for there to be a capitalist society where they do (e.g. collective labour contracts to perform a given job in a manner determined by those that do the contracting, such as harvesting a crop, building a house, planting trees), just so long as a few basic output criteria are met. In sum we must not confuse the question of 'operation' of the means of production with the question of 'control', any more than we can afford to confuse the question of determination by markets with the existence of capitalism. Socialism like capitalism is defined in terms of what class of people fundamentally control (not necessarily own or operate) the means of production (as well as the state).

Class and Social Class

Parallel to the differences between ownership and control are the differences between *class* and *social class.* Both the notions, control and class, are based solely on the idea of power, while the notions of ownership and social class add such ideas as legitimacy, consciousness, culture and traditions. By class is meant solely a set of people who have an essentially similar relation to the means of production, i.e. slaves or slave-owners, feudal lords or serfs, capitalists or proletarians, petty bourgeois independent producers, etc. By social class is meant a class which has a consciousness of itself as a class, with distinctive traditions and social customs manifested in high rates of inter-marriage within the class, and a high probability of passing one's class position on to one's children. To demonstrate that a society is a class society, it is sufficient to demonstrate that it has exploiting and exploited classes. It is not necessary to demonstrate that these classes have crystallized and consoli-dated into social classes. However, it should be noted that there is a universal tendency for such crystallization and consolidation of classes to take place. It follows that evidence of the existence of social classes, such as high rates of inter-marriage and close inter-generational linkages of social position where there are inequalities in income and decision making, can serve to indicate the existence of classes.

By *producing classes* or the *working people* I mean all those classes which primarily produce the goods and services required by society. By *non-producing classes* or the *owning/controlling classes* I mean all those classes that live off the labour of other classes (without themselves making an equivalent contribution to the needs of society), such as rentiers, 'coupon clippers', heirs of fortunes, landlords and the rich in general, as well as those engaged primarily in higher level supervision designed to ensure exploitation and domination, e.g. top corporate managers, most higher level state officials in class society, and higher level military officers.

In different types of society the producing classes have very different compositions, with one class normally being pre-eminent. In contemporary capitalist society the largest component of the producing classes is the proletariat or working class. This class lives by selling its labour power to those that own the means of production; they do not control the conditions of their labour. The working class has a number of sectors, the largest and most important of which is the industrial proletariat — those who mainly work with their hands in factories, mines, construction sites, transport and communication. The industrial working class, together with farm and service workers compose the manual working class. Other sectors of the working class include service workers who work in such places as restaurants or laundries, clerical and office workers, and sales workers. The petty bourgeoisie in advanced capitalist countries is a secondary class within the producing classes. It is composed of its traditional or independent sector ('the old petty bourgeoisie') comprising independent artisans and professionals, and small businessmen and farmers (all of whom have considerable control over the conditions of their labour); and the employed or salaried 'new petty bourgeoisie' comprising lower level managers, salaried professionals, teachers, engineers, scientists, etc. The new petty bourgeoisie can in turn be divided into its managerial strata composed of those engaged primarily in supervision (whether employed by enterprises or by the state), and its technical or professional strata composed of those who make a more direct contribution to providing goods and services. These latter two categories — the managerial strata and the technical and professional strata — are especially important in the analysis of societies such as the Soviet Union where they will be referred to respectively as the managerial intelligentsia (or stratum) and the professional (or technical) intelligentsia (or stratum).

It may be the case that the manual working class and the intelligentsia (managerial and professional) in socialist countries (but not, of course, in communist societies) have differences in their respective degrees of control over the conditions of their own labour comparable to those which exist in capitalist societies. However, in socialist societies the difference between the petty bourgeoisie of salaried managers, officials, professionals and experts on the one hand, and the working class on the other, must be defined in terms of the character of the work done, and not in terms of whether they receive a wage or a salary, or in terms of the varying degree of control of the two classes over the conditions of their labour. Thus in a socialist society we can speak of the following classes and sectors: the industrial sectors of the working class who work mostly with their hands in factories, mines, construction, transport and communications; the white collar sectors of the working class who do the menial work in offices and shops; the farm workers who do manual labour on the state farms; the highly educated technical sectors of the petty bourgeoisie (the technical or professional intelligentsia) who develop and disseminate knowledge and skills and who provide professional services; the managerial sector of the petty bourgeoisie, or intelligentsia, who are engaged primarily in supervision, planning and the overall guidance of institutions (e.g. enterprise managers, state officials and party leaders); and the peasants who either work on collective farms or for themselves.

Ruling Classes and Power Elites

Following a parallel discussion by G. William Domhoff in his *Who Rules America,* I will define a *'power elite'* as made up of those individuals who occupy command positions in the leading institutions of a society and who exercise day-to-day decision making power. A *'ruling class'*, on the other hand, refers to that class which controls the means of production (whether or not it owns them) and which dominates the state apparatus (whether or not it has a legitimate right to do so, and whether or not it exercises day-to-day operational decision making). There may be a coincidence between the ruling class and the power elite. On the other hand, the power elite may consist of individuals who are for the most part not members of the ruling class, but who are in the most fundamental sense under their control, and hence serve their interests. This could conceivably be the case in any type of class society, as well as in a socialist society. Logically, it is just as possible for a producing class to hire state officials both to run day-to-day matters and to take the initiative in formulating major policies, as it is possible for the owners of capitalist industry to secure officials to do exactly the same things. If one has power, one need not necessarily have to worry either about day-to-day detail or about coming up with policy proposals. One need only accept or reject basic policies and benefit from them. i.e. It is not necessary for a ruling class actually to be the first to come up with new ideas or policy proposals. It is only necessary for the policies that are implemented to be in this class's interests and for it to have the power to affirm or veto such policies. Ruling classes in all forms of class society have hired intellectuals, scientists, engineers, and experts of all kinds as well as officials, managers and top government leaders to come up with new ideas as well as carry them out. In fact most new ideas and policies in such societies come from people outside of the ruling class, e.g. U.S. Secretary of State Henry Kissinger's foreign policies during the 1970s. But such ideas and policies are always stamped with the interests of the class that controls the means of production and the state, and for whom these hirelings work. Thus state socialism, where the initiative as well as day-to-day operational decision making is in the hands of state officials, is just as much a socialist society as decentralized socialism, where initiative and day-to-day decision making are in the hands of the producing classes themselves. Whether or not a society is in fact socialist cannot be determined at the political level by whether or not there is a power elite which initiates policies and makes day-to-day decisions. It must be determined, instead, on the basis of whether or not the decisions made are in the interests of the producing classes, and whether or not the decision makers could have made any other decisions and still remained in their positions (i.e. whether or not the producing classes exercise effective control over them). If decisions are made in the interests of the producing classes, but the power elite could have gone against them and kept their positions, then the producing classes cannot be said to exercise control over the power elite. Thus, even if such a power elite can be considered to be humane and well intentioned, the society cannot be a socialist society since the producing classes cannot be considered to have power. Consequently, to prove that a society is *not* socialist, it is *not* sufficient to prove that it has a power elite which takes the initiative in policy formation and which makes day-to-day decisions. It must be further demonstrated that there is a *ruling class* which exploits the surplus labour of the producing class and uses it in its own interests.

Mechanisms of Popular Control

In the ideal model of fully decentralized socialism, all working people govern themselves through participation in workers' councils, selection of all leaders through frequent elections (with provision for immediate recall) and referenda or other votes on all the basic questions facing the society and its constituent parts. Further, the initiative in the decision making processes, as well as day-to-day operational control, in both the economic enterprises and in state bodies resides with the masses of working people. The existence of such structures and decentralized processes, however, is not a necessary condition for the rule of the working class, i.e. socialism can exist under much less stringent political conditions.

The existence of councils in which the members of the ruling class participate, and plebiscites or even elections for leading officials, are not necessary conditions for the rule of a given class; their existence is not a necessary test of whether or not a given class controls the power elite. This can easily be demonstrated by an examination of capitalist and especially pre-capitalist class societies. The leading officials of slave and feudal societies, for example, were not generally elected. Heredity and occasional conquests and uprisings were the mechanisms by which membership of the power elite of such societies was determined. Nevertheless, the leading state officials in feudal and slave societies did generally represent the interest of the classes which controlled the means of production in these societies. Likewise, in capitalist society, the rule of various fascist regimes in Europe and the widely prevalent military regimes in Asia, Africa and Latin America (which rely marginally, if at all, on elections) must also be considered, in most cases, to exemplify bourgeois and landlord control over the state. Clearly, there must be other channels by which a given class can exercise control over a power elite and thus constitute a ruling class.

Of course, even the selection of members of the power elite through elections and general votes on issues of public policy does not guarantee democracy for the productive classes. The example of plebiscites in Napoleon's France or Hitler's Germany, as well as the frequent elections in capitalist countries today, illustrates that merely holding elections does not provide real control over a power elite. There are numerous works that demonstrate the mechanisms of capitalist class control over the state in spite of popular elections.[5] Control, to be real, must be exercised through considerably more substantial channels than elections.

Just as it is possible for the capitalist class to exercise real control over the state in the absence of elections (or in spite of elections in which the number of its own votes is miniscule), so it is possible for the producing classes in a socialist society to exercise real control in the absence of such formal structures of control. The most important of such informal mechanisms include: (1) the original revolution by which the working people overthrew the old order and selected a revolutionary leadership; (2) the economic logic of the socialist mode of production which requires leaders to respond to the needs of the working people in order to promote production; (3) the threat of massive resistance and even another revolution in the event of a betrayal of the socialist ideal; (4) the effect of the recruitment of leaders from working class backgrounds; (5) the effect of the leaders' social integration into the working class by such means as participation in manual labour, living in working class neighbourhoods and taking part in popular activities; and (6) participation in a disciplined party which is predominantly working class. Let us examine each of these mechanisms in turn.

The ongoing importance of the original revolution, in which the masses of oppressed producers overthrew the old ruling classes and put new leaders and a new organization (e.g., a communist party) in power, should not be lightly dismissed. There is considerable inertia in people's attitudes, commitments and loyalties and − in the absence of such temptations as the old class society offered to, for example, trade union leaders − the revolutionary leadership can well be expected (at least for a considerable time) to remain loyal to the class which elevated it to power. Not only inertia, but also its conception of itself as a revolutionary leadership and sense of worth and accomplishment, are tied to its ongoing pursuit of the revolutionary idea.

The so-called 'iron law of oligarchy', developed in its most sophisticated form by Roberto Michels, is too easily accepted by cynics who believe that anyone in a position of power will more or less immediately and completely be corrupted by its exercise. While this may be true of many trade union officials in capitalist society, there is only scanty evidence that this 'law' can be more widely applied. On the contrary, the experiences of the Catholic Church and of military establishments, as well as of government officials in

all forms of class society, demonstrates the considerable strength of the ideological commitments of officials and their loyalty to the people from whom
they have emerged. The original revolution can thus be considered a valid
form of election, at least for a generation or so after the event, and perhaps
considerably longer, provided, early in the history of the new regime an
institutionalization of leadership selection is accomplished that can ensure the
promotion and selection of individuals of a similar mould to those first
selected by the working people in the act of revolution.

A power elite in a state socialist society is also not under the same pressures
to become self-serving as is a power elite in a class society. The very survival
and expansion of capitalists, and the promotion of corporate managers, lies in
their securing the greatest surplus from the workers. Failure to do so means
a lower rate of profit, eventual bankruptcy, or demotion. The case is similar
with slave owners or feudal lords. The inherent logic of these modes of
production requires them to act in such a way as to maximize the rate of
exploitation. This includes utilizing the state which they control to realize
their economic ends. Because of the class nature of production, this naturally
implies that the state will be used in the interests of one class against the
interests of another, since the very nature of slave, serf, peasant or capitalist
relations is based on conflicting class interests, (i.e. what is in the interests of
the ruling class is contrary to the interests of the producer class and vice-
versa).

No such logic applies in the case of non-class societies. The motive force
acting on a power elite in a socialist society moving it towards consolidating
its power, and advancing its own interests at the expense of the producing
classes would appear to be a diffuse psychologically based desire to get
more and more power for its own sake. This has nothing to do with any
requisites inherent in the mode of production, such as clearly exist in class
society. Any such psychological pressure must either be biologically determined or be a residue of conditioning inherited from class society. Given the
evidence of anthropology, the first alternative seems untenable. As for any
learned propensities for power and privilege on the part of a revolutionary
leadership, these are likely to be counteracted by the leadership's conception
of itself as performing a revolutionary duty and its own belief in the revolutionary ideas by which it achieved its position. There would seem to be
little structural pressure to undermine these ideals except that which comes
from the necessity to increase production, build social unity and defend the
revolution. Nevertheless there may be resistance to day-to-day operational
decisions being made by the masses and a desire to keep the initiative in
the leadership's own hands which stems from a feeling that it is best equipped
to make decisions and from the feeling of self-esteem when they are proved
right. In times of crisis, such as the 1920s and 1930s in the Soviet Union, this
feeling may well be valid.

While state socialism might well degenerate into state capitalism or even a
form of industrial state serfdom, the pressure for such a transformation
cannot be found in some inevitable biological or structural wish for power

amongst the revolutionary power elites, but must rather be sought in the structural logic of the social formation, such as may well occur at a low level of the development of the productive forces, or under extreme external or internal threats. A revolutionary power elite has no inherent interest in under-mining the position of the productive classes for its own sake. Indeed its feelings of accomplishment and self-esteem are best realized when greater popular participation and egalitarianism are achieved. This is not to say that a power elite does not attempt to achieve special privileges in the form of material benefits, as well as to secure political prerogatives in its hands. But it does not experience the same pressures to exploit the producing classes as do power elites in class societies. To the extent that the power elite succeeds in advancing the productive forces to the point where it need not suffer and the revolution is consolidated, and to the extent that it needs to validate the socialist ideology of the regime, a revolutionary power elite can at least be as much expected to move in the direction of communism, as towards state capitalism. The actual movement of the society will follow the structural logic of the social formation, not the subjective desires of its power elite.

Just as class societies have a logic of their own, independent of the will of their power elites, so does socialist society. (Only communist society is free of such a logic.) The capitalist state must act to maximize and guarantee profits and ensure the process of capitalist accumulation, regardless of whether representatives of the capitalist class or a proletarian party are occupying governmental positions. To act otherwise would result in a general economic collapse because of withdrawal of co-operation by the capitalist class (the so-called undermining of 'business confidence'). Thus, unless a socialist revolution is on the agenda, capitalist policies must be followed. There is a very limited number of options for the leadership of a capitalist state, as well as for the managers of capitalist enterprises, which in spite of appearances are not generally free to decide one thing or another. In practice, the laws of capitalist economic relations largely determine the decisions made and the probability of their successful implementation. Likewise, in a socialist society surrounded by a capitalist world; the necessity to develop industrially, to feed the people, to protect itself and catch up with the leading capitalist countries, imposes a fairly limited set of options on a socialist power elite. On a wide range of questions the decisions made by a socialist power elite or by the people as a whole would be much the same, since they are dictated by the situation.

There is no guarantee, however, that a power elite, once installed by the producing classes, will uphold its commitment to socialism indefinitely. A degeneration to state capitalism is a real possibility. State capitalism which does not rely on popular mobilization and enthusiasm to guarantee produc-tion is a real alternative to the necessity for such mobilization required by socialism. To prevent this degeneration there must be mechanisms by which the producing classes can exercise ongoing control over the power elite. One of the most important of these mechanisms, whether or not there are elections, is the threat of another revolution or uprising, or simply massive resistance and non-compliance in the event of the power elite moving towards becoming a ruling class. Such becomes a real possibility if arms are widely distributed and most of the working people have received military training. With revolutionary traditions alive from the recent revolution that installed the regime in power, and with the vitality and immediacy of the revolutionary ideology, this mechanism is far more real than in Western capitalist countries where bourgeois revolutionary traditions are ancient history and egalitarian ideologies are not used to legitimate the state. The claim that the power elite's position rests on its attaining progress towards communism can easily be discredited in the absence of such progress. Self-serving decision making and accumulated privilege among the power elite might be expected to result very soon in the delegitimation of any regime which bases its legitimacy on revolutionary egalitarianism and the achievement of communism, and would lead to massive resistance (at first passive but eventually probably actual uprisings). The Chinese Cultural Revolution is a leading case in point.

Socialist regimes must rely on massive grass roots participation if they are to work, especially since the control functions of markets do not operate. The productive classes must be mobilized and politically active. And such massive and authentic participation creates great pressures from below on the selection of officials (with or without real elections) and on policy formation (with or without formal voting on policies). In such a situation, blatant manipulation and lack of consideration for the sentiments and interests of the masses is ruled out since it would result in demoralization and depoliticization, a radical decline in productivity, the decay of the moral fabric of society and a general social breakdown.

Scholars who have analysed the mechanisms by which the capitalist class dominates the political process in formally democratic capitalist countries (specifically G. William Domhoff and C. Wright Mills) have argued that two of the most important ways in which the formally democratic structures are short-circuited are: (a) the sources of recruitment of the decision makers, and (b) their contemporary social networks. Analogous processes also operate in a socialist society as mechanisms of control, albeit in this case by the working people not the capitalists. Just as the capitalist class in bourgeois society can dominate the state by providing the personnel for top positions and integrating the brightest individuals from other classes through elite schools, so can the working class in a socialist society dominate the state by themselves providing the incumbents of the power elite and integrating the children of other classes via the educational process. Just as the capitalist class can dominate the state by integrating the power elite into the ruling class through social clubs, resorts, directorships, exclusive neighbourhoods and common leisure time activities, work life and friendship networks, so can the working class in a socialist society dominate the state by integrating the power elite through its participation in physical labour, living in working-class neighbourhoods and apartments, participation in working-class leisure activities, participation in grass roots political meetings, especially those of a disciplined party, and common friendship networks. Especially important is the role of a disciplined party which guides the process of the selection of leaders, using political criteria designed to ensure socialist policies, and which socially integrates the power elite with the working people, providing a channel through which the needs and ideas of common working people can be transmitted to the leadership. The question of the social composition of such a party, the degree of respect its working-class members have among other working people, and the degree of internal party democracy (formal and informal) are thus of central importance to the question of how much power the common working people have.

The various informal mechanisms discussed above are *possible* ways in which the working people can exercise real control over a power elite. They have their parallels in mechanisms used by owning classes to control feudal and capitalist societies, and can be expected to be real channels of power in socialist societies as well.

We can categorize a number of degrees of direct democracy through which the working people can impose their will on a power elite within socialist society. The most directly democratic socialism would be one in which policies were initiated by the masses, full discussion of the policies resulted in the formation of a popular will and the power elite merely passively implemented that will. The next most directly democratic would be where a power elite initiated most policies, but after full popular debate the working people passed, either positively or negatively , on them before they were implemented. The next most directly democratic would be where the power elite initiated most new policies and implemented them without a full popular debate, policy by policy, but where the leading members of the power elite were selected and dismissed by the working people on the basis of their politics and class stand. Finally, in the absence of any of these three formal mechanisms for controlling decision making, a society can still be socialist so long as any of the *informal* mechanisms outlined above ensure real control over the power elite by the working people. Whether any or all of the formal or informal mechanisms, or some combination of them, in fact operate to guarantee real control over the power elite by the productive masses in any given country is an empirical question which can only be resolved by concrete investigation.

The various mechanisms by which a socialist power elite can be effectively controlled by the working people can be negated by the tendency for a new state bourgeoisie to emerge out of such an elite. Material conditions might be such that those who are selected by the revolutionary masses to occupy power elite positions are gradually transformed into the controllers (and eventually owners) of the means of production and come to control the state (becoming the beneficiaries of such control at the expense of the working people). Both political ideology and behaviour can come to adapt themselves to one's social position. Thus those who are in the command posts of society can gradually, under the proper conditions, without admitting it to themselves, slip into objectively bourgeois roles. The road from a state socialism, where a power elite has the political initiative and decision making is centralized, to a state capitalism where the elite uses its initiative and decision making rights in its own interests without being controlled by the working people, is both continuous and without distinctive markers. Whether or not a socialist society travels down it is a product of the objective material conditions of the society: e.g. external threats, the level of the productive forces, the extensiveness of popular enthusiasm for the system and the degree of internal opposition to socialism.

We cannot rule out the very real possibility of a degeneration of socialism into state capitalism. There is, of course, no *a priori* process by which we can determine whether or not a given society that claims to be socialist, e.g. the Soviet Union in the 1930s, Cuba in the 1960s, China from 1955 to 1965, Romania in the 1970s, the Democratic People's Republic of Korea in the 1970s, etc., is in fact socialist, or state capitalist, or state feudalist or yet some other social form. Only a scientific study of its concrete reality can resolve such questions.

The Marxist argument about the function of a vanguard class is relevant in this discussion. Marx argued that the bourgeoisie during the period of the French Revolution served the general interest of all classes (except the old feudal lords) because its interests coincided with the general interest. Similar arguments were made by Marx and Engels in relation to the ruling class of every form of class society during its early period. The proletariat, according to Marxist-Leninist theory, plays a similar role even in societies where it is a small minority such as in most Third World countries. Its interests represent the interests of lumpen elements, peasantry, petty bourgeois and even national bourgeois. The vanguard class serves the interests of other classes independent of any formal or even informal mechanism of control by the other classes over the leading class. It is purely a matter of the interest of the working class coinciding with the interest of the ruling class at a given level of the development of the productive forces.[6]

Thus even if it were demonstrated that the Soviet Union were not socialist, i.e. that the producing classes did not exercise formal or informal control over the power elite and the state, it would not necessarily follow that the policies pursued by the power elite (which must in such a case be considered a ruling class, whether or not it was also a crystallized social class) are to the detriment of the producing classes (even if the latter were being exploited). Marx and Engels justified the exploitation of slaves, serfs and proletarians during the early phase of slave, feudal and capitalist society as being in the real interest of the slaves, serfs and workers (e.g. Engels argued that the alternative to slavery for war captives, who were the source of slaves, was death by torture).[7] Thus it could well be the case that a ruling class of the Soviet Union could be serving the authentic interests of the producing classes. Consequently, proof that the producing classes benefit (but not whether or not they benefit relative to the power elite) is not evidence that they rule, and thus not support for the thesis that a society is socialist. However, if it can be demonstrated that the producing classes do *not* benefit, then this would seem to be sufficient proof that they do *not* rule. Likewise, if it can be shown that the power elite does *not* benefit, but that the producing classes do, this would appear to be substantial evidence in favour of the hypothesis that the producing classes rule and that such a society is socialist.

There is thus a possibility of a society which, while not socialist, would serve the interests of the working class along with those of a ruling class. We might call such a society a benevolent bureaucratism which must be categorized as capitalist (although of a most peculiar variety), if wage labour is the predominant form by which the ruling class appropriates the economic surplus (which it then dispenses in such a fashion as to benefit the masses of producers). Calling such a society capitalist, however, stretches this concept to its outer limits since, because of the absence of both markets and self-interested exploitation, it would bear almost no resemblance to contemporary Western capitalism. Such a benevolent form of state capitalism might even have the inherent possibility of transforming itself into a form of socialism *without a revolution* if the power elite was required to move in the direction of increasing popular involvement in order to justify and legitimate its position (e.g. the need to make credible an egalitarian ideology which justifies the leading role of the elite). Whether or not such a society could exist in the real world must be decided by empirical investigation.

Forms of Socialism

There are many different types of socialism. Perhaps the most fundamental distinction between the forms of socialism lies in the degree of collective operation of the means of production and the locus of initiative in decision making. We will use the term 'decentralized socialism' to refer basically to all those varieties of socialism where the producers exercise direct day-to-day operation of the means of production and tend to initiate decision making processes. 'Decentralized socialism' may be considered to have two basic sub-cases: (a) *market socialism*, where the collectives of producers who make the day-to-day decisions relate to one another primarily through markets; and (b) *communal socialism*, where the producers' collectives eschew market relations in favour of collective agreements and understandings motivated by a consciousness of the interest of the whole. Perhaps Yugoslavia comes the closest of any presently existing society to the first, while 1967-76 China comes the closest to the second.

We will use the term 'state socialism' to refer to those social formations where the means of production are not operated directly by the producing class (although they may well play an important secondary role) and where therefore state officials typically play the leading role in initiating decisions. It has been claimed by many sympathizers that the Soviet Union — for some until the mid-1920s, for others until the mid-1950s, and for still others until today — is the prototype of such a social formation. We may usefully distinguish four sub-types of state socialism: (a) *State Market Socialism* where day-to-day operational decision making resides with managers (ultimately controlled by the producing classes) and where the enterprises relate to one another through markets (perhaps it could be argued that Hungary is becoming an example); (b) *Charismatic State Socialism,* where day-to-day decision making power and overall initiative resides with a small body of leaders such as the political bureau of the Communist Party, but where real ultimate control rests with the producing classes (some would argue that Cuba is, or has been, an example of such a type of society, others would argue that China during the 1950s, or the Soviet Union from the 1920s until the 1950s were other examples); (c) *Bureaucratic State Socialism,* here although ultimate control resides in the hands of the producing class, a rather large body of state and party officials maintain the initiative and day-to-day operational decision making, and use their position to a considerable degree in their own interests (this is similar to Trotsky's view of the Soviet Union in the late 1920s and 1930s); and (d) *Technocratic Socialism,* where a sizeable group of people with scientific and technical training motivated largely by concerns for efficiency, science and progress maintain both the initiative and day-to-day decision making power.

Socialism means the collective ownership and control of the 'means of production by the working people or producing classes (these two terms are used interchangeably). Since there are a number of different producing classes, we can also define a number of types of socialism in terms of their specific class nature. Traditionally Marxists have talked primarily about *proletarian socialism,* where the industrial working class owned and controlled the means of production and dominated the state. But Marx and Engels (e.g. in the *Communist Manifesto* and in *Socialism: Utopian and Scientific*) discussed a number of other forms of socialism such as 'Christian Socialism', 'petty bourgeois socialism', and 'utopian socialism'. Beside proletarian socialism it might today be most useful to distinguish *peasant socialism* and *petty bourgeois socialism:* they are those forms of socialism in which the centre of gravity of political power and control over productive enterprises resides respectively in the hands of the peasants who control the land through collectives or communes or in the hands of petty bourgeois engineers, professionals, scientists, economists, lower level managers, etc. employed by the state or collectives. Any actual socialist society may well contain significant components of all three types. The main question here is which of the three producing classes plays the leading role in a given socialist social formation.

A given society of course need not fully correspond to any of the various types of societies laid out in the above schema. Societies can be intermediate between two or even three of the forms. Societies may also be in relatively rapid transition from one form to another. Nothing in the schema is meant to rule out any of these possibilities. Yugoslavia for example may well be a case of a society intermediate between market socialism and market capitalism, and in transition from the former to the latter.

Transformation of Socialist Societies

There is a strong tendency for competitive capitalism to evolve into monopoly capitalism, for monopoly capitalism to evolve into state capitalism and for the contradictions of monopoly capitalism to explode and a socialist society of one or another type to develop out of its ashes. Either charismatic socialism or communal socialism would seem to be the most likely immediate forms. Communal socialism has a tendency in turn to evolve either into state socialism with initiative and day-to-day decision making passing to state officials, or into communism. Communal socialism may evolve either towards bureaucratic or towards technocratic state socialism depending on whether state officials or technical experts come to assume more and more of the initiative in response to the serious problems of industrialization, protection from foreign and domestic enemies, etc. Charismatic socialism, as revolutionary energies become institutionalized, tends to evolve towards any of the other forms of socialism, depending on the leaders' evaluation of the domestic and local situation.

Decentralized market socialism tends to evolve towards state market socialism because the imperatives of profit making imposed by markets force the producers to give up their autonomy in order to survive in the competitive struggle. State market socialism in turn also has a tendency to regress to private capitalism for the same reason. Managers who were originally given authority by the workers in order to make a profit for the collective tend to accrue more and more power and prerogatives to themselves until they eventually have *de facto* control over both production and the state.

Bureaucratic state socialism has a tendency to regress to state capitalism as state and party officials, under pressure from domestic and internal opposition, as well as the logic of industrialization, accrue more and more prerogatives to themselves until eventually it can be said that they form an exploiting class with *de facto* control over both the means of production and the state, control that they are able to exercise securely even against the interests and will of the producing classes. The smoothest road to communism (a stateless social formation without a fundamental division of labour) is clearly from communal socialism. Roads to communism from either variety of market socialism and from bureaucratic state socialism would appear to have major roadblocks because of the degenerative forces inherent in these forms.

The other two possible roads to communism would appear to be through charismatic and technocratic socialism. Since it appears that not very long after the revolution charisma is inevitably routinized, it does not seem that the life of this form would ever be sufficient for the full transition to communism. Whether or not technocratic socialism can give birth to communism is still an open question, although the lack of initiative and day-to-day decision making powers on the part of the masses raises real questions about the probability of such a path without an intervening cultural revolution of the Chinese type.

The greatest question of our time may well be the relative potentials of one or another type of socialism for either regression back to market or state capitalism or for moving forward to communism. The Chinese in the late 1960s put forth a very different model of transition from the Soviets. The rest of this investigation will attempt to throw some light on a major aspect of this general problem.

References

1. See Paul Sweezy's contribution in Ronald Hilton, (ed.), *The Transition from Feudalism to Capitalism,* (London: New Left Review, 1976); Andre Gunder Frank, *Capitalism and Underdevelopment in Latin America,* (New York: Monthly Review Press, 1967); and Immanuel Wallerstein, *The Modern World System,* (New York: Academic Press, 1974).
2. See Paul Sweezy in Paul Sweezy and Charles Bettelheim, (eds.), *On the Transition to Socialism,* (New York: Monthly Review Press, 1971), p.4.
3. Martin Nicolaus, *Restoration of Capitalism in the U.S.S.R.,* (Chicago: Liberator Press, 1975), pp.97-98.
4. See Maurice Dobb's contribution to Ronald Hilton, (ed.), *op. cit.;* Charles Bettelheim in Paul Sweezy and Charles Bettelheim, (eds.), *On the Transition to Socialism, op. cit.;* Ernesto Laclau, 'Feudalism and Capitalism in Latin America', *New Left Review,* No. 67, (May-June 1971); Alex Dupuy and Paul Fitzgerald, 'A Contribution to the Critique of the World System Perspective', *Insurgent Sociologist,* VII:2, (Spring 1977); and Robert Brenner 'The Origins of Capitalist Development', *New Left Review,* No. 104 (July-August 1977).
5. See for example G. William Domhoff, *Who Rules America,* (Englewood Cliffs: Prentice Hall, 1967); and Ralph Miliband, *The State in Capitalist Society,* (New York: Basic Books, 1969).
6. See for example the discussion of capitalism's progressive role in Karl Marx and Frederick Engels, *The Communist Manifesto,* Part I.
7. Engels discusses the progressive role of slavery in *Anti-Duhring,* Part II, Ch.4.

3. The Role of Market Forces

In both the principal definitions of capitalism given in the previous chapter markets are considered central. By one definition, capitalism is essentially equated with a market economy (i.e. the predominance of capital, labour and commodity markets) while in the other, the predominance of wage labour markets together with the existence of an exploiting class, is considered to be the defining characteristic. This chapter will examine the extent to which markets, especially wage labour markets, predominate in the U.S.S.R. This will help answer the question of whether the country is capitalist (by either definition).

In this chapter I will systematically look at: (1) the relative role of profits and the central plan in guiding the Soviet economy, examining especially the significance of the Liberman-Kosygin reforms; (2) the role of commodity markets and the factors determining commodity prices; (3) the role of capital (or producer) goods markets; (4) the role of labour markets; and (5) any tendencies generated through the operation of markets to produce either a declining rate of profit or an increasing surplus.

Since, of all these points, the question of the existence of labour markets is the most important (because the traditional Marxist definition of capitalism centres on the concept of labour power as a commodity, along with the existence of a controlling and exploiting class), three separate aspects of this question are examined: (a) the allocation of labour power; (b) the remuneration of workers, especially the role (if any) of unemployment in setting wages; and (c) the extent to which workers' self-management of enterprises exists. If it can be shown that labour is fundamentally allocated by, and wages determined by, unemployment and the reserve army of labour (operating openly or in a hidden form through the plan), and that workers are treated merely as labour power in the factories (i.e. have no real control over the conditions of their labour), then the hypothesis that labour markets do predominate in the Soviet Union (a necessary, but not sufficient, condition for the existence of capitalism) will have been demonstrated.

Profit and the Plan

The essence of the 'new system' being pushed ahead so vigorously by the Soviet revisionist leading group under the cloak of 'economic reform' is to practise in an all around way capitalist management in all fields of the national economy, completely disrupt the socialist relations of production and thoroughly break up the socialist economic base. The enforcement of the 'new system' has resulted in abolishing the former system of unified economic planning by the state and setting profit above all. It authorizes the enterprises to decide independently on their production and management plans and gives them free rein to seek high profits as in capitalist enterprises. It provides the leaders of the enterprises with more and bigger privileges and endows them with the power to deal freely with matters concerning production, finance and personnel in the enterprises. (Hsinhua, 29 October 1967)

Contrary to this Chinese claim, in the Soviet Union today the most important production and allocation decisions are still made through the central plan. The initiative for the goals of the plan comes from the Central Committee of the Communist Party which establishes the basic priorities. The State Planning Commission (GOSPLAN) then formulates control statistics for about 250 product groups which fulfil these priorities. GOSPLAN negotiates with the various industrial ministries and sends the tentative annual target figures to the enterprises. Enterprises evaluate the GOSPLAN proposals and communicate back to the central agencies the extent to which they feel they can fulfil the annual plan. GOSPLAN then puts it all together, checking the consistency of the various inputs and outputs to ensure a 'material balance' (e.g. that the amount of steel that the steel industry is targeted to produce in fact equals the demand from steel consuming industries). Finally, it sends the modified plan to the Council of Ministers for approval and then sends the finalized annual production targets to individual enterprises. Only the basic commodities are fully planned in this way. Large numbers of minor commodities are not explicitly planned by the central planning agencies, but because their production depends on the output of the basic planned commodities, the plan greatly influences their production as well. Each enterprise is presented with about 14 annual targets to fulfil, the most important of which is the total output actually sold.[1] Enterprises are controlled by the central authorities not only through the physical plan from which they receive their necessary material inputs, but also through the financial plan. This controls their wages bill, credit, planned cost reductions, etc. And, to the extent the enterprises have to borrow from the central bank to finance investment, they are controlled through the central state banking system as well.[2] The state bank oversees enterprises in their fulfilment of the plan, and audits their operations in order to check on any deviations from the tasks assigned by the planning authorities. While it is true that the intermediate level five year plans often embody only general targets rather than fully worked out goals for each enterprise, over the entire five year period it is certainly also true that planning is the dominant force. This planning takes the form of the annual establishment of targets and the central allocation of resources, as well as the central establishment of prices and wages and centralized investment decisions. As a result, very little actual autonomy lies with individual enterprises or associations.[3]

Contrary to some people's preconceptions, profit in the Soviet Union, while it is one of the planned targets of enterprises and a criterion on which the central planning commission evaluates performance, is not in command. Profit, rather than being the sole determinant of production and distribution decisions (as it is in private capitalist economies) is in the Soviet Union merely a lever by which the central planning authorities attempt to increase productivity, efficiency and compliance with planned production targets. Gross realized (sold) output is the primary indicator of managerial success, *not* profits.[4]

A number of differences between profits in the Soviet Union and profits in market capitalist societies should be pointed out: (1) Profits cannot be increased in the Soviet Union by restricting production since all prices are centrally determined. (2) Profits are not owned or even very much controlled by private persons. Profits are shared out by the state and the enterprises according to criteria established by the state. Only a very, very small proportion accrues to the managers in the form of bonuses. Thus, unlike in the West, the profits of an enterprise do not lead to great differences in people's social positions. (3) Profits are not necessarily an objective measure of efficiency since the state very often fixes prices below their values (in the case of many basic necessities) or above their values (in the case of many luxury goods). (4) Differences in profits do not necessarily determine the distribution of investment since basic investment decisions are centrally determined on the basis of complex criteria. These depend on the state's decisions as to the relative priority of competing long-term goals, such as emphasis on heavy industry, building up the military, decreasing inequality, raising consumption levels and, recently, promoting agriculture. (5) The flow of Soviet capital to foreign countries is not determined by profit maximization or the inability to invest profits at home (under-consumption).[5]

The Liberman/Kosygin Reforms:
Much of the Chinese argument that capitalism was restored in the Soviet Union in the 1960s rests on an interpretation of the 1965 Liberman/Kosygin reforms. The Chinese argue that these reforms transferred fundamental control over the economy to the individual enterprise managers who now essentially relate to one another through markets. Such an interpretation cannot be substantiated.

The debate about the proposals put forward by Liberman in the early 1960s, proposals which called for an increasing reliance on markets and decentralization of economic decision making, gained central attention because of the slowing down in Soviet growth rates at that time. Liberman never called for giving enterprises autonomy (as is the case in Yugoslavia).

Instead he argued only for a decrease in the number of targets given by the central planning authorities to the enterprises, in order to increase their flexibility and initiative, and also for the use of profitability as one indicator of the efficient use of resources.[6] He never proposed that basic decisions concerning the quantity, composition and prices of output should devolve from the central planners.

> All the basic levers of centralized planning — prices, finances, budget, accounting, large capital investments — and finally all the value, labour and major natural indices of rates and proportions in the sphere of production, distribution and consumption will be determined entirely at the centre.
> Their fulfillment will be assured and guaranteed because obligatory annual control figures on all important indices will be presented to the economic councils (and to the executive committees of local Soviets). The economic council would no longer be just an intermediate agency . . . but a centre or hub at which all the lines of planning converge.[7]

The actual reforms implemented in 1965 (referred to as the Kosygin reforms) were actually considerably less far reaching than even those actually proposed by Liberman. These Kosygin reforms were quite modest and amounted to no fundamental change in the Soviet system of planning, enterprise management or incentives. The reforms were implemented in an attempt to reverse the lagging performance of the economy by countering tendencies of the enterprises to hoard, become self-sufficient in inputs and be particularistic in outlook. They were an attempt to use resources more efficiently, improve the quality of output, get enterprises to adopt higher plan targets, introduce new technology, increase productivity and decrease costs. They used the traditional Soviet method of reliance on material incentives while decreasing the complexity of drawing up and implementing the central plan, a task which had been made all the more difficult by the growing complexity of the advanced Soviet economy.[8]

> . . . conditions must be created under which the enterprises will be able to solve their problems of improving production independently, and that they will be interested in utilizing to the utmost the fixed assets assigned to them for increasing output and the amount of profit they receive . . .
> . . . on the basis of the cost accounting system, it is necessary to provide material incentives for the entire collective and every shop and section of the enterprise to make them interested in fulfilling not only their own individual assignments but also in improving the overall results of the enterprise. In doing this, incentives must be organized so that enterprises will be interested in working out and fulfilling higher planned assignments, and in the better utilization of internal resources.[9]

The 1965 Kosygin Reforms reduced the number of planned targets assigned to enterprises from between 20 and 30 to eight. These were: (1) the total quantity of goods to be produced and sold, (2) the main assortment of these goods, (3) the size of the wage fund, (4) the amount and rate of profit, (5) the payment to and allocation from the state budget, (6) the volume of investment and exploitation of fixed assets, (7) the main assignment for improving technology, and (8) the allocation of material and technical supplies. In addition it should be remembered that all wage rates and prices, as well as interest rates and the main distribution of credit, remained centrally determined. The number one indicator of success by which managers were judged (and so their bonuses decided and their future careers determined) was 'realized output' i.e. the actual material quantity of goods sold.[10]

The other main aspects of the 1965 reforms were: (1) The introduction of an interest rate on borrowed capital and an increased reliance on the central bank for financing investments. (2) The establishment of a production development fund which received a share of enterprise profits and money from sales of redundant equipment. (Investment funds, bonuses for managers and bonus payments for workers were all tied to this fund, and thus to enterprise profits.) (3) Increased bonuses for managers tied to fulfillment of planned targets for sales, profits, profitability and physical output. (4) Price reforms that allowed many more enterprises to be profitable under normal conditions of operation. (5) Increased reliance on accounting and enforcing contracts among enterprises.[11]

Limited as the Kosygin reforms were, they were in any case largely rescinded in favour of increased centralization in the early 1970s. Because of undesirable enterprise behaviour under the somewhat more flexible and decentralized conditions, a series of new reforms were implemented between 1971 and 1973 that restored a number of the previously dropped planned targets for enterprises, raising the total from eight to fourteen or fifteen. Rigid regulations were instituted which governed the size and use of the enterprise incentive fund, thereby making decentralized investment more difficult. The size of the incentive fund is now centrally determined and is a function of the enterprise's fulfillment of the output, profitability and pro-ductivity targets, as well as of the overall plan for consumer goods and plans to change product quality and what products are produced. Things are now structured so that the higher the targets for output, profitability and labour productivity, the better off is the enterprise. Limits have been placed on the rate of growth of managerial bonuses which themselves have been tied to sales, profitability and the product mix plan. The percentage of profits to be allocated by each enterprise for various uses is now also set by the ministry. The centrally planned enterprise targets which have been added are in the fields of: (1) labour productivity, (2) gross output, (3) consumer goods, (4) quality, (5) economy in the use of material and fiscal resources, and (6) the size of the incentive fund.[12]

Since 1971 then, there has been a move, away from the use of 'levers' to motivate managers to fulfill the plan, and back towards direct state tutelage over enterprises to improve economic performance. This change of direction coincided with improved methods of central planning which have been based on much greater use of computers, with a resultant increased ability to use refined statistical indicators to evaluate and monitor enterprise performance, as well as to establish output targets.[13] In sum, the Soviet economy today is as dependent on centralized planning of inputs and outputs, central administration of prices and wages, and centralized allocation of investments, as it has ever been. Commodity and capital markets play as little role today as they have at any time since the late 1920s.

Another reform occurred in 1973 which coincided with the re-centralization of authority over enterprises and which was probably its corollary. Facing the continuing problem of the geometrically growing complexity of central planning and the problems of decentralizing authority, individual enterprises are being consolidated into multi-enterprise associations. Each association either links enterprises which perform similar functions or links those that are closely integrated economically with each other (typically they are in close physical proximity). Thus considerable decision making power is now vested in this middle level between the enterprise and the ministry. Centrally planned targets are now given only to the association which in turn allocates its responsibilities to its various constituent units, thereby considerably simplifying the job of the centre without losing any fundamental control. The average number of enterprises per association is three to five with usually around 4,000 employees per association.

The objects of establishing these intermediate level associations were to improve industrial performance by increasing productivity and quality, increasing specialization and concentration of production, developing reliable supplier-customer ties, increasing co-ordination between research and production, speeding up the introduction of technical improvements, simplifying the administrative structure, achieving economies of operation, decreasing the cost of management, decreasing the incentive to hoard, and facilitating the transfer of knowledge among firms.[14]

Commodity Markets and Prices

> The core of this 'new system' is to use every means to encourage the enterprises to seek profit and to promote production by material incentives. It means expanding the autonomous power of the management of enterprises, energetically carrying out the practice of adjusting production according to market prices . . . (*Renmin Ribao,* 8 November 1967)
> In this period, the Soviet revisionist clique also lifted all restriction on the prices of agricultural produce and livestock products in the free markets and vigorously developed capitalist free markets and free competition, leaving the door wide open for private merchants. (*Hsinhua,* 29 October 1967)
> Inflation and soaring prices have brought more difficulties to working people in the lower income category. (*Peking Review,* 16 May, 1975, p.19)

In spite of statements like these, commodity markets are not hegemonic in the Soviet Union. Their logic does not exert any appreciable influence on the

Soviet economy. The central plan, however, does utilize some devices developed first in market economies in order to secure compliance by enterprises and consumers with the goals of the plan. Consumption goods are allocated through markets, but markets which are structured by the central plan and state regulations, rather than by the laws of commodity production and autonomous market forces.

In all market economies, the law of value operates autonomously to determine the level of prices. Even in monopoly capitalist economies, the law of value is only distorted in its operation. In planned economies — whether of the state capitalist, state socialist or decentralized socialist types — the extent that the law of value operates is determined by the planners who may or may not elect to make prices reflect the labour time that goes into producing them.

In the Soviet Union retail prices are set by the state to clear the market. If there is too much demand for a commodity, its price is raised; if too little, it is lowered. If the government wants to encourage consumption, as is the case with basic consumption goods, it sets their price artificially low; retail prices for food, for example, are maintained at a fairly low level to ensure a low cost of living for industrial workers.[15] On the other hand, if the state wants to discourage consumption, as in the case of luxury goods, it sets prices very high.[16] As in the West the state subsidizes agricultural production, but unlike in the West it does this to lower, rather than raise the price of food.[17] There is normally a considerable difference between the wholesale and retail prices of a commodity, the difference going to the state as a form of turnover tax which represents a major source of state income (until the mid 1960s *the* largest single source of state funds). Wholesale and retail prices thus often move in opposite directions from one another. To encourage the production and consumption of a commodity, the state may raise its wholesale price while at the same time cutting its retail price in order to stimulate both production and consumption. Such a phenomenon is most unlikely to occur in a market economy. Wholesale prices in the Soviet Union thus do not perform allocation functions; they are primarily accounting prices which serve as a means of control and evaluation of enterprise performance, while retail prices serve primarily to allocate consumption goods.[18] The central planning body attempts to meet consumers' private preferences up to the point where they do not interfere with what it considers to be the overall, long term interest of society.[19] The only rationing of consumer goods is for automobiles, housing and certain consumer durables. These relatively few consumer goods are rationed in order to keep their prices lower than what they would be in a free market (in which those with the most money would bid their prices up to where only the better off could afford them). This also makes their distribution fairer than would be the case if they were distributed to those with the greatest purchasing power.[20] The laws of commodity markets clearly do not operate to determine the distribution of goods.

The fact that the laws of commodity markets do not prevail in the Soviet Union is shown by the absence of inflation and erratic price movements in the economy. The index for retail prices for all commodities barely changed from 1955 to 1975. There was a slight tendency for food prices to rise during this period, but at the same time there was an equivalent tendency for non-food commodities to decrease in price. This suggests that there has been a movement away from state subsidization of necessities such as food and also away from artificially high prices on non-necessities such as washing machines and television sets (see Table 3.1).

Table 3.1
Indices of Soviet Retail Prices, 1955-1975   (1955=100)

Commodity Group	1955	1958	1962	1963	1967	1971	1975
All Commodities	100	103	103	103	101	101	101
Food	100	104	107	107	106	107	108
Non-Food	100	99	98	96	93	93	92

Sources: Morris Bornstein, 'Soviet Price Theory and Policy' in Morris Bornstein and Daniel Gusfeld (eds.), *The Soviet Economy* (4th edition),(Homewood, Illinois, Richard Irwin Inc., 1974), p.109; and United Nations, *Statistical Yearbook*, 1976, Table 181.

Producer Goods Markets

[Managers and directors] are entitled to 'take possession, use and dispose of' the property of the enterprises, buy or sell the means of production, fix plans for production and sales and freely produce goods that can bring in high profits. . . (*Peking Review*, 18 July 1975).
The 1965 measures, in sum, wiped out the legal and financial barriers that had kept the emerging market in means of production underground during the Khrushchev years. The exchange of means of production as commodities — hard to finance, illegal, but widespread under Khrushchev — became respectable, universal and amply supplied with liquidity. (Martin Nicolaus, *Restoration of Capitalism*. p.22).
This stagnant economy reflects the moribund dying nature of Soviet social-imperialism and all imperialism . . . the anarchic development of production under capitalism means that some products are always, in effect, over-produced while others are shortchanged. Not only do these factors produce the periodic crises of capitalism, they also tend to permanently depress the rate of profit, stagnating economic development. Thus, all imperialists are driven by the internal logic — the fundamental laws of their system — to seek new markets for their commodities, but, more important, for the investment of their capital. (Revolutionary Union, *How Capitalism Has Been Restored*, p.57.)

Just as commodity markets are not a leading force in determining production and allocation of goods, so capital markets are not the leading force in determining investment. Basic investment decisions are made outside of the enterprise by central agencies on a co-ordinated and planned basis. Neither rates of interest nor profit are allowed to determine the size and broad distribution of accumulation, although since 1965 both have become important *measures* of efficiency. Enterprise funds for investment come from three sources: (1) the state budget, (2) loans from the state bank, and (3) the enterprise's own production fund to which a share of its profits are allocated. Funds are allocated from the state budget for investment on the basis of numerous rules including the capital/output ratio, the productivity of labour, the profitability of the enterprise, the importance of the product for the economy and the political goals of the planners. The enterprise's own production fund is also rather strictly guided by the central authorities. Not only is the amount of profit planned, but the share of profits that must be allocated to the production fund and the proportion of the production fund which must be reallocated to investment is also centrally determined. Since most capital goods are allocated centrally and since most means of production cannot be bought nor labour recruited outside of planning channels, these constitute another set of restrictions on the managers' ability to reinvest out of the production fund. It should be noted that managers have the right to sell surplus equipment and allocate much of the proceeds to the enterprise production fund, but that the total of such sales each year represents less than one per cent of the total transfer of productive equipment in the Soviet economy.[21] Additional funds for reinvestment can be obtained from the state bank which not only monitors the enterprises' fulfillment of the plan and the overall efficiency of the enterprise but requires repayment at an interest rate centrally determined by the state (between one and five per cent). Not only the rate of interest charged by the state bank (charged in order to promote the efficient use of scarce resources), but also the broad distribution of bank investments are centrally determined (in order to realize the investment priorities of the state plan). As the Soviet economy becomes more complex the banks are coming to play an increasingly important role in relation to the ministries and GOSPLAN.[22]

The absence of market forces in determining capital allocations is reflected in the data reported in Table 3.2 on the annual rates of economic growth and capital accumulation (See Table 3.2).

From Table 3.2 it can be seen that, in the ten year period 1966-75, the Soviet rate of economic growth was 2.4 times that of the American (while in the 1958-65 period it had been 1.7 times more). In the 1966-75 period the annual fluctuations in the American rate of growth were 280 per cent that of the Soviet Union's (while in 1958-65 the American annual fluctuations were 175 per cent that of the Soviet Union's). These figures show that: (1) the Soviet economy is growing considerably more rapidly than that of the U.S.A.; (2) the differential in performance of the two economies is increasingly in favour of the Soviets; and (3) the Soviet economy is considerably less subject to market-like fluctuations than the American. In sum the contrast with the U.S. economy is so great that it is most unlikely that market forces can be predominant in the U.S.S.R.

Table 3.2
Fluctuations in Rate of Growth of Net Material Product and Gross Fixed
Capital Formation, 1958-1975

	U.S.S.R. Annual Rate of Growth in N.M.P.	Annual Gross Fixed Capital Formation/ N.M.P. *	U.S.A. Annual Rate of Growth in G.N.P. ***
1958	11.7%	26.8%	−1.1%
1959	6.2	28.5	6.0
1960	6.1	28.9	2.4
1961	5.2	28.6	1.9
1962	7.1	27.9	6.2
1963	2.5	28.6	3.8
1964	7.4	29.0	5.2
1965	6.7	29.5	5.9
1958-1965 Average	*6.6 (.36)***	*28.5 (.027)***	*3.8 (.63)***
1966	7.2	29.4	6.1
1967	8.7	29.3	2.4
1968	8.2	29.2	4.7
1969	7.3	28.1	2.5
1970	10.7	28.3	−.4
1971	5.2	28.9	3.2
1972	2.8	30.1	5.8
1973	7.5	29.2	5.6
1974	5.0	28.7	− 1.6
1975	2.5	27.7	− 1.6
1966-1975 Average	*6.5 (.38)***	*28.9 (.023)***	*2.7 (1.05)***

* The figures for Gross Fixed Capital Formation for the U.S.S.R. from 1958
to 1962 were adjusted to make them compatible with the comparable figures
for the period 1963 to 1975.
** Standard deviations of the annual rates of growth for the period divided
by the mean rate of growth for the period.
*** Gross National Product is approximately the same as Net Material
Product plus the cost of 'services' and depreciation.

Sources: *UN Yearbook of National Account Statistics,* 1967 and 1976, Vol II,
(tables 2A, 2B, 4B).

It is also interesting to examine the differences between the 1958-65 and the 1966-75 periods. According to many of those who claim that the Soviet Union is now a market capitalist country, the Kosygin reforms in 1965 mark the introduction of market principles and 'putting profits in command.' If the Kosygin reforms resulted in a significant modification of the Soviet economy in the direction of giving market forces and pursuit of profits free rein, we should expect to see a considerable difference between the pre- and post-1965 periods in the size of the fluctuations in growth rate of the Soviet economy. There should be a similar difference in the size and fluctuations of gross fixed capital formation (since enterprise managers now allegedly have considerable authority over investment decisions). Yet as Table 3.2 shows, rather than a great increase after 1965 in the fluctuations in the rates of growth and gross fixed capital formation as a percentage of Net Material Product (N.M.P.), which we would expect if market forces were given greater rein, there was actually no significant change in either the fluctuations in the rate of growth or in the rate of gross fixed capital formation between the earlier and later periods. Likewise the ratio of gross fixed capital formation and rate of economic growth was more or less the same during the two periods. Consequently, there is no empirical evidence that the Kosygin reforms in fact 'put profits in command' or installed market forces as the guiding principle of the Soviet economy. It would thus seem that the plan, not the pursuit of profit in markets, remains the guiding principle of Soviet economics.

The Labour Market

Since one of the two essential components of the traditional Marxist definition of capitalism is the existence of wage labour markets in which labour power is sold by a proletariat (the other component being the existence of an exploiting class which controls the means of production), the question of whether or not a wage labour market exists in the Soviet Union in the same sense as it does in the Western capitalist countries must be examined very closely. In this section I will look in turn at the mechanisms of labour allocation, the payment of labour and the role of workers in determining what happens in the enterprises.

The Allocation of Labour Power

Unemployment in the capitalist world is caused mainly by the capitalists' insatiate desire for profits and massive layoffs. This is also the case in the Soviet Union (*Peking Review,* 20 February 1976).
The conversion of labour power into a commodity has . . . brought about a large-scale labor market from one end of the country to the other . . . (Nicolaus, *op cit.,* p.113).
Under the 'reform, the Soviet workers are reduced exactly to the position of sellers of their labour power to capitalist exploiters.

When we examine what life is like for workers in the Soviet Union today, a very different picture emerges. One of its 'highlights' is the re-emergence of the free labor market . . . (Revolutionary Union, *op cit.*, pp.10, 48).

Labour power, like consumption goods, is distributed through markets, but markets which are structured by the plan, rather than by their own autonomous logic, i.e. the price and allocation of labour power is centrally determined rather than determined by the operation of a reserve army of labour, the differential productivity of labour and the rate of exploitation. Wage labour is the overwhelmingly predominant form of employment in the Soviet Union. Peasants on collective farms still share in their collective product rather than receiving a wage (although the difference in this regard is diminishing as the differences between state farms and collectives decrease), and a very small number of artisans continue to work for themselves. Workers are free to quit and seek new employment any time they like (with a few minor and not rigorously enforced restrictions). The great labour shortage in the Soviet Union makes finding alternative employment very easy. No one, including the state, has any rights of ownership in their bodies nor are they tied to the land or their place of work or residence (although, again, there are some restrictions on moving to a few over-populated areas).[23] The predominance of the wage form is compatible with capitalism as well as with the basic kinds of socialist social formation. But it is incompatible with any form of slave or feudal society (the Soviet Union being a restoration of 'oriental despotism', as Wittfogel claimed or Schactman suggests, is thus ruled out); for the same reason it is equally clear that the U.S.S.R. is not a communist social formation. Whether the Soviet Union is capitalist or socialist, then, must hinge on whether wage labour is exploited by and in the interest of a non-producing class *or* whether wages are merely the form in which the producing class assigns itself to jobs, motivates the economic performance of individuals and allocates consumption goods to its members (according to the Marxist principle 'from each according to their ability, to each according to their work').

The Soviet Union has had an endemic and increasingly severe labour shortage, or (conversely) job surplus for years. As a result there is no significant unemployment.[24] Anyone can easily get a job or change jobs and be retrained. The amount of labour required is largely decided outside of enterprises, by the central planning agencies which also establish the industrial wage rates. Basic rates are established for each type of industry, each type of occupation within each industry, and for different regions of the U.S.S.R. Standard incremental scales are also set for each. The various scales are established and modified in order:(1) to channel labour into those industries, occupations, job training programmes and regions where it is most required, and (2) to realize the planner's conceptions of social justice.[25] The total wage payments for the economy, as well as their distribution by region, industry and occupation, are determined by the central plan rather than by the enterprise managers, the trade unions or collective agreements between

47

them. Thus the decisions of who gets what are made centrally according to the plan rather than through an *ad hoc* process where the stronger bargaining groups get more and the weaker unions gets less, and with the most profitable enterprises paying higher wages than the least profitable. The process of central wage determination also allows a balance to be struck between total consumer purchasing power in the economy and the total value of consumer output, thus preventing either inflation or underconsumption. In other words wage determination is not done by the autonomous workings of a labour market but rather by plan. This means that the tendencies of wage markets to perpetuate and generate inequality, as well as a reserve army of labour functioning to keep the level of wages down, are not manifested. Since wages are centrally determined, they can be set at a level sufficient to allow adequate reinvestment funds without the need to force wages down by means of the unemployed threatening to take away the jobs of the employed. The mechanism of central wage determination thus allows the economy both to avoid all structural unemployment (i.e. a reserve army of labour) and to accumulate sufficient investment funds.

In a market economy (whether socialist or capitalist) the permanent labour shortage would produce a rapid increase in wages and reduction in profits to the point where many marginal businesses would go bankrupt and the surviving businesses would introduce new labour saving technology to replace workers. Large numbers of workers would then be laid off, swelling the reserve army of labour. Millions of workers desperately seeking work would then allow the enterprises to reduce greatly the wages of the employed under threat of being replaced by members of the reserve army. No such logic operates in the Soviet Union.

The structural labour shortage implies considerable opportunities for changing jobs since, according to one estimate, the rate of job turnover in the Soviet Union is 20 per cent less than in the U.S., and since laying off and dismissing workers is far less prevalent in the Soviet Union than in the U.S., it is clear that the rate at which Soviet workers voluntarily change jobs is significantly higher.[26]

To meet the structural labour shortage, measures have been taken in recent years which encourage people of pensionable age to continue to work, and housewives have been increasingly drawn into the labour market.[27] The social norm in the Soviet Union is that all able-bodied adults should work and that everyone is entitled to a job. But there are no formal laws which fully embody either the duty or the right to work. There are 'anti-parasite laws' which make it illegal to live off exploitative income such as rents, speculation, blackmarketeering or buying other people's labour power; but there are no laws against living off relatives, friends or savings (although there is considerable social pressure against these ways of life).[28] Most new jobs in the Soviet Union have until very recently been obtained through newspaper, radio and television ads, posted openings at factory gates and by word of mouth.[29] In the 1960s about 90 per cent of all 'new hires' were directly negotiated between the enterprises and workers.[30] The major exception to complete

freedom of job seeking has traditionally been the requirement that graduates
from institutions of higher education must work for three years at a job
determined by the state (to be selected by the candidate from a list of
positions that need filling). In fact, however, even this requirement is not
strictly enforced and it is quite common for recent graduates to refuse their
assignments or to leave them without penalty. The second traditional
exception to a totally free labour market has been the punitive use of com-
pulsory job assignments in lieu of jail, especially for minor criminals. The
official ideology here is that productive labour is a good cure for anti-social
behaviour and works far better than confinement. In any case, these two
latter forms of labour recruitment play only a small part in assigning people
to jobs.

It was not until 1966 that the Soviet Union set up republic wide (not
Union wide) commissions for placing workers with enterprises that needed
labourers, and thus began to allocate individuals to jobs on an organized
basis. In addition to serving as labour exchanges where a worker or enterprise could go to find out what openings or what workers were available, these
commissions were charged with systematically providing job information,
organizing recruitment of wage labour, developing proposals for the use of
persons not currently employed, participating in the development of locations
for new industries and developing measures for locating and utilizing the
labour reserve.[31] By the early 1970s about one half of all new hires came
through these commissions rather than by direct contact between the enterprises and workers. The operation of these labour exchanges, by greatly
facilitating the process of finding desirable jobs, has reduced the average time
between jobs from approximately 28 days to 12 to 15 days in the Russian
Republic and to shorter periods in other regions. The purpose of establishing
these commissions was to rationalize the whole process of matching jobs with
workers and thereby to reduce: (1) the cost to society of underemployment
and over-manning, (2) the time between jobs, (3) wasteful geographical
mobility, and (4) unnecessary retraining.[32] It is rather surprising that the
Soviets did not adopt such a system far earlier. Perhaps the reason lies in their
reluctance to admit that anything resembling unemployment could ever exist
in the Soviet Union.

The layoff or dismissal of workers is far rarer in the U.S.S.R. than in
capitalist economies. On the one hand, the structural labour shortage has
motivated enterprises to hoard labour, even if all workers are not being
efficiently employed (because at some future time the enterprises may need
labour which would be unobtainable), and on the other because there are
considerable legal and customary constraints on the manager's ability to
dismiss workers. Through most of the post-war period, and still in most
enterprises today, the following have been the legally permissible reasons for
dismissing workers: 1) a worker refusing a transfer, 2) liquidation of the
enterprise, 3) the worker's unfitness for his or her job, 4) the systematic non-
fulfillment of duties, 5) criminal acts, 6) excessive absenteeism, 7) long-term
disability, and 8) restoration of a predecessor to a job.[33] Workers can be

dismissed by managers, however, only with the agreement of the factory and local trade union committees (with a few exceptions). Further, in the event of a dismissal with the trade union's concurrence, the worker can appeal to the courts for restoration of his or her job. Empirical evidence indicates that about one-half of workers who so appeal are reinstated by the labour courts.[34]

Beginning in 1967-68 in selected enterprises, managers have been given expanded authority to dismiss workers they consider to be redundant in order to raise productivity and release workers to other enterprises where they are needed. The Shekekino Plan (as this experiement is called) gives the enterprise an incentive to use labour more efficiently by allowing it to keep the same size wage fund even though workers are dismissed (with the difference going to the remaining employees in the form of increased wages). As of 1972, 300 enterprises in the Soviet Union were operating according to this system.[35]

In selecting workers to be released, the following factors must be considered: seniority, family circumstances, number of dependents, pregnancy, single motherhood etc. Managers must moreover find other jobs for displaced workers, jobs of a similar kind to those previously held. In lieu of being able to do this, the dismissed worker's former enterprise must pay 100 per cent of the costs of retraining the worker for another job of comparable skill and provide him or her with a stipend during the retraining process.[36]

Enterprises remain reluctant to dismiss workers even if they are redundant. There has been considerable discussion in the Soviet press and other institutions about guaranteeing protection for dismissed workers, e.g. giving six months notice, increasing severance pay, etc. Dismissed workers are presently entitled to two weeks pay regardless of the length of their termination notice.[37] One study found that only about 40 per cent of dismissed workers took more than 10 days to find a comparable job.[38] All in all, the limited managerial right to dismiss workers includes so many guarantees and protections for dismissed workers that it can hardly be considered a decisive step towards making labour power a commodity or constituting a threat hanging over workers to ensure their subordination to management. It would appear, given the extreme labour shortage in the Soviet Union and the very real problem of increasing productivity (which has been aggravated by the tendency of enterprises to hoard redundant labour), that something like these measures were dictated by the situation and thus cannot be considered as measures which enhance the power of the managerial stratum over the working class. In a perfect model of an industrial socialist society, provisions would still have to be made to separate redundant workers from an enterprise that introduces labour saving technology so that other collectives which are short of manpower will be able to recruit them. The real question is not dismissal of workers, but who has ultimate control over dismissal policies and whether such dismissals are purely technical or are instruments of the power of one class (or incipient class) over another.

Remuneration

With the implementation of the 'new system', the principle of socialist distribution, i.e. 'from each according to his ability, to each according to his work', was entirely discarded. The income gap between the leaders of enterprises, engineering and technical personnel, and high-ranking staff members on the one hand and the workers on the other become wider and wider. A small handful of men of the privileged stratum gets richer and richer while the broad masses of workers become poorer and poorer. (Renmin Ribao, 8 November 1967)

. . . inequality is growing; rich and poor have emerged and the rich are becoming richer and the poor poorer.(Nicolaus, *op. cit.*, p.171).

In the Soviet Union today, the distribution of wealth has grown increasingly uneven and the ruling class is in every respect a privileged elite. Expanding differentials in income are coupled with cutbacks in social services. (Revolutionary Union, *op. cit.*, p.82).

If labour markets operate in the Soviet Union (as they do in the Western capitalist countries) to establish the price of the commodity labour power, i.e. wages, then we should expect both the distribution of wages, salaries and the income of managers/owners of productive enterprises to be more or less comparable in the two types of society, and for the trends over time either to reflect a growing inequality (as capitalism became consolidated in the U.S.S.R.) or at the very least to maintain already existing inequalities.

Table 3.3 reports the average wages of various sectors of the Soviet labour force in 1965 and 1973. From this table it can be seen that the highest paid people are industrial, engineering and technical personnel who in 1973 earned an average of 1.27 times the wages of industrial workers. The lowest paid group were the collective farmers who earned 0.60 times the wages of industrial workers. In 1973 no group other than industrial engineering and technical personnel earned more than industrial workers. In 1973 the spread between the highest and lowest paid groups was a factor of 2.12, while in 1965 it had been a factor of 3.20. The eight year trend from 1965 to 1973 shows a very clear tendency for the highest paid occupations in 1965 to have the slowest rate of growth in wages, while the lowest paid occupations have the most rapid rate of growth. The major exception to this trend would appear to be industrial workers who were rather well paid in 1965, but nevertheless received the highest increase in wages of any non-agricultural group. Very clearly, then, there appears to be a rather egalitarian wage structure, a strong tendency towards further egalitarianism in wages, and also a tendency for industrial workers to be favoured.

The trend towards wage equalization has been a long-term one. In 1940 engineering and technical workers earned 2.13 times as much as manual workers, while in 1960 they earned only 1.48 times as much.[39]

A thorough disucssion of income levels and trends, as well as of

Table 3.3
Changes in Average Wages in the U.S.S.R., 1965-1973

Category of Wage-earners	1965 (in rubles)	1973	Increase (%)	Ratio of Wages to Industrial Workers' Wages (1973)
Employees of the state apparatus	106	126	19	0.83
Industrial engineering and technical personnel	148	185	25	1.27
Education and culture employees	94	121	29	0.83
Trade and service employees	75	102	36	0.70
Industrial white collar workers	86	119	38	0.82
Industrial workers	102	146	43	1.00
State farm workers	72	116	61	0.79
Collective farmers	49	87	78	0.60
All workers and employees (excluding collective farmers)	97	135	39	0.92

Source: Jerry Hough, 'The Brezhnev Era: The Man and the System', *Problems of Commnism*, November-December 1974, p.13.

non-monetary forms of income, accruing to different groups in the Soviet Union,is contained in Chapter Four (the section entitled 'The distribution of material rewards'). To summarize the data presented here, as well as the much more comprehensive data presented later, it is obvious that the income spread in the Soviet Union is far more egalitarian than it is in the U.S. This is especially true in the very highest income ranges since there are no equivalents in the U.S.S.R. of the owners of industry in the U.S. (e.g. the Rockefellers, Mellons, Duponts, etc., who earn tens of millions of dollars each year from their stocks and bonds) and because the top Soviet managers (the leading officials of the economic ministries) average only three or four times as much as skilled workers compared to ten to fifty times as much in the U.S. Finally, the trends in income in the Soviet Union are decisively in the opposite direction from that predicted by the defenders of the thesis that a new capitalist class is consolidating its privileges in that country. Rather than increasing income inequality, there is a strong trend towards increasing income equality.

Worker Participation in the Day-to-Day Operation of Enterprises

The regulations empower the managers to fix or change the wages, grades and bonuses for the workers and staff at will, to recruit or dismiss workers and mete out punishment to them, and to determine themselves the structure and personnel of the enterprises. Thus, the enterprises of socialist ownership have been turned into capitalist undertakings owned by a bourgeois privileged stratum, and broad sections of working people in industry and agriculture into wage slaves who have to sell their labour power.(Hsinhua, 29 October 1967)

. . . the power to handle and use the means of production in the enterprises and the power of distribution and personnel all rest in the hands of the agents sent there by the bureaucratic-monopoly bourgeoisie . . .(*Peking Review,* 18 July 1975)

There is near consensus among non-Marxist Anglo-Saxon social scientists who seriously study the Soviet Union that workers' participation in industrial management goes considerably beyond that found in American firms and that workers have a real say in enterprise decision making.[40]

Strikes are illegal in the Soviet Union. This is justified by the Soviets on the grounds that no segment of the working class has the right to strike against the working class as a whole. Strikes, according to the Soviet theory, would give workers with the strongest unions and those in the most strategic locations an unjustified advantage over the weaker and less strategically placed segments of the work-force, as well as reducing the output of the economy and undermining the rationality of the plan. If in fact the Soviet Union is really a socialist society in which the working class rules and benefits, the Soviet theory makes considerable sense. If on the other hand the system is not a proletarian socialism, then the no-strike rule is a front for greater exploitation of the working class. Whether the Soviet theory underlying the no-strike rule is valid must then be based on our analysis of the class nature of the Soviet Union. Striking for one's own economic benefit (as opposed to striking against bureaucracy and for political demands) would result in economic inequality and the accumulation of privilege as well as undermining the overall democracy of working-class rule in any authentically socialist country.

Although strikes are illegal, in a situation of extreme labour shortage such as exists in the Soviet Union, the use of widespread resignation from jobs in response to adverse conditions and/or unsympathetic management or bureaucratized trade unions is a very powerful weapon. There have been well publicized cases in which discontented workers simply left *en masse*.[41] The mere threat of this happening is probably as potent as a strike in dealing with bureaucratic management.

Trade unions play a strong and growing role both nationally and in the enterprises. Especially since 1956 the role of unions as defenders of workers' interests has been emphasized. [42]   The basic functions of Soviet trade unions include: 1) taking part in drafting, discussing and examining the production plan of the enterprise; 2) participating in drafting new systems of wages and fixing wage scales, 3) establishing obligatory safety rules and norms; 4) participating in drafting legislation on labour conditions; 5) promoting active forms of worker participation in solving production problems; 6) encouraging workers' initiative in the introduction of new techniques, inventions and rationalization of production; 7) managing much of the social insurance and welfare programmes including funeral allocations, help with childcare, free legal aid, subsidies for special diets, places in sanatoriums, sickness benefits, retraining expenses and housing; 8) organizing cultural, recreational and sports activities including tourism (the unions own and manage resorts for their members), musical events, dances, artistic programmes, films, educational programmes, lectures, etc.; 9) organising meetings of workers in the enterprise at which management must report and be scrutinized; 10) approving or rejecting the dismissal of workers; 11) discussing the correct use of work time and personnel, and methods for increasing labour discipline and productivity; 12) establishing collective agreements with management on production quotas, methods of production, allocation of workers, etc.; and 13) checking up on management's compliance with the collective agreements and labour laws.[43]

The Soviet view of trade unions is that they should perform the dual role of directly representing the interests of production workers and advancing the quality and quantity of production for the benefit of the working class as a whole. If in fact the Soviet Union is a socialist society, there is no antagonistic contradiction between the interests of the state and management on the one hand, and the workers on the other. Therefore both goals can be realized at the same time. Thus an evaluation of the union's role in advancing the interests of production hinges on one's evaluation of whether there exists in the Soviet Union an exploiting class that derives a disproportionate benefit from increases in production at the expense of the working class as a whole.

Beginning in 1957 (after being suspended in the 1930s) the trade unions once again have come to sign collective agreements with the enterprise management. Because all wages are centrally determined, these annual collective agreements do not set wages. However, they do establish work norms, quotas, standards of labour productivity, ways in which the plan will be fulfilled, and the uses of enterprise funds. It is not clear how the terms of the collective agreement are arrived at in the event of disagreement between the manager and the trade union. The managers of the enterprise must, by law, live up to both labour regulations and contractual agreements. A manager found in violation of either can theoretically be dismissed and sentenced to up to five years in confinement. Union and management meet together on grievances and the decisions they reach must be unanimous and based on labour legislation and the labour contract. If unanimity cannot be reached at the first stage of a grievance procedure, the plant committee of the union is empowered to make the final decision. Management can appeal the decision of the union plant committee only on the grounds that the union's decision was in conflict with the law. Grievances seem to run the full gamut of possible issues. While the managers are bound by law to fulfil the conditions of the collective agreements, the obligations of the unions are purely moral, i.e. they cannot be enforced in the courts.[44]

About 95 per cent of all workers in the Soviet Union belong to trade unions (which exist in all enterprises). For one reason or another, several million workers abstain from union membership (which is voluntary) inspite of the great material benefits accruing to members.[45] Regular meetings of rank and file trade union members are held in each enterprise. All union organs from the bottom up are elected by union members and are accountable to the majority and subordinate to higher union organs. Factory trade union committees are assuming increasing rights and responsibilities for enterprise management, while the national trade unions are assuming increasing responsibility for the management of welfare programmes.[46] The official explanation for the widening powers of the trade unions is that this represents part of the process of the withering away of the state.[47]

A second major means by which production workers take part in the day-to-day management and operation of their enterprises is through production conferences. These institutions, although they played an important role throughout the 1930s and 1940s, were revitalized in 1957. The members of the production conferences are elected at general meetings of all workers and are composed of representatives of the plant trade union committee, the Party, the Young Communist League, the scientific and technical societies in the enterprise, the employees, etc. The conference of an enterprise in turn elects a presidium of five to fifteen members. There is frequently a high level of worker participation at the general meetings (which must be held at least once every six months). The permanent production conference members must report to the general meetings. Members of the conferences can be recalled at any time. The functions of the production conferences include taking part in the drafting and discussion of production plans, examining questions concerning the organization of production, wage rates and labour allocation, increasing the efficiency of equipment, introducing new machinery, protecting workers and increasing labour discipline.[48] The evidence seems to be that they are both a real instrument of workers' participation and have resulted in increasing production.[49]

General meetings of all workers are also held where the managers are required to report and submit themselves to questioning from the floor. Finance, procurement, production schedules and according to one pro-U.S. business observer 'everyone and everything' is fair game for the workers. These sessions are apparently a real ordeal for the managers who must answer all questions put to them. Attempts by managers to suppress criticisms can be punished by dismissal or even legal action.[50] The evidence seems to indicate that workers have a real and meaningful say in enterprise decision making. It is also apparently the case that the enterprise is normally managed in an atmosphere of authentic co-operation between the union, production conferences, general workers' meetings and managerial personnel.

The third major mechanism by which production workers have an important input into the day-to-day management of a firm is through the plant committees of the Communist Party whose members are selected by the Communist Party members in the plant. In 1957 the local party was greatly strengthened in relation to plant management.[51] The chairman of the plant party committee, according to many observers, seems to have power equal to that of the plant manager.[52] Although *de facto* responsibility for results lies with the manager appointed by the state ministry, the Party also holds the party plant committee responsible for results. Local party branches attempt to guide the general policies followed by the enterprise, while avoiding too detailed interference with management prerogatives. The precise role of the local party branch in enterprise policy making has been a matter of periodic public debate and struggle.[53] It would appear that real power in the typical enterprise is shared between the manager appointed from above, the party committee elected by party members but influenced by higher party bodies, and the trade unions and production conferences representing all the workers in the enterprise. It would seem that, although all three centres of power have a real impact on the outcome of decisions, more power resides with management and the Communist Party apparatus outside the plant than with rank and file workers within the plant. The question of whether the working class in the last analysis can be considered to control production must then rest on the resolution of the question of whether they control the party and state (which is a question examined in Chapter Five).

The feeling of having influence in one's enterprise varies in accordance with occupational group. A study of feelings of influence over collective affairs made around 1970 in three areas of the U.S.S.R. found that the proportion of managerial personnel and specialists who felt they had no influence on the affairs of their work collectives ranged from 13 to 24 per cent, while the range among machine operators was 32 to 45 per cent, skilled manual workers 32 to 67 per cent and low skilled and unskilled manual workers from 67 to 68 per cent.[54] Such feelings are probably a function of actual influence (but not this alone). It would thus seem that managerial personnel do in fact have more influence over enterprise decision making than do manual workers, and that among manual workers the relatively high status occupations have more influence than the low status ones. It should be noted that the majority of those in the relatively higher status occupations felt they had some influence on enterprise policies. But it must also be noted that the percentage who felt they had no influence would seem to be incompatible with direct day-to-day control of the enterprise by its workers as a whole (although not of course incompatible with considerable influence coming from the Party members or the most skilled workers who may well dominate the organs of worker participation).

In conclusion, although experts and specialists, both in the plant and in those bodies which supervise the enterprises from above, appear to play the pre-eminent role in operational decision making, worker involvement in the running of industrial enterprises would appear to be too great to consider workers as merely embodying labour power (i.e. a commodity bought and sold like any other by the entrepreneurs who manage industry). Very significantly, workers' involvement in industrial decision making is increasing (not decreasing as the proponents of the thesis of a recent capitalist restoration and consolidation must maintain). This increasing self-managing role for workers would appear to be thoroughly incompatible with the idea that labour power has recently become a commodity.

Tendencies in the Rate of Profit

There is some disagreement among Marxists about whether under conditions of monopoly capitalism there is a tendency for the rate of profit to decline or to rise over time.[55] According to Marx, at least under classical competitive conditions, the organic composition of capital (the ratio of labour time incorporated in the raw materials and means of production consumed in the labour process, to the amount of active labour time it takes to transform the raw materials into finished products) tends to grow over time. This is both because of the increasing productivity of more and more advanced industrial techniques and, more importantly, because of the competitive pressure among capitalists which forces each to reinvest most of their profits in ever more marginally efficient technology in order to produce more cheaply than their competitors (or face the immediate threat of bankruptcy in an increasingly glutted market). The rate of profit can be expressed as the ratio of the rate of exploitation of labour power (which grows in proportion to increases in productivity in the wage goods sector) to the organic composition of capital. It can thus be seen that, since the organic composition of capital increases in proportion to both improvements in technique and in proportion to the competitive pressure among capitalists, while the rate of exploitation increases only in proportion to improvements in technique, the rate of profit should tend to decrease over time.

Baran and Sweezy argue that this tendency is specific to competitive capitalism, and does not operate under conditions of monopoly, where the competitive pressure to reinvest almost all profits has been neutralized by collusion among giant corporations to invest only when there is sufficient return to rationally justify doing so (there is now an implicit prohibition against cut-throat price competition designed to drive competitors out of business). Instead, under monopoly capitalism, there is a tendency to compete by reducing costs. This, combined with the tendency for prices to rise (due to collusion in price setting), tends to result in the economic surplus (more or less the equivalent concept to Marx's profits — both include interest, undistributed profits, rents, payments to sales personnel, etc.) rising over time. This book is not the place to resolve empirically whether Baran and Sweezy are correct or whether there is a tendency for the rate of profit to decline even under monopoly conditions.

The important point to make is that the Soviet economy has neither a tendency for the rate of profit to decline nor a tendency for the rate of surplus to rise. Instead the level of profits and surplus are a product of the plan, not of any inherent logic of the system. There is no tendency for the organic composition of capital to rise more rapidly than justified by purely technological considerations. Because all prices are centrally determined and basic investment decisions are made by the central authorities, there is no competitive pressure to reinvest profits at a rate more rapid than required by pure criteria of efficiency. Such purely rational criteria for investment, by the way, often dictate the introduction of more efficient machinery which utilizes less raw material than the old process and/or incorporates fewer labour hours in its construction (i.e. capital saving innovations). On the other hand, there is no inherent tendency for the rate of exploitation (the number of hours a worker labours and is paid for, divided into the number of hours worked, but not paid for) to increase. This is because decisions about both direct pay and social benefits, and the proportion of the value of the worker's product to be reinvested and allocated to the non-productive classes, are made centrally on the basis of a rational plan; this plan may, or may not, depending on the criteria of the planners, increase or decrease the share of the product going to workers and the share going to reinvestment and non-productive workers. The rate of profit can be expressed by the ratio of the rate of exploitation to the organic composition of capital. We see that there is no inherent tendency for this quantity to move one way or the other.

Similarly with any tendency for the rate of surplus to rise. Since there is no systematic inflation in the Soviet Union, prices have no inherent tendency to rise. Although costs of production are continually being reduced through increases in efficiency, rather than these reduced costs of production being expressed in reduced prices, they are manifested in increased wages and social benefits. They are definitely not expressed (as they are in the U.S.) in growing sales expenses (e.g advertisements), or wasteful government expenditures (such as unjustified military expenses, highway construction, etc.) [For a discussion of Soviet military expenditures, see Chapter 6.] There is a sharp tendency for wages of productive workers to rise in relation to those of non-productive workers and for the level of free social benefits, which disproportionately benefit the productive classes, also to rise (see Chapter Four). This indicates that the surplus is not increasing. In looking for any tendency for the surplus to rise, the role of social benefits appears to be key. It is probably the case that in the Soviet Union the ratio of productive to unproductive workers (i.e. the ratio of peasants, industrial and farm workers to sales, clerical, medical, educational, scientific, professional, managerial, etc., personnel) is decreasing. Whether this means that there is a tendency for the surplus to rise must be judged by the extent to which the growing non-productive sector is providing authentic services for the productive strata, as opposed to merely allowing the system to go on functioning (as well as in the wage trends of the two groups). Since there is a sharp tendency for the wages of productive workers to rise relatively faster than for non-productive workers, and since it appears that productive workers are increasingly benefiting from social services, there does not appear to be any evidence for a rising economic surplus. The Soviet economic system generates neither a declining rate of profit, nor a rising rate of surplus. Whether such tendencies empirically occur then is a product of policy not necessity. This makes the Soviet economic system very different from market capitalism, or even market socialism, where the logic of markets produces its own law of profits independent of the intentions of the class which has power. Lastly, it should be emphasized that the absence of any inherent tendency in relation to profits or surplus speaks only to the question of the role of capital and commodity markets, *not* to the question of the relations of production.

Conclusion

This chapter has shown that market forces do not operate in the Soviet Union to structure its economy, and specifically (and very importantly) that labour power is not a commodity. Thus the Soviet Union does not fit either the classical Marxist or the neo-Marxist definitions of capitalism. If we had merely shown that capital and commodity markets do not predominate, then, according to the classical Marxist definition, we would have only demonstrated that the U.S.S.R. is not a market capitalism. But the fact that we have also shown that labour power is not a commodity rules out even the further possibility of the Soviet Union being a state capitalism. The next two chapters will examine a different dimension — the question of social classes and political decision making — in search of evidence for and against the notion that the U.S.S.R. is a capitalist society.

References

1. Paul Gregory and Robert Stuart, *Soviet Economic Structure and Performance,* (New York: Harper and Row, 1974), Ch. 5 and pp.353-9.
2. *Ibid.,* pp.150-2.
3. On the role of the five year plans see Gregory Grossman, 'An Economy at Middle Age' in *Problems of Communism,* Vol. 25 (18-33), November-December, 1974.
4. Howard Sherman, *The Soviet Economy,* (Boston: Little Brown and Co., 1969), p.316; and Gregory and Stuart, *op. cit.,* pp.349-50.
5. J. Wilczynski, *The Economics of Socialism,* (Chicago: Aldine Publishing Co., 1970), Ch. 3.
6. Sherman, *op. cit.,* pp.308-11 and Gregory and Stuart, *op. cit.,* pp.346-8.
7. E.G. Liberman, 'The Plan, Profit and Bonuses', *Pravda,* 9 September 1962, reprinted in Alec Nove and D.M. Nuti, (eds.), *Socialist Economics,* (Baltimore: Penguin, 1972), p.313.
8. Gertrude Schoeder, 'Recent Developments in Soviet Planning and Incentives' in Morris Bornstein and Daniel Fusfeld, (eds.), *The Soviet Economy: A Book of Readings,* (4th edition), (Homewood, Illinois:

Richard Irwin Inc., 1974).

9.   A.N. Kosygin, *Report to the CPSU Central Committee*, 25 September, 1965. Reprinted in Nove and Nuti, *op cit.*, pp.324-5.
10. Schoeder, *op. cit.*, and Gregory and Stuart, *op. cit.*, Ch.10.
11. *Ibid.*, and Sherman, *op. cit.*, Ch.13.
12. Schoeder, *op. cit.*, pp.514-8 and Gregory and Stuart, *op. cit.*, pp.357-9.
13. Schoeder, *op. cit.*, p.519 ff, and Gregory and Stuart, *op. cit.*, p.359.
14. Alice Gorlin, 'Socialist Corporation: The Wave of the Future in the U.S.S.R.', in Bornstein and Fusfeld, *op. cit.*
15. Wilczynski, *op. cit.*, p.121.
16. *Ibid.*, p.166 and Gregory and Stuart, *op. cit.*, pp.152-67.
17. *Ibid.*, p.260.
18. *Ibid.*, pp.152-67 and Bornstein, 'Soviet Price Theory and Policy', *op. cit.*
19. Wilczynski, *op. cit.*, p.89.
20. *Ibid.*, p.90.
21. *Ibid.*, pp.85-7, 149; and Gregory and Stuart, *op. cit.*, Ch.10., and the Revolutionary Union, *How Capitalism Has Been Restored in the Soviet Union and What This Means for the World Struggle*, (Chicago; the Revolutionary Union, 1974) p.50.
22. George Garry, 'Finance and Banking in the U.S.S.R. in Bornstein and Fusfeld, *op. cit.*, and Wilczynski, *op. cit.*, pp.143-8.
23. Robert Osborn, *Soviet Social Policies: Welfare, Equality and Community*, (Homewood, Illinois: The Dorsey Press, 1970).
24. Gregory and Stuart, *op. cit.*, pp.202-3; Sherman, *op. cit.*, p.233; and Osborn, *op. cit.*, pp.139-40.
25. Gregory and Stuart, *op. cit.*, pp.193-211.
26. *Ibid.*, p.203.
27. Murray Feshbach, 'Manpower Management' in *Problems of Communism*, November-December, 1974.
28. Osborn, *op. cit.*, p.141.
29. *Ibid.*, p.141ff.
30. Feshbach, *op. cit.*, p.29.
31. *Ibid.*, p.30.
32. Emily Clark Brown, 'Continuity and Change in the Soviet Labor Market' in Bornstein and Fusfeld, *op. cit.*
33. Robert Conquest, *Industrial Workers in the U.S.S.R.*, (New York: Praeger, 1967), p.19.
34. *Ibid.*, p.20.
35. Brown, *op. cit.*, p.182.
36. *Ibid.*, p.192.
37. *Ibid.*, p.183.
38. *Ibid.*, p.183.
39. Robert Lane, *The End of Inequality: Stratification Under State Socialism*, (Baltimore: Penguin, 1971).
40. David Granick, *The Red Executive*, (Garden City, N.Y.: Doubleday, 1961), Ch. 13, Conquest, *op. cit.*, Ch.5, and Wilczynski, *op. cit.*, p.209.
41. Osborn, *op. cit.*, pp.138-9.
42. Conquest, *op. cit.*, pp.157-59.
43. *Ibid.*, Ch.5; Granick, *op. cit.*, Ch.13; Sherman, *op. cit.*, pp.163-6; and Wilczynski, *op. cit.*, pp.100-2.

44. Conquest, *op. cit.,* Ch.5.
45. *Ibid.,* p.174.
46. *Ibid.,* Ch.5.
47. It is of interest to note that at the All Union Congress of Trade Unions in 1961, 36 per cent of all delegates were full-time union officials and 40 per cent full-time workers. This suggests considerable rank and file influence in the unions. See Conquest, *op. cit.,* pp.161-2.
48. *Ibid.,* pp.182-5.
49. David Brodersen, *The Soviet Worker: Labor and Government in Soviet Society,* (New York: Random House, 1966).
50. Granick, *op. cit.,* p.199.
51. Merle Fainsod, *How Russia is Ruled,* (Cambridge: Harvard University Press, 1963), pp.514-5.
52. Granick, *op. cit.,* Ch.12.
53. Fainsod, *op. cit.,* pp.240, 514-8.
54. I.V. Arutiunian, 'The Distribution of Decision Making Among the Rural Population of the USSR', in Murray Yanowitch and Wesley Fisher, *Social Stratification and Mobility in the USSR,* (White Plains, N.Y.: International Arts and Sciences Press, 1973), pp.113-4.
55. See Karl Marx, *Capital,* Vol.III, Part 3, for the presentation of Marx's own argument on the question of the falling tendency of the rate of profit. See Paul Sweezy, *The Theory of Capitalist Development,* (New York: Monthly Review Press, 1942), Ch.6 for a critical discussion. See Paul Baran and Paul Sweezy, *Monopoly Capital,* (New York: Monthly Review Press, 1966), Ch.3 for the presentation of the argument that the surplus has a tendency to rise under monopoly capitalism.

4. Social Classes

This chapter will examine the evidence for and against the thesis that social classes have formed or are forming in the Soviet Union. I will examine two aspects of the question of inequality in the Soviet Union: the differentiation in terms of material rewards amongst those with different types of jobs, and the tendency for the different strata of Soviet society to crystallize into distinct social classes on the basis of differences in income or occupation.

The closely related questions of whether the Soviet power elite has become a class, and more generally whether any classes exist in the Soviet Union is only partially dealt with here. In this chapter we will not examine actual power relationships within enterprises or in society as a whole. (The question of political power is dealt with in Chapter 5). Here will will only look at the distribution of material rewards as an indicator of the relative power exercised by the power elite, intelligentsia and working people. On the reasonable expectation that people with power will exercise it in their own interest, the distribution of material rewards — as well as the trends in that distribution — are good indicators of the distribution of power over the means of production (i.e. of the relationships of production and the control over labour power) in a society.

This chapter will also examine whether distinctive social classes have tended to form in the Soviet Union by looking at the major indicators of social class: distinctive customs and life styles; common friendship and inter-marriage patterns; and the tendency to pass one's position on to one's children.

I should also point out at the outset that I use the term 'intelligentsia' to mean all people in teaching, scientific, technical, managerial, engineering, etc. roles, as well as those holding government posts and party or mass organization offices. In this chapter, when discussing the intelligentsia, I focus on the scientific-technical intelligentsia (scientists, academics and other technical specialists), sometimes referred to as the technical or professional intelligentsia, and on the managerial-political intelligentsia (those with formal positions of authority and leadership in the production enterprises, the state, party, or mass organizations such as trade unions), sometimes referred to as the managerial strata. I will attempt to determine the degree of homogeneity between these two strata as well as their differential social integration with the working class.

The Distribution of Material Rewards

In 1973 about 61 per cent of the economically active people in the Soviet Union were manual workers, about 10 per cent were non-professional white collar employees and service workers, about 16 per cent 'intelligentsia' and about 14 per cent peasants on collective farms.[1] The manual working class (which was 33 per cent of the total in 1939 and 48 per cent of the total in 1959) is the most rapidly growing section, while the collective farm peasantry is shrinking fast.[2]

Table 3.3 reported the average wages of various sectors of the labour force in 1965 and 1973. As was seen, the highest paid people are industrial engineering and technical personnel who in 1973 earned an average of 1.27 times the wages of industrial workers. In 1973 it was only this group that earned more than the industrial workers. The spread between the highest and lowest paid groups was 2.12 times, while in 1965 it had been 3.20 times. The eight year trend from 1965 to 1973 shows a clear tendency for the highest paid occupations in 1965 to have the slowest rate of growth in wages while the lowest paid occupations had the highest rates of growth. The major exception to this trend would appear to be industrial workers who were rather well paid in 1965, but who nevertheless received the highest increase in wages of any non-agricultural group.

Perhaps a better idea of the wage spread in the Soviet Union can be got from data on occupations within the same industry. In 1965 the average wages of machine building personnel in Leningrad (a key industry in a major manufacturing city) showed that the highest paid category of workers, the executives of labour collectives and of public and state organizations, earned 1.60 times the wages of skilled operatives. (See Table 4.1)

Table 4.2 reports the basic monthly rates, in rubles, for production and non-production personnel in the construction industry in 1969. From this table it can be seen that the highest paid managers and specialists earn about 1.46 times as much as time-rate workers in the highest pay grade. (See Table 4.2).

It should be noted that the average earnings of production workers in certain segments of Soviet industries exceed those of engineering and technical personnel in many industries. For example, in 1969, steel workers averaged 145 rubles a month, lumber workers 143 and coal miners (the highest paid) 210. This compared with monthly earnings of 138 rubles for engineering and technical personnel in light industry and the same group's average monthly salary of 172 rubles in Soviet industry as a whole.[3]

There appears to be a strong tendency towards egalitarianism in wages and also a tendency for industrial workers to be favoured. The trend towards wage equalization has continued since the 1940s.[4]

The highest paid people in the Soviet Union are prominent artists, writers,

Table 4.1
Average Wages of Surveyed Machine-Building Personnel in Leningrad, 1965
(in rubles per month)

Groups of Employed Personnel	Average Wage	Ratio to Skilled Machine Workers
Personnel in unskilled manual labour and low-skilled nonmanual labour without special training	97.5	0.90
Personnel in skilled nonmanual labour without special education	83.6	0.78
Personnel in skilled, primarily manual labour, employed on machines and mechanisms	107.5	1.00
Personnel in skilled, primarily manual, hand labour	120.0	1.12
Personnel in highly skilled work combining mental and manual functions	129.0	1.20
Personnel in skilled mental work	109.8	1.02
Highly skilled scientific and technical personnel	127.0	1.18
Executives of labour collectives, public and state organizations	172.9	1.60

Source: O.J. Shkaratan, 'Social Groups in the Working Class of a Developed Socialist Society', in Murray Yanowitch and Wesley Fisher, *Social Stratification and Mobility in the USSR,* (White Plains, N.Y.: International Arts and Sciences Press, 1973), p.8.

leading university administrators, professors and scientists. In the mid 1960s the president of the Soviet Academy of Sciences made 1,500 rubles a month and leading university presidents 1,200.[5] A few famous artists and performers have incomes in the same range. In the 1960s leading government officials earned about 600 rubles a month, about four times the wages of industrial workers, and leading enterprise directors from 190 to 400 rubles a month, (exclusive of bonuses), which was about 1.3 to 2.7 times workers' wages.[6]

In 1956 the ratio of the wage exceeded by the top 10 per cent of Soviet employees and workers (excluding only collective farmers) to the wage exceeded by 90 per cent was 4.4; in 1964, 3.6; in 1970 3.2; and in 1975 (if the intentions of the plan were fulfilled) 2.9.[7] Again the rather strong egalitarian trend in the Soviet Union can be seen. In the U.S. in 1974, the similar spread was roughly 6.2 times.[8] In 1956 the ratio of the average wages of the 10 per cent highest paid to the 10 per cent lowest paid was 8.1; in 1975 it was only 4.1. In the United States in 1974, the similar ratio was roughly 12.[9] Even those whose conceptualization of income distribution is

Table 4.2
Basic Monthly Rates of Production and Non-production Personnel in
Construction, 1969
(in rubles per month)

Position	Basic Wage or Salary Rate
Within a trust:	
Chief of production department, also chief specialist	160-190
Chief of planning and economic department	150-190
Chief of personnel department	135-170
Within an administration:	
Chief of administration	170-190
Chief of supply office, chief of production department	150-190
Chief of planning and economic department	150-180
Senior work superintendent	180-200
Work superintendent	160-180
Foreman, shop mechanic	135-150
Engineer	120-160
Technician	100-125
Accounting and related personnel	90-145
Typist, clerk, cashier, and similar positions	78-80
Time-rate worker in the 6th (highest) grade	137
Time-rate worker in the 1st (lowest) grade	76

Source: Robert Osborn, *Soviet Social Policies,* Homewood, Ill.: The Dorsey
Press, 1970), p.176.

designed to make Soviet income distribution look as non-egalitarian as
possible, have been forced to conclude that it is about twice as egalitarian as
the American.[10]

When, as such critical authors do, the ratio of the lower limits of the upper
decile are compared to the upper limits of the lower decile the Soviet income
differentiation looks somewhat less egalitarian than it really is, because the
absence of very high incomes in the Soviet Union is not taken into account.
The very highest incomes in the Soviet Union (of which there are very few)
are ten times more than the average industrial wage, while the wages of the
highest level state ministers and enterprise managers are about 2.7 to 4.0
times the average industrial wage. The ratios of the very highest to the average
industrial wage must be compared to the equivalent income distribution in
the United States. In the U.S. in 1973, there were about 1,000 individuals
who had an income of at least a million dollars a year, while the annual wage
in manufacturing was $8,632.[11] Assuming (very conservatively) a million
dollars a year as the highest income level in the U.S., this is a ratio of roughly
115 times compared to the Soviet ratio of approximately ten times. In the

U.S. the pay of top managers (including income from stock options) in the leading corporations in the mid 1970s was around a million dollars a year. For example, in 1970 the president of I.T.T. earned $1,242,000, the president of Xerox $1,032,000 and the president of Atlantic Richfield $972,000.[12] Again, comparing such incomes to the income of U.S. production workers, we have a ratio of roughly 115:1 compared to the equivalent Soviet ratio of about 2.5:1 between the best paid managers and the average industrial wage, and a ratio of about 4:1 between the heads of ministries and the average industrial wage. Thus when we compare the highest incomes with the average income, we see that the Soviet Union is far more egalitarian than the U.S.

Furthermore, while there has been no appreciable decrease in income inequality in the last generation in the U.S., in the twenty years between the mid 1950s and the mid 1970s, the Soviets have eliminated about half of the inequality in their income distribution (reducing the ratio of the highest decile's to the lowest decile's average wages from 8.1 to 4.1) – a radical reduction in inequality in a very short time.[13] Such a reduction provides strong evidence against the Chinese claim that a 'new capitalist class' of either state bureaucrats or managers assumed control of the Soviet Union in the 1960s, since if this were the case they would have undoubtedly used their new power to increase, not decrease, their relative material advantage.

In the United States in 1973, male self-employed professionals earned on average $20,490 a year while salaried physicians and surgeons earned $23,360.[14] The ratio of these earnings to the average industrial wage in the U.S. in 1973 was 2.4:1 and 2.7:1 respectively. This is approximately the same as the ratio in the Soviet Union of the highest managerial incomes to the industrial wage, and considerably less than the average managerial wage to the average industrial wage. Thus the spread between top management and production workers in the Soviet Union is more or less the same as that between petty bourgeois professionals and industrial workers in the United States. This suggests that the leading stratum in the Soviet Union is, at least in income terms, similar to the U.S. professional petty bourgeoisie, rather than to the American capitalist class (of either corporate managers or multi-millionaire wealthy).

It should also be noted that family income distribution in the Soviet Union is considerably more egalitarian than the distribution of average monthly wages because of differences in the number of wage earners and dependents per family.[15] The lowest paid occupations have relatively more wage earners and fewer dependents than do the highest paid families. While the spread of average monthly wages is from 74 to 169 rubles (a factor of 2.28) between unskilled workers and managerial personnel, the spread in average monthly family income per capita was only 62 to 81 (a factor of only 1.31). (See Table 4.3).

Soviet data on wages are complicated by two factors. On the one side, they underestimate the income of managers and directors by leaving out bonuses earned over and above wages (bonuses average about 25 to 30 per cent

Table 4.3
Soviet Wages and Per Capita Family Income, c.1966

	Average Monthly Wage of Head (rubles)	*Average Monthly Income per capita according to Occupation of Head (rubles)*
Unskilled and low-skilled workers	74	62
Skilled workers	111	69
Highly skilled workers	144	72
Employees in management positions	169	81
Teachers, scientific, medical and other specialists not in the sector of material production	110	81
Engineering-technical personnel and other specialists in the sector of material production	117	78
Employees without specialized education	84	66

Source: L.A. Gordon and E.V. Klopov, 'Some Problems of the Social Structure of the Soviet Working Class', in Yanowitch and Fisher, *op. cit.*, p.42.

of managerial wages), as well as their privileged access to fringe benefits such as automobiles, summer houses, etc.[16] On the other hand, the state provides a wide range of free and heavy subsidized goods and services which disproportionately favour the low income groups.

State pricing policy sets the price of basic necessities such as basic food-stuffs below their value and luxury goods above their value.[17] This means that a wage spread of 3:1 is actually considerably less than this, when measured against the actual value of the goods and services purchased by the high and low wage earners. Most of the lowest wage earners' income goes to purchase goods and services obtainable below their value (or cost of production) while a good share, if not most, of the income of the highest wage earners purchases goods at a cost considerably above their value (e.g. automobiles and personal luxury goods).[18]

Besides the equalizing effect of the pricing policy on necessities and luxuries, another major equalizing effect comes from social welfare services often referred to as the 'social wage'. Such benefits available to all include free medical care, free education at all levels including college, heavily subsidized housing (rents are set at the level required to maintain housing), subsidized child care, generous pensions, paid maternity leave, etc., all of which considerably increase family income for manual workers in particular.[19] The relative proportion of the social wage in total worker compensation has risen over the last generation. As a percentage of individual earnings it rose from 23 per cent in 1940 and 29 per cent in 1950, to 34 to 35 per cent through the 1960s.[20] Because the social wage adds about the same absolute amount to each household, it has a considerable equalizing effect on total family income. In 1968 it has been estimated that free goods and services averaged about 46 per cent of the income of the lowest paid strata, but only 12 per cent of the income of the highest paid. In heavy industry the spread of about two to one in take-home wages is reduced to about 1.5 to 1 because of the egalitarian effect of services provided on the basis of need.[21] In addition to trends towards reducing wage differentials and increasing free goods and services, in recent years the minimum wage and pensions have been greatly increased, and also income tax used increasingly to promote equality.[22]

While it could be that higher paid strata in the Soviet Union have far easier access to scarce goods such as cars and housing, thus manifesting far greater inequality in possession of material goods than is suggested by the income distribution, this does not appear to be the case. The relative egalitarianism of income *is* reflected in the distribution of housing. Most housing in the Soviet Union is built by either the state or the trade unions. Rents (including utilities) are set at a level necessary to maintain the housing, rents thus consuming on average about 7 per cent of workers' income (compared to over 20 per cent in the U.S.).[23]

A study done in the mid 1960s showed that the quality of housing for higher professionals was, on average, about 1.6 times better than that of semi-skilled workers. Another study found that socio-occupational status only correlated about 0.1 with the amount of housing space per family.[24] There is no consistent pattern of neighbourhoods differentiated by income level. There are, for example, some exclusive neighbourhoods in Moscow where leading officials of the Communist Party and its employees live, but there are also many cases (for example) of janitors and full professors at leading universities living in the same apartment building. It is normal for government and enterprise officials to live in the same apartments as production workers.[25]

Similar, but not quite as egalitarian, results have been found for automobile ownership. Studies show that enterprise directors and leading professional people have about a 2.5 times higher probability of owning an automobile than do manual workers.[26] Thus, the chances of owning a car are roughly proportional to the income differential between the highest paid managers and the production workers, and do not reflect any special access to automobiles by the intelligentsia strata beyond that accounted for by their higher incomes.

In summary, although it certainly is true that managers receive bonuses averaging 25 to 30 per cent of their income (workers receive bonuses as well) and have access to special privileges such as the automobiles belonging to the enterprise, the weight of the evidence leads us to conclude that such effects, when set against the generous subsidies to the lower paid strata, do not make the distribution of material goods more unequal. In fact the evidence, at least for housing, suggests that the distribution of material goods may even be more egalitarian than the income statistics indicate. In conclusion it would appear that the difference in material living standards between managers and government ministers in the U.S.S.R. and industrial workers come close to the difference between professionals and industrial workers in the U.S. Nothing like the gap between millionaires and workers that exists in the U.S. can be found in the U.S.S.R.

Tendencies Towards the Formation of Social Classes

While there are no strata in Soviet society comparable in income to the top managerial and property owning classes in the capitalist countries, as we have seen above, there is a stratum comparable in income to the professional middle classes in the capitalist countries. Here we will examine the extent to which this stratum may be forming into a distinctive social class.

If such a class is forming in the Soviet Union, we would expect to find three things: (1) a high correlation of customs, life style and leisure patterns with occupation; (2) a high rate of intermarriage and friendship patterns within each occupational group; and (3) a higher inter-generational correlation between parents' and children's occupational levels. We will examine data on each of these factors in turn.

Life Style
A number of studies have been done by Soviet sociologists on the material goods possessed by different types of Soviet families. A study done around 1970 in the Lukhovitskii District of the Moscow region found that 61 per cent of the intelligentsia, 26 per cent of white collar employees, 23 per cent of machine operators and 10 per cent of low skilled and unskilled workers possessed a library. The figures for radio ownership were 94 per cent, 88 per cent, 95 per cent and 55 per cent respectively and for TV ownership 73 per cent, 65 per cent, 68 per cent and 41 per cent. A study done of Leningrad machine building personnel in 1965 showed that 2.5 per cent of production workers own both an automobile and a piano compared to 5.6 per cent of the executives of production collectives and 6.8 per cent of the engineers.[27] Another study done in Akademgorodok in the late 1960s showed that 22 per cent of the directors of institutions and senior research personnel had either an automobile or motor boat, compared to 8 per cent of low skilled workers, 68 per cent of the former compared to 80 per cent of the latter had television sets, 90 per cent of the former and 75 per cent of the latter had washing machines, 85 per cent of the former and 52 per cent of the latter had a refrigerator.[28] Some significant differences between workers and the intelligentsia emerge from these findings.

Studies of leisure patterns among members of various occupations also show there to be significant differences. Among the intelligentsia 55 per cent preferred to spend their free time with fellow employees, compared to 30 per cent of operatives and 25 per cent of manual workers. On the other hand, 63 per cent of these unskilled workers, compared to 50 per cent of operatives and 23 per cent of the intelligentsia, preferred to spend their leisure time with their relatives and neighbours.[29]

One Soviet sociological study on leisure activities in different regions of the U.S.S.R. in the late 1960s found some significant differences in the use of leisure time by occupational groups. This study showed that the high level intelligentsia (higher managers, state officials, top scientists, etc.) are much more likely to be engaged in self-education and reading in their spare time than are manual workers. They are also more likely than manual workers to spend their time watching TV and listening to the radio. On the other hand, manual workers are more likely simply to spend their time resting than are the higher level intelligentsia. These, however, would seem to be the only areas in which there is a significant difference between the leisure time activities of the two groups. There are no consistent differences between them in relation to housework, spending time with children, going to films and dances, playing dominoes or cards, engaging in sport, hunting, fishing or participating in other hobbies.[30]

A study of the Leningrad machine tool industry showed that 56 per cent of the unskilled labourers, 80 per cent of the skilled and 85 per cent of the executives were regular newspaper readers.[31] Twenty per cent of unskilled workers read one or more books a week, compared to 35 per cent of the skilled and 29 per cent of the technicians, scientists and directors. Also, 80 to 85 per cent of low paid workers attended theatres and concerts at least once a month, while among highly paid workers only 58 per cent did. This would indicate no great differences in life style between the more skilled workers and the managers.

Recently, studies of Soviet customs broken down by occupation have appeared. One showed that there was no great difference by occupation in attitudes towards using physical punishment on children or towards marriage between people of different nationality groups. This study did find, however, that professional and managerial people are less likely than manual workers to believe that wives should, if the possibility existed, engage only in housework.[32] The overall difference, however, was relatively small.

Most Anglo-Saxon non-Communist scholars are of the opinion that there is relatively little class snobbery in the Soviet Union. Most believe that, compared to the situation in Western capitalist countries, there are relatively few cultural differences between people in various urban occupations. There appears to be little in the way of a distinctive class culture, accents or mode of dress.[33] However, there are some differences in status and life styles.[34] Evidence about whether elite members regard themselves as part of a distinctive status group is conflicting, but it is clear that any such status consciousness is considerably less than in the Western capitalist countries.

In summary, although differences in life style between the professional and managerial strata and the production workers are, for the most part, not very great as measured by consumer goods, leisure patterns and attitudes, significant differences do exist in relation to book ownership, possession of automobiles and pianos, and engaging in study. While differences in life style seem to be relatively small, they do reflect some differentiation of strata, although certainly nothing on the scale existing in the Western countries between managers or owners and production workers.[35]

Intermarriage and Friendship Patterns

A study of graduating secondary school students in Estonia in 1966 showed that 79 per cent of their fathers who were manual workers in enterprises employing more than 50 workers were themselves married to other manual or office workers. Manual fathers married to women in the professions or in leading positions in trade unions, Soviets and other organizations represented only 2 per cent of the total. On the other hand, 29 per cent of the fathers who were scientists and 74 per cent of the fathers who were leaders in trade unions, Soviets, and other organizations were married to women who were manual or office workers.[36] In sum there did not appear to be all that much difference in the marriage patterns of manual workers and of leaders of trade unions, Soviets and other organizations. The most significant difference here appears to be among scientists who have a high rate of intermarriage to other professionals.

Another study found that among male employees at a Pskov automatic telephone exchange plant in 1967, 87 per cent of unskilled manual workers, 66 per cent of skilled manual workers and 83 per cent of machine operatives were married to manual or unskilled white collar workers, while only 33 per cent of personnel in skilled mental work (including scientific and technical work) and 36 per cent of labour collective executives were married to women who were manual workers or unskilled office workers. Thirty-six per cent of executives and 24 per cent of personnel in skilled mental work were married to women who had a specialized higher education, compared to only four per cent of the unskilled manual workers, nine per cent of skilled, manual workers and nought per cent of operatives.[37] This study showed no significant difference between the professional and managerial strata.

Another Soviet sociological study found a correlation of +0.66 between the educational attainment of spouses, and discovered that 93 per cent of men with higher education had wives with middle or higher education, while 65 per cent of men with only an elementary education had wives at the same educational level.[38] A study of friendship patterns showed that about two-thirds of workers say that their best friend is another manual worker and that only about five to eleven per cent have a best friend who is an engineer or someone else with higher education. On the other hand, about 10 per cent of the professional intelligentsia and 21 per cent of the managerial personnel have best friends who are manual workers, while 50 per cent of the professional intelligentsia and 42 per cent of the managerial personnel have best friends who are engineers or others with a higher education. There seems to be a clear pattern for people of similar occupations to associate with others of their own kind with this tendency being most pronounced among the professional intelligentsia.[39]

The evidence from intermarriage and friendship patterns that there are distinctive social strata (based on different relations of production) is stronger than that based on life style and consumption patterns. There clearly is a distinctive social stratum of professional intelligentsia differentiated from the production workers, while the managerial stratum seems to be more socially integrated into the working class than are the professional intelligentsia.

Education and Social Mobility

A higher proportion of Soviet youth go through higher education than in any other country of the world except the United States and Canada. The system of part-time, night and adult education programmes is probably the most extensive in the world. In general the Soviet working people are among the best trained anywhere.

Stipends to cover living and school expenses are provided for higher education students who maintain a 'B' or better average. All I.Q. and general aptitude tests are barred. Admission to higher education is on the basis of passing standardized examinations in specific subjects. Among applicants for positions in institutions of higher education, preference is given to those with two or more years work experience. Special preparatory courses are available for students with at least one year of work experience who fail university entrance examinations. Adult education is encouraged and facilitated by enterprises and trade unions. There are no guidance counsellors in Soviet schools to push working class children into prescribed life channels. All these aspects of the Soviet educational system encourage children from the manual working class and peasantry to get into higher education and thereby to provide the personnel for the higher level positions in society.[40]

In spite of these considerable efforts to equalize educational opportunity for all, children of the intelligentsia are considerably more likely to complete higher education successfully. Through the 1960s children of manual workers and unskilled staff represented roughly 40 to 50 per cent of all higher education students although they made up approximately 60 per cent of the population.[41] Children of the intelligentsia also accounted for about 40 to 50 per cent, while students from the collective farm peasantry represented approximately 10 per cent. Studies of the differential probability of secondary school graduates going on to higher education generally find that children of the intelligentsia have a 1.5 to 2 times greater chance of beginning higher education than do the children of urban workers.[42] However, the trend in the last generation is away from the over-representation of children of the intelligentsia in institutions of higher education. For example the ratio of children of production workers to children of employees (both intelligentsia and non-professional staff) amongst first year students in the day-time division of six Sverdlovsk higher educational institutions was 0.52 in 1950, 0.57 in 1957, 0.70 in 1965 and 0.94 in 1969.[43]

Although all higher education is free, students are given stipends to support themselves, and admission is on the basis of standardized examinations, occupational position still tends to be passed on through two mechanisms (which operate in Western capitalist societies as well): (1) differential

aspirations to become members of the intelligentsia, and (2) differential
ability to do well in school and examinations. Both are products of the degree
of cultural stimulation of the child by parents. One study in the Novosibirsk
Oblast in 1962-63 showed that 71 per cent of children of the intelligentsia
– compared to 60 per cent of children of workers in industry and construction
– aspired to become part of the intelligentsia, while only 25 per cent of
children of the intelligentsia, but 35 per cent of children of industrial and
construction workers aspired to be workers.[44]

A 1966 study in the Sverdlovsk region showed that 94 per cent of the
intelligentsia compared to 65 per cent of workers were planning a higher
education for their children.[45] In 1970, 71 per cent of students who passed
entrance examinations for Novosibirsk State University had parents with a
higher education, while only 33 per cent of applicants passed whose parents
had merely a primary education, and 42 per cent of applicants passed whose
parents had a general secondary education.[46] Performance in school is also
associated with parents' occupations. A study of Leningrad eighth grade
graduates in 1968 showed that 89 per cent of the children of the intelligent
sia compared with 69 per cent of the children of skilled workers had an
overall grade average of at least 3.5.[47]

In order to put this data in perspective, it is necessary to look at the
capitalist countries. Around 1960 the percentage of university students of
working-class origins in Britain was about 25 per cent, in Sweden 16 per cent,
in France 8 per cent and in West Germany and the Netherlands only 5 per
cent (compared to approximately 40 per cent in the Soviet Union).[48] In the
U.S. in 1950 children of manual workers were about 8 per cent of total
college graduates and in 1965 about 25 per cent of college students.[49] One
U.S. study reported that, of 1957 high school seniors, 14 per cent of the
children of working-class families had graduated from college by 1965
compared to 42 per cent of the children from the upper middle class.[50]
Thus it appears that the differential probability of working-class children
going to college in the Soviet Union is higher than that of any capitalist
country and a lot higher than most. This indicates that the relative privilege
(in terms of ability to pass on occupational position) of higher groups in the
Soviet Union is less than that of higher groups (both professionals and
capitalists) in the West. But children of the Soviet intelligentsia are still three
times more likely than working-class children to be at college.

Because there is no inheritance of productive property or any other linkage
between the generations except those which operate through unequal
educational opportunities, upward mobility in the Soviet Union is very high.[51]
Nevertheless, because of this educational factor, there is a significant linkage
of occupational positions from generation to generation. A 1965 study of
heads of family in Leningrad showed that only 35 per cent of highly skilled
scientific and technical personnel and 63 per cent of executives from labour
and state organizations came from manual or peasant families.[52] This same
study showed that 20 per cent of the adult children of managerial personnel
and 26 per cent of the children of highly skilled scientific and technical

workers were in the intelligentsia compared to about 10 per cent of the children of manual workers and 14.3 per cent of the children of skilled workers. Another Leningrad study found that in 1970 42 per cent of specialists had manual working-class fathers while 31 per cent had fathers who were also specialists.[53]

Most studies of Soviet mobility show that working-class children are the major source of recruits for administrative positions while the scientific-academic intelligentsia has an especially high rate of recruitment from the intelligentsia. The inter-generational continuity of intelligentsia status is most pronounced among those with advanced academic degrees.[54] The proportion of senior party and government leaders from the working class is much higher than among the leading segments of the professional intelligentsia, again suggesting that there is a tendency for something like a social class to be forming around the roles of the professional intelligentsia but not around managerial-administrative jobs.

Of the 47 government ministers of the U.S.S.R. (the nearest Soviet equivalent to the richest owners and top managers of corporate wealth in the West) 40 per cent in 1966 had manual working-class parents, 27 per cent had parents who were peasants, 15 per cent had parents who were low level white collar workers, and only 18 per cent had parents in the intelligentsia. i.e. About 80 per cent came from humble origins.[55]

The two leading bodies of the Communist Party, the Central Committee and the Politburo, are also predominantly composed of people from lower status non-intelligentsia backgrounds. For example, a study of the 1966 Central Committee showed that, of the 74 per cent on which information could be found, 36 per cent had manual working-class parents, 47 per cent peasant parents and only 16 per cent non-manual (i.e. either intelligentsia or low level white collar) parents.[56] i.e. About 90 per cent of leading Party members came from humble origins. This information on the social background of both the economic and the political elites leads us to conclude that the differential rate of inter-generational working class versus intelligentsia recruitment into the highest managerial and political positions is no different than into the intelligentsia as a whole. Further, working class recruitment to the power elite is greater (i.e. more favourable to the lower strata) than into the scientific-technical segment of the intelligentsia.

The intelligentsia are able to give their children a good chance of not going into manual occupations (i.e. avoiding downward social mobility), but at the same time children of manual workers have a fairly good chance of rising into the intelligentsia. The amount of upward mobility into all levels of Soviet society is considerable. Although children of the intelligentsia have a better chance of becoming managers than children of manual workers or peasants, the majority of managerial personnel at all levels are not children of the intelligentsia.[57]

The children of the intelligentsia have twice as great a chance as manual workers of making it into the intelligentsia (either as a whole or into the top managerial positions). Let us compare this Soviet situation with the Western capitalist countries. In the latter, children of manual workers are more likely to retain the manual status of their parents than to become non-manuals by a factor of roughly three. In the U.S., for example, it is 2.7, in France 2.5, in Japan 3.0, in Britain 2.3, in West Germany 3.6, and in Sweden, 2.8.[58] Since the category 'non-manual' in the West includes even low level white collar workers such as clerks and sales people, while the Soviet category of intelligentsia used here excludes them, the differential between the two types of society is in fact considerably greater than the data reported here suggests.

The greater upward mobility of workers in the Soviet Union than in the capitalist countries is clear enough when comparing recruitment into the intelligentsia as a whole. But it becomes qualitatively different when comparing mobility into the elites, especially into the highest level economic positions. The differential in access between the intelligentsia and manual workers to the highest level economic positions in Soviet society is about two to one; this compares with a ratio in the West of middle class versus manual worker access to a broadly defined elite of 3.6 in France, 4.2 in Britain, 4.4 in Sweden and 5.5 in West Germany.[59] A study of U.S. business elites in the mid 1950s showed that, of the businessmen born from 1891 to 1920, only three per cent had manual parents compared to 74 per cent who had wealthy parents.[60] This compares to the approximate 40 per cent of Soviet economic ministers who are from manual working class backgrounds, a difference of more than 10 times in favour of the Soviets.

In capitalist countries, like the U.S., ownership of economic wealth is passed from generation to generation through inheritance. If one's parents were corporate wealthy, the probability approaches 100 per cent that one will be as well. Thus the Rockefellers, Fords, Mellons, Duponts, etc. accumulate wealth from generation to generation, assuring each new generation of tremendous fortunes. Further, the members of boards of directors of leading corporations tend to come predominantly from those who inherit large sums of wealth. A study of 50 of the largest U.S. corporations in 1963 showed that 53 per cent of their 884 directors were hereditary members of the U.S. upper class while most of the rest had middle-class backgrounds.[61] Furthermore, the top hired managers of the corporations, while not generally being part of the hereditary capitalist upper class, are recruited mostly from urban middle-class, not manual working-class or rural, backgrounds. There is nothing like this in the Soviet Union where access to the highest level economic positions shows no inter-generational linkage and hence no tendency whatsoever for a social class of top managers to form. There is no significant tendency for leading governmental, enterprise or party officials to pass on their positions. At best they can give their children only membership in the intelligentsia as a whole. There are virtually no cases of any Soviet leaders successfully passing on a top level position to their children. Each generation of top managers and political leaders is recruited afresh from the lower levels of the intelligentsia (no more than a quarter) and the manual working class (at least a third), as well as from the peasantry and white collar workers. This is qualitatively different from the Western capitalist countries.

75

In summary, the data on social mobility in the Soviet Union shows that this society is far more open, especially in its highest reaches, to children from the manual working class than are contemporary capitalist societies, but that children from the intelligentsia (especially the professional intelligentsia in contrast to governmental, party or managerial personnel) have a significantly higher probability than working-class children of becoming members in their turn of the intelligentsia. Although status boundaries are considerably more fluid in the Soviet Union than in the West, there is a tendency for the scientific-technical intelligentsia to crystallize as a distinctive social stratum, separate from both the manual working class and the managerial-political intelligentsia (who appear to be significantly more working class in origin than the former group).

Summary
The evidence on social class formation seems to parallel that on the distribution of material rewards. While there is no social class corresponding to the wealthy corporate owning and managerial class in the Western countries (i.e. the Soviet power elite does not form a distinctive social class), there does tend to be a significant differentiation in life style, marriage patterns and inheritance of position, roughly comparable to the differences between the petty bourgeoisie and the manual working class in the U.S. The most distinctive tendencies toward social class formation occur within the scientific-technical section of the intelligentsia who appear to have the most distinctive life styles and inter-marriage patterns and the highest probability of passing on intelligentsia status, while the managerial-political stratum of the intelligentsia appears to be somewhat more socially integrated into the working class.

Conclusion

The evidence on income distribution as well as on social class formation shows that: (1) there is no wealthy class which has an income remotely comparable to that of the economic elite in the capitalist countries; (2) no elite privileged social stratum exists with its own highly distinctive life style, exclusive intermarriage patterns and virtual certainty of passing on its positions to its children as is the case in the capitalist countries; (3) there is an income differential in the Soviet Union between the higher level managers and the scientific and technical intelligentsia on the one hand and the manual working class on the other, roughly similar to that between the higher professionals and manual workers in the U.S.; (4) there are distinctive life style and intermarriage patterns as well as inter-generational linkages among the scientific and technical intelligentsia which tend to make them a social stratum distinct from the working class; (5) tendencies for the scientific-technical or managerial-political intelligentsia to crystallize into a social class are significantly weaker compared to the class divide that exists in the capitalist countries between the economic elite and the manual workers (nevertheless the gap between the professional stratum and the working class in the U.S.S.R. is roughly equivalent to that existing between professionals and manual workers in the U.S.); and (6) unlike the capitalist countries, the incumbents of decision making positions in the economy and state apparatus are not integrated into the technical intelligentsia. Rather the managerial stratum appears to be significantly closer to the manual working class than is the scientific-technical intelligentsia.

References

1. Murray Yanowitch, *Social and Economic Inequality in the Soviet Union,* (White Plains, N.Y.: M.E. Sharpe, 1977), p.111.
2. Mervyn Matthews, *Class and Society in Soviet Russia,* (New York: Walker & Co., 1972), p.35.
3. Yanowitch, *op. cit.,* p.32.
4. Robert Lane, *The End of Inequality?* (Baltimore: Penguin, 1971), p.73.
5. Matthews, *op. cit.,* pp.91-3.
6. *Ibid.*
7. Jerry Hough, 'The Brezhnev Era: The Man and the System', *Soviet Studies,* 25:2, (October 1973), p.12.
8. Computed from data reported in the 1975 edition of the U.S. Department of Commerce, *The Statistical Abstract of the U.S.,* p.393.
9. *Ibid.,* and Yanowitch, *op. cit.,* p.25.
10. Peter Wiles, *Distribution of Income: East and West,* (New York: American Elseview Publishing Co., 1974), p.48.
11. U.S. Department of Commerce, *op. cit.,* pp.233, 366.
12. Howard Tuckman, *The Economics of the Rich,* (New York: Random House, 1973), pp.44-5.
13. U.S. Department of Commerce, *op. cit.,* p.392.
14. *Ibid.,* pp.366, 370.
15. In addition to Table 4.3 see Robert Osborn, *Soviet Social Policies,* (Homewood, Ill.: The Dorsey Press, 1970), p.50.
16. Paul Gregory and Robert Stuart, *Soviet Economic Structure and Performance,* (New York: Harper & Row, 1974), pp.189-90 and 399.
17. J. Wilczynski, *The Economics of Socialism,* (Chicago: Aldine Publishing Co., 1970), p.121.
18. Morris Bornstein, 'Soviet Price Theory and Policy', in Morris Bornstein and Daniel Gusfeld, (eds.), *The Soviet Economy: A Book of Readings,* (4th edition), (Homewood, Ill.: Richard Irwin, Inc., 1974), p.109.
19. Osborn, *op. cit.,* p.50.
20. *Ibid.,* p.32.
21. *Ibid.,* p.48.
22. Frank Parkin, *Class Inequality and Political Order,* (New York: Praeger, 1971), p.144; and Gregory and Stuart, *op. cit.,* p.198.
23. Gertrude Schroeder, 'Consumption in the U.S.S.R.', in Bornstein and Gusfeld, *op. cit.,* p.281.
24. Lane, *op. cit.,* p.78.

25. Osborn, *op. cit.,* Ch. 6 and Schroeder, *op. cit.,* pp.279-82; Yanowitch, *op. cit.,* p.40; and Vladimir Voinvich, 'Oh for a Room of My Own', *New York Times Magazine,* 20 June 1976.
26. O.I. Shkaraton, 'Social Groups in the Working Class of a Developed Socialist Society', in Murray Yanowitch and Wesley Fisher, *Social Stratification and Mobility in the USSR,* (White Plains, N.Y.: International Arts and Sciences Press, 1973), p.95; and Yanowitch, *op. cit.,* p.45.
27. Shkaraton, *op. cit.,* p.95; and I.A. Arutiunian, 'Culture and the Social Psychology of the Soviet Rural Population', in Yanowitch and Fisher, *op. cit.,* p.120.
28. Yanowitch, *op. cit.,* p.45.
29. M.V. Timiashevskaia, 'Some Social Consequences of a City-Building Experiment', in Yanowitch and Fisher, *op. cit.,* p.144.
30. Arutiunian, *op. cit.,* p.124.
31. Shkaratan, *op. cit.,* p.86.
32. Arutiunian, *op. cit.,* p.132.
33. Parkin, *op. cit.,* p.157.
34. Lane, *op. cit.,* pp.79-86.
35. See for example August Hollingshead and Frederick Redlich, *Social Class and Mental Illness,* (New York: John Wiley, 1958), Appendix Three.
36. M.K. Titma, 'The Influence of Social Origins on the Occupational Values of Graduating Secondary School Students', in Yanowitch and Fisher, *op. cit.,* pp.192-3.
37. Shkaratan, *op. cit.,* p.309.
38. Lane, *op. cit.,* p.101.
39. O.I. Shkaraton, 'Social Ties and Social Mobility', in Yanowitch and Fisher, *op. cit.,* p.290.
40. Osborn, *op. cit.,* Ch. 4 and Matthews, *op. cit.,* Chs. 9 and 10.
41. *Ibid.,* p.297; Yanowitch, *op. cit.,* pp. 89, 90; and M.N. Rutkevich and F.R. Filipev, 'The Social Sources of Recruitment of the Intelligentsia', in Yanowitch and Fisher, *op. cit.,* p.248.
42. Yanowitch, *op. cit.,* p.86.
43. M.N. Rutkevich and F.R. Filippev, 'The Social Sources of Recruitment of the Intelligentsia', in Yanowitch and Fisher, *op. cit.*
44. Matthews, *op. cit.,* p.263.
45. Yanowitch, *op. cit.,* p.71.
46. L.F. Liss, 'The Social Conditioning of Occupational Choice', in Yanowitch and Fisher, *op. cit.,* p.286.
47. Yanowitch, *op. cit.,* p.71.
48. Parkin, *op. cit.,* p.110.
49. Seymour Martin Lipset and Reinhard Bendix, *Social Mobility in Industrial Society,* (Berkeley: University of California Press, 1964), p.97; and Daniel Rossides, *The American Class System,* (Boston: Houghton Mifflin Co., 1976), p.211.
50 Lucile Duberman, *Social Inequality,* (Philadelphia: J.B. Lippincott Co., 1976), p.208.
51. For a thorough review of the literature on social mobility in the U.S.S.R. see Rich Dobson, 'Mobility and Stratification in the USSR', *American*

Sociological Review, 1977, No. 3. Reprinted in *Annual Review of Sociology.*

52. Shkaraton, 'Social Ties and Social Mobility', *op. cit.,* p.294.
53. *Ibid.,* p.300; and Yanowitch, *op. cit.,* p.109.
54. Dobson, *op. cit.,* p.309; and Yanowitch, *op. cit.,* pp.108-14.
55. Jeremy Azreal, *Managerial Power and Soviet Politics,* (Cambridge, Mass.: Harvard University Press, 1966), pp.157-67; and Lane, *op. cit.,* p.126.
56. T.H. Rigby, 'The Soviet Politburo', *Soviet Studies,* 24:1, (July 1972), p.11; and Lane, *op. cit.,* p.122.
57. See also David Granick, *The Red Executive,* (Garden City, N.Y.: Doubleday, 1961), Ch.3; and John Hardt and Theodore Frankel, 'The Industrial Manager', in Bornstein and Fusfield, *op. cit.,* p.155.
58. S.M. Miller, 'Comparative Social Mobility', in Celia Sheller, (ed.), *Structured Social Inequality,* (New York: Macmillan Co., 1969), p.330.
59. *Ibid.,* p.334. The definition of elites used here refers to the top 2.5 to 4.5 per cent of the population.
60. Lipset and Bendix, *op. cit.,* p.122.
61. G.W. Domhoff, *Who Rules America,* (Englewood Cliffs: Prentice-Hall, 1967), pp.151-2.

5. Political Processes

There is considerable and highly polarized debate about the role of the Soviet working people in the decision making processes of Soviet society. The anti-communists of the West, the Chinese Communist Party and their supporters throughout the world, claim that the Soviet state is the instrument of a small minority of state bureaucrats, or 'state capitalists', who use it as their instrument against the interests of the Soviet people.[1] The Soviet working people thus are seen as excluded from the real decision making processes. Further, this is largely the result of developments from the death of Stalin in 1953, to 1965, when, they claim, capitalism was restored in the Soviet Union. The Soviets and their supporters, on the other hand, maintain that the Soviet Union is a popular democracy in which the masses of working people are integrally involved in making the decisions that affect their lives, and that the Soviet state is an instrument of their interest and their will.[2] It would be hard to imagine two more opposite positions on any question.

To prove that a society is socialist, in addition to showing that the producing classes benefit economically relative to the power elite or to any owning or controlling class that is hypothesized to exist, it must also be shown that such groups are in fact the ruling class, i.e. that the role in the political process is the primary factor which determines the role of the state in society.

There are numerous possible ways, it must be remembered, by which the producing classes can determine state policies. Amont these are as we argued earlier, the initial revolution by which the producing classes overthrew the old regime and selected a new leadership. Because there is considerable inertia in people's commitments, this 'election' might well be expected to determine the class content of policies for some time. Again, as we saw, this initial 'election' is reinforced by the real possibility that a politically mobilized people would be inclined to overthrow a leadership that betrays its original revolutionary commitments, i.e. would revolt once again if necessary, to ensure that policies were in the popular interest. These two factors will not, however, guarantee that a group of leaders, once installed by the working people, will indefinitely uphold their original commitments, unless there also exist ongoing mechanisms by which the masses of people can affect state policies. A country cannot be considered socialist, even if state policies disproportionately benefit the productive

80

classes, unless the working people are involved on an ongoing basis in running the state.

Since approximately two generations have passed since the Bolshevik Revolution, claims that the Soviet Union is a socialist country where the working classes rule, based only on evidence that the working people disproportionately benefit and that these classes installed the leadership of the Bolshevik party in power in the 1917-1920 period are insufficient to prove that the U.S.S.R. is still socialist. Whether the working people of the Soviet Union can be considered to rule must depend on whether structures and processes of the kind outlined in Chapter Two predominate. Thus, as part of our attempt to determine whether the Soviet Union is a socialist country, we will examine the processes of elections and decision making in state bodies, public debates and public opinion formation, participation in state and economic enterprise administration and decision making, the role of the working people in the Communist Party, the social origins of, and integration of, the leadership with the masses of working people, and finally, the structural constraints which ensure that decisions made benefit the masses of working people.

The Formal Political Structure
The Electoral Process
Even though the number of candidates on the ballot papers in Soviet elections is equal to the number of positions open, the electoral process in the U.S.S.R. must be taken seriously as one means of exerting influence on the decision making process. At the final stage of the election process (in a secret ballot on election day) the voter (over 99 per cent of Soviet adults normally vote in elections) checks a 'yes' or 'no' after the various candidates' names. If the majority of voters reject a candidate, he or she is not elected and another candidate must be nominated and is in turn subject to the possibility of being vetoed by a majority vote. In 1965, 208 candidates for local Soviets were rejected by the voters at the final stage of the election process, and in 1969 there were rejections in 145 districts.[3]

But, since virtually all candidates nominated get elected, it is clear that most of the negotiation and politicking takes place at the nomination stage. (This is not so unlike how primaries and general elections produced successful candidates in the old one party system of the South of the U.S.A.) Considerable attention is given in the Soviet Union to producing a slate of nominees who represent the community, support Communist Party policies and can win election. The actual final elections serve mostly to express solidarity and energize people, rather than to make decisions. The very real decision making process occurs before the final casting of ballots. Candidates are nominated at meetings of workers and members of mass organizations after sounding out their opinions and evaluation of the candidates by local election committees and Communist Party members. Anyone at a meeting has the right to propose or oppose a candidate.[4] Wide and thorough discussion of the qualifications of

81

candidates at these meetings is said by official sources to exist. Regrettably, I could find no hard evidence on the extent to which the nomination process was authentically democratic. But it is relevant to point out that the election process in China, formally at least, is the same as in the Soviet Union, China having adopted the latter's system.

The fact that there is only one candidate per post at the final stage of the election procedure and that almost all candidates nominated get elected cannot be considered *ipso facto* evidence against the thesis that the producing classes rule in the Soviet Union. Whether this is the case must be decided on the basis of a study of their role in the selection of nominees, the political positions of nominees, and in their control over the nominees both directly and through their influence on the Communist Party.

Legislative Bodies

Western sovietologists agree that there has been a significant increase both in the political role of the Soviets and in popular participation in them since the mid 1950s.[5] The standing commissions of the Supreme Soviet (which has authority over all aspects of Soviet society) initiate and draft proposals to be submitted to its general meetings. They also operate as a permanent watchdog on social institutions, and supervise and assist state organs in implementing the acts of the Supreme Soviet and its Presidium (which is empowered to make decisions when the Supreme Soviet is not meeting). In addition, the Supreme Soviet establishes other commissions whose members visit localities for investigations and hold on-the-spot public meetings. These commissions continually check the state of administration in their areas. There is an expanding policy of bringing in experts in various fields for consultation with the standing commissions and Presidium of the Supreme Soviet (which suggests the growing power of professionals).

The City and Republic Soviets have responsibility for checking up on the work of all enterprises and organizations within their territorial jurisdiction. Such Soviets focus on matters like public eating facilities, public health and public transport, education, anti-'social parasite' activities, working conditions, pensions, etc. Careful studies of the operation of local Soviets by Western sovietologists conclude that these institutions play a real and active role in local decision making; that a considerable diversity of views is put forward in their internal discussions prior to adopting legislation; that they actually make rather than just 'rubber stamp' decisions previously agreed on by Party organizations; and that they do influence broader political processes in the direction of popular responsiveness.[6]

As for the general meetings of the Supreme Soviet which are open to the public, these serve the function of expressing unity and solidarity behind policy decisions already hammered out in public debate, the commissions and the Party, rather than actually formulating state policy. It should be noted that the National People's Congress in the People's Republic of China functions in exactly the same manner. Both national bodies meet for only a few days a year, obviously not enough time to do anything other than listen to some speeches and give legitimacy to decisions which have already been made. No real debate normally occurs in either body. Again, it should be noted that there is nothing especially unique about such a situation. For example, in the U.S.A., the Democratic and Republican party conventions, Congressional votes on major foreign policy questions (e.g. the declaration of war in 1941 and the Gulf of Tonkin Resolution in 1964), the brief perfunctory debates about Department of Defense appropriations and for that matter most major legislation before the U.S. Congress, all indicate that most of the hammering out of policies occurs in private and before general public meetings. The actual process of voting in the U.S., as in the Soviet Union and China, very often serves primarily to generate public support behind a decision already reached. In none of these countries does the relative absence of real decision making in the public general sessions of their leading legislative bodies indicate that their ruling class does not participate in a thorough and wide ranging process of debate, negotiation and compromise before making decisions. The unanimity of Supreme Soviet votes then cannot be taken as evidence against the producing classes actually controlling the state. Whether this is the case depends on their involvement in processes prior to taking the final public votes.

Public Debate and Public Opinion Formation

Authentic democracy within a ruling class implies the real opportunity for conflicting ideas to confront one another on a more or less equal basis so that members of the ruling class can form valid opinions without being 'brainwashed' through hearing only one viewpoint expressed. Fully developed and genuine socialism must then institutionalize the structures for full and authentic debate among the producing classes on questions of public policy.

There is very little public debate either in the open meetings of the Supreme Soviet or in candidates' election campaigns for state office on the pros and cons of the various issues facing the Soviet people. But this does not mean that freewheeling and wide ranging public debate on the basic issues facing the Soviet Union does not occur, or that such debate does not influence the decisions made, or that elections and the Supreme Soviet play no real role in decision making.

In the Soviet Union, unlike the Western capitalist countries, the major forums for public debate, criticism, and public opinion formation are the mass media, together with specialized journals and conferences. The media are the major forum for opposing views with *Pravda* and *Izvestia* ranging more freely as social critics than the local weeklies.[7] The Soviet press is full of public debates on a very wide range of issues: literary policy, economic and legal reform, military strategy, the relation between the Party and the military, city planning, crime, pollution, farm problems, the role of the press, art, women's role in the economy, access to higher education, incompetent economic management, bungling bureaucrats, etc. The only issues that are more or less immune from open, concerted criticism in the press, whether readers' commentaries or official editorials, are the Communist Party as an institution (as opposed to concrete abuses by party officials), the existence of the military (though not military strategy and the political role of the military), socialism as a system and communism as an ideal (though again not specific practices of the Communist Party), the idea of the unity of the Party and the people (but not flaws in its concrete manifestations), and the persons of the current top political leaders (but not lower and intermediate level officials, and not the ideas and programmes of the top leaders). All but the last of these taboo subjects represent the fundamental assumptions of Soviet society.[8] These issues are considered to have been settled once and for all and public discussion of them is considered by the regime to be potentially disruptive of popular rule. Other than these few basic assumptions of Soviet society there appears to be no official policy that is immune from questioning and criticism in the press.[9] Even in the sensitive areas of foreign and nationality policy, where advocacy of basic changes is permitted only in veiled form, a lively public debate goes on under the guise of discussions on the actual facts of the present situation.[10] The consensus among those who follow the Soviet media seems to be that the area and depth of public debate has been growing and that in recent years there has been virtually no proposal for gradual change in the policy of the Communist Party which has not been aired in the mass media.

Observers otherwise hostile to the Soviet Union claim that the public debates, struggles and criticisms are reaching deeper and deeper into the social structure as policy making becomes more and more decentralized and the number of participants increases.[11] There is considerable freedom of discussion and there exist sharp differences of opinion on a wide range of issues.[12] Basic policies are increasingly formulated, discussed and challenged in public speeches, forums and editorial statements in newspapers and periodicals.[13] The different Soviet papers and periodicals more or less openly take sides on public issues. This appears to be especially the case with proposed new welfare policies, each of which has been debated vigorously by specialists and ordinary citizens alike in professional journals and the public press. Public debate on proposed legislation has for the most part become an institution. A law is proposed, a period of wide ranging debate takes place, and a revised version of the law is finally promulgated which incorporates the results of the public criticism.[14]

Letters to editors of the Soviet press, which very often amount to guest editorials or articles, play a very significant role.[15] This institution provides a major forum for the producing class to present its opinions and participate directly in the sharp confrontation of conflicting ideas. Many discussions are thus initiated from below. Letters to government agencies, Party organs, etc. also play a very important role in initiating public discussion and influencing the decision making process. It appears that group opinion, as expressed in letters and the media, exerts a significant influence on the course of events.[16]

All the mass media have letter departments which keep letters received on file and forward them to the appropriate government agency. By law any agency against whom a complaint or suggestion is directed must respond within 15 days and the sender must be notified of the results. The state takes very seriously the channelling of complaints and grievances to collection points where they can be processed. The press thus serves the function of ombudsman for the masses. In 1970 Pravda handled about 360,000 letters a year and Izvestia 500,000. Obviously the press cannot publish all the letters it receives, but all must be processed and referred to the agencies against which a complaint is directed.[17]

The press itself does more than provide a forum for public debate and opinion formation. It also actively performs the role of social critic (although not of the basic premises of Soviet society listed above). The newspapers actively search out corruption, managerial incompetence, inept government and flaws in social organization. They investigate allegations of injustice, inefficiency, bungled planning and highhanded bureaucracy. Pravda and the other major papers, in particular, systematically engage in public exposures. The press maintains public surveillance over official programmes, checks the performance of social institutions and promotes creative solutions to complex problems of Soviet society. It encourages citizens to take an active part in criticizing everyone who may be abusing public trust, except the persons of the top leaders.[18] Complaints, many of them originating from readers, have produced criminal prosecutions or disciplinary action against Communist Party members.

Soviet citizens are becoming increasingly active in working with the press. It is common for volunteers working with a paper to 'raid' a factory or government installation and produce a sharp critique for the paper.[19] And Soviet newspaper editors are rewarded for representing public opinion and taking a critical stance towards inefficiency, bureaucracy and other abuses. That the press at least some of the time does its job effectively is attested to by attempts by bureaucrats to suppress criticism, attempts which themselves have been exposed by the press.[20]

It may be useful to mention some of the **specific** issues which have involved considerable public discussion: Khrushchev's attempt to proletarianize higher education from the late 1950s until 1965; the ongoing and sharp debates about the greater access of children of the intelligentsia to higher education (and the consequences of this for the creation of a privileged stratum); the debate over the role of the Communist Party in the military which occurred between 1958 and 1962; continuing discussions on the role of writers and artists; the question of centralization versus decentralization of economic decision making; environmental protection issues (the debate over Lake Baikal being the most famous example); discussion over whether the birthrate can best be increased by paying mothers a wage for staying at home or by improving day care services (prominent in the mid 1970s); and discussions over whether enterprise managers should be elected by workers in the plants (also a public issue in the mid 1970s).[21]

Public debates over legal reforms have also taken place in universities, legal research institutes, jurists' associations and factories, as well as in the public press and journals (e.g. around the reform of Civil Law in 1961). They have often produced considerable changes in the original drafts offered for public discussion.[22]

The professional intelligentsia, especially economists and jurists, seem to exert considerable influence on public decision making through their specialized papers, journals, conferences and other institutions. These professionals, through these media, set out various public policy options and seek to convince their colleagues and the public through debate at meetings and the written word. Especially important channels of influence are the Soviet Academy of Sciences and the universities.[23]

Various groups of the intelligentsia generally — particularly economists, journalists, military officers, managers, scientists, party officials, state officials, etc — are active in presenting their interests and opinions to the public. Their associations and periodicals play a disproportionate role in public debates, and they have a disproportionate influence on both the outcome of public debates and the actual decisions reached (by influencing both the public and the behind-the-scenes aspects of the decision making process). In contrast, the trade unions and the Young Communist League have not traditionally played as active and as autonomous a role in public opinion formation. However, the trade unions in recent years are coming to play an increasingly active role in public debates especially at the regional and factory levels.[24]

Another Soviet institution which provides a forum for public discussion and criticism is wall newspapers (which the Chinese have adopted and made a vital part of their own political life). These papers are issued by shops and sections of industrial enterprises, as well as by collectives and state farms, educational institutions, etc. Every worker has the right to participate by having their ideas and criticisms put up for public scrutiny. There is a right to criticize the heads of trade unions, enterprises, etc. through this medium.[25]

The organs of public policy making in the Soviet Union — the mass media, the Soviets, public meetings and the Party — seem to be the forums in which various interest groups fight it out within the broad assumptions of the system.[26] There appear to be systematic differences over major policy decisions among various interest groups. One of the principal interests seems to be the 'experts' (scientists, academics, engineers, jurists, etc.), many of whom tend to favour such policies as greater inequality and more decision making power for enterprise directors and other professionals, as well as favouring purely technical criteria for admission to institutions of higher education. On the other hand, the working class organizations, most party officials and the Young Communist League have tended to favour such contrary policies as greater egalitarianism and limits on the powers and prerogatives of enterprise directors and experts, as well as class criteria in admission to institutions of higher education. As we will see in a later chapter, it was a split along similar lines that engulfed Czechoslovakia in 1967-68 and precipitated the intervention, for good or ill, of the Soviet army.

During the 1960s the intelligentsia and experts who became increasingly dominant in the Czech party pushed harder and harder for greater inequality *vis-a-vis* workers. Novotny, leader of the anti-liberal faction, appealed to the industrial workers for support against the intelligentsia (indeed several strikes in large factories did occur against the Czech reforms).[27]

In summary, there appears to be very widespread involvement both among the professional intelligentsia and the working class in the formulation and discussion of public issues, as well as in criticisms of state and Party perform- ance. But although considerable influence over the course of public policy seems to be exercised by the working class, it does appear that greater influ- ence is exerted by the professional intelligentsia. The Soviet political process seems to be considerably biased in favour of the highly trained employees.

Popular Participation in State Bodies

Popular institutions include the system of comrades courts which were set up in 1959. The judges of these courts are local citizens elected by local mass organizations. They deal with minor crime, violations of work discipline and rules of behaviour in apartment blocks, neglect of safety regulations, im- proper behaviour in public places, failure to bring children up properly, 'parasitism', 'hooliganism', drunkenness, etc. The courts are empowered to impose penalties including banishment, transferring people to lower paying jobs, reprimands, ordering apologies and imposing fines. There are also com- mittees elected at general meetings of all residents in apartment blocks which regulate, improve living conditions and assign living quarters.[28]

The Soviets have People's Control Commissions whose sole function is to inspect enterprises and public institutions and to expose abuses. They were reinvigorated in 1962 (although they have a history dating from the revolut- ion). The commissions are set up and co-ordinated with the local, regional, republic and supreme Soviets. They have state authority behind them in their investigations. Their officers are elected for two year terms.[29] In 1963-64 about 4.3 million people, mostly volunteers, were working on these control bodies; in 1975-76, 9.4 million.[30]

People's police units and a popular militia have been given increasing responsibilities since the 1950s. Around 1970 the popular militia had six million volunteers. In 1964-65 there were 5.5 million people's auxiliary policemen; in 1975-76, 7.0 million.[31]

As for legislative bodies, although the intelligentsia are considerably over- represented, workers and peasants are increasingly involved in them. Workers increased their share of all local Soviet deputies from 10.6 per cent in 1954- 55 to 39.3 per cent in 1972-73 and their share of Supreme Soviet positions from 14 to 42 per cent.[32]

There appears to be a clear increase in popular participation in the Soviet Union. The levels of public debate and participation (and the nature of the socialist ideology which is hegemonic) indicate that public opinion and participation play a major role in policy decisions.[33] It seems to be the case, however, that the considerably greater participation of the professional intelligentsia in Soviet institutions gives them disproportionate political influence compared to the manual working class.

There seems to be virtual consensus among Western sovietologists — most of whom are of course, neither Marxists nor sympathizers of the Soviet regime — that there is widespread support for the Soviet system among the people as a whole and the working people in particular. Even harsh domestic critics of the system bemoan the fact of the unpopularity of their own ideas among working people.[34] Although workers' opposition has periodically made itself felt on specific economic issues, there is no evidence of widespread working class support for oppositional tendencies. For example, an analysis of names on petitions calling for liberal reforms found that only 6 per cent of the names were those of workers.[35] While the apparently high level of support for the Soviet system amongst the working class is not proof that they rule (after all, a high percentage of U.S. working people support capitalism), it is certainly compatible with the position that they are the ruling class. Conversely, if there had been significant evidence (which there is not) that most workers were disenchanted with the Soviet system, this would constitute strong evidence that they don't rule.

The Communist Party

The most important institution in Soviet society is the Communist Party. Its influence and guiding role are all pervasive. An examination of the social composition of its rank and file and its leadership, as well as of its processes of decision making, can therefore be expected to give us a good idea of the power of various social groups in both the party apparatus itself and society as a whole.

Social Composition

In 1976, 41.6 per cent of the membership of the Communist Party were manual workers (including workers on state farms), 13.9 per cent were peasants on collective farms and 44.5 per cent were white collar workers and intelligentsia. In comparison with the occupational structure of the Soviet Union in 1973, these figures reflected an under-representation of manual workers by a factor of 0.69 and an over-representation of white collar persons and the intelligentsia by 1.71.[36] Trends in the social composition of the Party over time are reported in Table 5.1.

Table 5.1 reflects the fact that during the 1930s and 1940s white collar workers and intelligentsia were heavily favoured in the Party's recruitment policies. By the mid 1950s they were actually the majority of party members while manual workers represented less than one-third of the total membership. Since the mid 1950s, however, there has been a steady tendency for the proportion of white collar workers and intelligentsia to decrease and that of manual workers to increase. Through the early 1960s manual workers were about 45 per cent of all new recruits to the Party.[37] Since the 23rd Party Congress in 1966, well over half of all new recruits have been industrial workers and in the major industrial areas the number has been between 60 and 70 per cent. In the most recent period (1971-76), manual workers have been 57.6 per cent of all new party members.[38] 'Specialists' (i.e. the professional intelligentsia), on the other hand, were only 24.2 per cent of recruits in 1971-72, compared to 27.3 per cent in 1962-70 and 26.4 per cent in 1952-55.[39] There is no evidence that manual workers are being pushed into the background in the C.P.S.U.

In 1976, enterprise directors and top level state officials were four per cent of all party members, while 10.8 per cent were scientists, teachers, artists and medical professionals, and 17.8 per cent were agricultural specialists, engineers and technicians.[40] The policy is to maintain, if not increase, the relative number of specialists being admitted into the Party (engineers, technicians, agronomists, doctors, teachers, economists, etc.) and to decrease recruitment from administrative positions.[41] Official Soviet literature proudly emphasizes the recruitment of scientists and other professionals.[42]

Decision Making Within the Party

In the 1920s, fundamental and often bitter debate occurred at the plenary sessions of the Party Congresses. From the 1930s to 1950s the plenary sessions came instead to serve the function of expressing the solidarity and unity of the Party and boosting the Party's and country's morale. Votes became unanimous and debates perfunctory. The real debates and decision making occurred in committees, the Politburo, the press and through the other institutions already outlined. Recent evidence indicates that the Party Congress is once again a genuinely deliberative body where real decisions are made.

The principal decision making organs of the Party are its Politburo (with about 15 full members, it normally seems to be the more important organ) and the Central Committee which elects the Politburo. But the Central Committee seems to be becoming an increasingly central decision making body. A telling event which demonstrated the power of the Central Committee was the attempted removal of Khrushchev in 1957. After a majority of the Politburo voted to dismiss him as secretary of the Party, he refused to resign, taking his case instead to the Central Committee which upheld him.[43]

Since the 1950s there has been renewed emphasis on democratization and wider participation in the Party, and more frequent meetings of Party bodies, some of which had fallen into disuse (e.g. there were no Party Congresses between 1939 and 1952). Rank and file initiative has been increasingly stimulated and broader participation encouraged.[44] There is considerable evidence that inner party democracy exists and that it includes wide ranging criticism and self-criticism. This fills the party press and is expressed at party meetings and public gatherings.[45] The percentage of delegates to Party

Table 5.1
The Class Composition of C.P.S.U. Membership: 1924-1976

Percentage of All Members and Candidates

	1924	1930	1932	1956	1961	1966	1971	1976
Manual workers	44.0%	65.3%	65.2%	32.0%	34.5%	37.8%	40.1%	41.6%
Peasants	28.8	20.2	26.9	17.1	17.5	16.2	15.1	13.9
White-collar workers and others	27.2	14.5	7.9	50.9	48.0	46.0	44.8	44.5

Source: T.H. Rigby, *Communist Party Membership in the USSR*, p.327 and *The Current Digest of the Soviet Press*, 29 September 1976, p.3.

Congresses who are workers and peasants has increased significantly. At the 1952 Party Congress these groups represented only 15 per cent of all delegates, but in 1959 they comprised 31 per cent.[46] On the other hand, it must be pointed out that in 1966 higher level party and government officials (i.e. full-time members of the party or state apparatus), who represented only 2.1 per cent of all party members, were 40 per cent of all delegates to the 23rd Party Congress, and 81 per cent of all those elected to the Central Committee.[47]

New rules passed in the 1960s stipulate that party officials must rotate in office. At the Central Committee and Politburo level, one-fourth of the membership must turn over at each Party Congress (held every four years); at the lowest levels one-half must turn over at each election; and at inter- mediate levels one-third. Further, members of executive Party bodies cannot be elected more than three times. There can, however, be exceptions to these rules for those who receive more than three-quarters of the vote.[48] In practice, however, from 1966 to 1971 there was no turnover among the full members of the Politburo, although there was a 24 per cent turnover in the Central Committee, a 21 per cent turnover of Republic first secretaries and a 43 per cent turnover of Obkom first secretaries.[49]

Party rules also guarantee the formal right of any member to criticize any Party leaders.[50] The draft of the Party Programme on political, economic and cultural issues is put up for nation-wide preliminary discussion before it is revised and adopted by the Party. The Party units in institutions also mix all strata of the population. For example, in institutions of higher education, Party committees include full professors, administrators, junior instructors, graduate students and undergraduate students. This has a definite demo- cratizing influence on the Party.[51]

The Party, to guide Soviet society, relies heavily on its moral prestige, on setting an example, inspiring people and persuasion. Party members have no special privileges except undoubtedly an enhanced chance of promotion. They carry a considerable extra burden in being expected to set standards of exemplary conduct, volunteer for public service activities and otherwise behave like the 'new Soviet man'.[52] Even the harshest Western academic critics of the Soviet Union almost all agree that the Party does command the popular support necessary for the system to function effectively.

In summary, there is substantial evidence that a considerable degree of internal party democracy exists, that the Party has considerable support in the working class, and that the two-thirds of its members who are ordinary working people play an active and influential role in party affairs. Nevertheless, it is almost certainly the case that the one-third of the Party who are professionals — teachers, engineers, technicians, managers, officials, scientists, economists, agronomists, etc. — do exert influence greatly out of proportion to their numbers, thus in considerable degree reducing the influence that the manual classes can exert on Soviet society through the Party.

Social Background of the Leaders

Another very important mechanism of popular control can be the immersion of the power elite in the producing classes, especially the manual working class. To the extent they are recruited from this class, maintain close contacts with it and are socially, culturally and ideologically integrated with the working people, they must be heavily influenced by them. Common origins, in a society in which there is no property owning class to attract them, and thus separate working people from their origins, are a strong force bringing the leaders to think and act like the common people from which they come. Common life style, participation in physical labour, shared friendship patterns, close immersion in popular activities, and exposure to the same ideas are important forces which can make the decisions of the power elite those of the people.

The Central Committee of the C.P.S.U.
Of all 360 (full and candidate) Central Committee members in 1966, 42 per cent were engaged in full-time party work, 28 per cent were in the government apparatus, 14 per cent were in the military or police, and 4 per cent (15 members) were full-time workers. However, most of the 360 had working class or peasant backgrounds. Twenty-seven per cent were children of manual workers, 35 per cent children of peasants, 12 per cent children of non-manual workers and for 26 per cent no information could be found. It would appear then that at least two-thirds of Central Committee members and probably more (considering that many low level white collar jobs are counted as non-manual and many of those for whom no information was available are probably from poorer backgrounds) are from the lower strata.[53]   Comparing Central Committee members between 1917 and 1951 with those in the period 1966 to 1971 shows that very little has changed.[54] The overwhelming majority continue to come from humble origins.

One further point. In 1956, only six per cent of the Central Committee also held jobs as industrial officials and only 20 per cent were ever industrial managers.[55] Thus industrial management is not the route to top positions in the Party.[56]

The Politburo of the C.P.S.U.

Of the 15 full members of the Politburo of the C.P.S.U. in 1971, ten (i.e. 66 per cent) had at some point in their careers been manual workers (the mean average experience of all Politburo members in manual labour was two years). On the other hand, the same percentage also had had experience as managers (with an average experience of 3.3 years). This represented an increase in both categories over the 1951 Politburo where 45 per cent had had experience as manual workers and 18 per cent as industrial managers. It should be noted however that, while the number with experience as manual workers has increased, the average experience as manual workers has declined. The over-riding tendency would seem to be for Politburo members to more and more be career party people.[57] The typical career pattern of 1971 Politburo members includes a period as a manual worker in their youth, a diploma course in a technical school followed by a managerial job in industry, then a position in the party apparatus which includes a period as regional party secretary. The Party leaders tend then to be generalists rather than specialists and have had a wide range of experience.

Government Ministers

There seem to be rather distinct differences in career pattern separating leading Party officials, industrial directors and economic ministers, and senior government officials (other than economic ministers). Most economic ministers and top managers, while they are usually Party members, do not have experience at full-time Party posts.[58] Heads of economic ministries tend to have had careers in industry. Likewise very few Party officials transfer to government jobs. From 1950 to 1970 a total of only five government ministers switched between Party and government jobs.[59] One study showed that only two per cent of Party officials are ever transferred to Union level government jobs and only 15 per cent to Republic government level jobs.[60] Recruitment to both top managerial and governmental positions appears to be determined by education, qualifications, performance and politics; and promotion seems to be on the basis of merit and politics.[61]

Perhaps more importantly, and as was seen in the previous chapter, of the 47 government ministers of the U.S.S.R. in 1966 40 per cent of those for whom information was available had manual working class parents, 27 per cent were of peasant origin, 15 per cent had parents who were in lower level white collar positions and 18 per cent grew up as children of the intelligentsia.[62]

Enterprise Directors

A study in Kazan in 1967 showed that 75.3 per cent of the executives of economic enterprises and state organizations came from manual and peasant backgrounds and that only 8.6 per cent of their parents had higher education.[63] The clear majority of managerial personnel thus are not children of the intelligentsia, although the latter do have a better chance of becoming managers than

do the children of manual workers or peasants.[64] Industrial managers seem
generally to come from much the same types of background as do Party
officials, i.e. they tend to have parents who were peasants, manual workers and
unskilled employees.[65]

In 1967 about 68 per cent of directors had a higher education, mostly at
engineering institutes.[66] The career pattern of enterprise directors starts on the
shop floor as an assistant foreman and involves a series of promotions through
production jobs.[67] Both because of their engineering training and their direct
production experience throughout their careers, Soviet managers are considerably more familiar with production processes than are Western capitalist
directors.

There is considerable managerial turnover, with transfers decided on by
the ministries to which an enterprise is responsible. Thus any tendency to
develop proprietary attitudes towards (let alone proprietary rights in) a given
enterprise is undermined. Managerial security of tenure has, however,
increased a lot since 1940.[68] Recruitment and promotion depend on qualifications, performance and political loyalty to the principles of Marxism-
Leninism as interpreted by the C.P.S.U. Top enterprise directors must normally be trusted Party members who are active politically and accept the leadership of the Party.[69] There is no evidence that managers pass on their prerogatives to their relatives.

Training in Marxist principles plays an important part in the education of
managers.[70] In-depth interviews have shown that managers take seriously
their belief in industrialization, patriotism and service to their fellow human
beings.[71] They seem to be motivated by a combination of material and
moral incentives which include genuine dedication to socialist principles.

After the death of Stalin in 1953, one of the leading contenders for the top
leadership position, Malenkov, tended to articulate the interests of Soviet
managers and in turn received their support. Khrushchev, however, who was
the representative of the Party apparatus and an articulator of proletarian
rhetoric, decisively defeated Malenkov.[72] During the period that followed
(1957 to 1965), the managerial stratum was clearly subordinated to the Party
which made it very clear that the managers were in a subordinate position.[73]
While the position of managers improved somewhat after 1965, they remain
clearly subordinate to the Communist Party which closely directs their
activities.[74] Although the managerial stratum consistently pushes for greater
autonomy in the running of their enterprises, they show very little interest in
or ability to assume leadership of Soviet society as a whole.[75] On the
contrary, if only because of the effectiveness of training and promotion
policies, and because of their close supervision by the Communist Party, they
seem to accept the political leadership of the Party.

Inheritance of Top Positions
There is no tendency for there to be any inheritance of government, party or
managerial positions. I have never come across any evidence that there is a
tendency to pass on higher government, Party, or enterprise office to one's

relatives. (Of course there is a passing on of enhanced probabilities of making it into the intelligentsia as a whole). Neither Lenin, Stalin, Khrushchev, Brezhnev, Kosygin or any other top officials have ever, as far as I could determine, successfully passed on top governmental, managerial or party prerogatives to their children or other relatives (even Khrushchev's attempt to put his son-in-law in a leading position proved short-lived). This fact makes the Soviet Union very different from Western capitalist, or feudal and slave societies where those who control property are virtually certain to pass on their positions to their children.

In summary, there appears to be no tendency for the power elite of Party, government and economic enterprise officials to be self-perpetuating across the generations. In each generation the majority of incumbents starts life in humble positions. Further, there is no significant exchange of positions between the top managerial and the top governmental and party personnel. In both these respects, the Soviet Union differs fundamentally from Western capitalist countries. The data presented in this section is fully compatible with the thesis that the productive classes exercise control over the state, Party and enterprises through providing the majority of incumbents of the leading positions in all three sectors.

Structural Determinants of State Policies

Socialist, like capitalist, societies have a structural logic operating independently of the will of their power elite. The capitalist state is forced to behave in certain ways regardless of the ideology of top political office-holders because of the structural necessity to guarantee profits, ensure ongoing capital accumulation, and in general to maintain business confidence. The decisions reached and the probabilities of their successful implementation are in a large measure a product of the laws of capitalism, in the sense that an economic collapse would result if the leaders of the state followed anything other than one of a very limited set of options which are viable within the capitalist logic. Parallel factors operate in a socialist society still surrounded by a capitalist world. A rather limited set of options are imposed on its power elite by the necessity to develop industrially in order to feed the people, to satisfy the aspirations of the people for a comfortable living standard, and to defend the society. Since they are dictated by the structure of the situation, decisions made by a socialist power elite, or directly by the people as a whole, would to a large extent be the same.

Barrington Moore and Herbert Marcuse argue that, independently of the direct mechanisms that exist for popular control over the Soviet state, the power elite's decisions must conform to the ideology which gives the system and their positions legitimacy.[76] This argument appears valid. In order to maintain the legitimacy of the system, the power elite must operate within the framework of Marxist-Leninist values, or face massive popular resistance (passive perhaps at first, but eventually active). The system requires massive active participation to function, and this cannot be compelled, although of course it can to a considerable degree be directed. Attempts to use terror or intimidation, or even purely economic incentives, to produce the enthusiastic participation that the system requires — being, as it is, a complex industrial society not dependent on markets and inheritance — would result in demoralization, resistance and social disintegration (as has happened in right-wing dictatorial regimes such as Portugal, Greece, Iran, etc.). It is a necessity to preserve the legitimacy of a system which has Marxism-Leninism as its guiding ideology. For this ideology is far more specific in its analysis and goals than Western liberal capitalist ideology. This necessity not only sets limits on the freedom of action of the power elite, but also forces it to take concrete measures towards egalitarianism and decentralization of decision making. Marxist-Leninist ideology requires movement towards the withering away of the state and the reduction of class distinctions. Only the extreme emergency of the 1930s and 1940s, when the imminent danger of foreign invasion and domestic subversion was most real, could justify, in the popular mind, movement in the opposite direction. But, once conditions settled down, and the threat of foreign intervention had subsided, and the basic industrialization of the country had been completed, anything other than a reversal of the course followed in the 1930s and 1940s would have produced a widening gulf between the Marxist-Leninist ideology, which was used to justify the position and decisions of the power elite, and the reality of life among the producing masses. Therefore, in order both to preserve their position (i.e. to avoid a legitimation crisis) and to realize their own self-conceptions (since it appears that the power elite for the most part takes Marxism—Leninism seriously and believes in its mission to strive towards communism), the power elite is required to take concrete steps towards communist transformation. i.e. It has to decrease wage differentials, increase popular involvement in decision making, raise social mobility and devolve state functions to mass organizations.

Summary and Conclusion

There appears to be a high level of political participation in the Soviet Union, both through formal governmental channels and through the process of public opinion formation in the mass media. Public debate on a wide range of topics is real and growing in depth and significance. Support for the regime is especially high amongst the working class. Manual workers are playing a greater and greater role in the self-management of enterprises. The Communist Party is becoming increasingly proletarian and democratic. Most leading officials and managers come from the ordinary working people. The pressures to maintain legitimacy push the power elite to take egalitarian and democratic measures. In sum, there appear to be numerous mechanisms by which real control is exerted by the producing classes over the power elite. The only important qualification to this statement is that the centre of gravity of power within the producing classes lies with the skilled workers and the technical and professional intelligentsia who seem to play a disproportionate role in public debates, the Communist Party, the government apparatus and the decision making processes in economic enterprises. While democratic life in the Soviet Union seems to be real, it is not dominated by the peasantry, and unskilled and semi-skilled workers; but rather by the upper levels of the working class and professionals and experts of various kinds.

While it is clear that major steps have been taken towards democratization since the mid 1950s (and that the Chinese thesis of the coming to power of a group of 'state capitalists' is not valid), it is not clear that such measures will continue in a linear fashion until there is full equality among occupational strata, and all state functions devolve to mass organizations and all people are active politically. It may well be that a considerable residue of privilege will be maintained by the power elite who will insist on maintaining the means to keep the initiative. Only the future can reveal the course that will be followed. But the high and growing level of popular involvement in Soviet institutions, the fact that Marxism-Leninism is taken very seriously by wide segments of the population and that clear steps are being taken in the direction of greater economic equality and political democratization (which of course creates rising expectations of further measures), and the growing economic prosperity of the country *vis-a-vis* its own past as well as *vis-a-vis* the Western capitalist countries (which reduces the credibility of appeals for sacrifice), are all important forces leading the working class to push effectively for still more equality and decentralization of decision making.

The formal institutions of the Soviets, and their auxiliary commissions and control bodies, the Communist Party with its increasing membership of workers and apparently growing internal decentralization of initiative, and the increasingly significant system of public debate and criticism, all appear to be becoming more and more central in the process of decision making. Given this mass participation, devolution of decision making and the increasing egalitarianism, there would seem to be a definite momentum which should increasingly reinforce these tendencies. It is possible that at some point the power elite and the professional intelligentsia will attempt to reverse the egalitarian trend (as they were able to do temporarily in Czechoslovakia in the mid 1960s). They may at least put the brake on further egalitarian and democratic measures (as they did in China in the periods before the Great Leap Forward, before the Cultural Revolution, and perhaps again since the death of Mao Tse-tung). But in such a case it is likely that something like a Great Proletarian Cultural Revolution could occur in the Soviet Union, since it seems unlikely that the working class would passively accept a recentralization of decision making and a movement towards greater inequality, without a struggle.

References

1. As examples of the Chinese and pro-Chinese positions on the Soviet state, see *How the Soviet Revisionists Carry Out All-Round Restoration of Capitalism in the USSR*, (Peking: Foreign Languages Press, 1968); *Down with the New Tsars, (ibid.* 1969); Yenan Books, (ed.), *Social Imperialism: Reprints from Peking Review*, (Berkeley: Yenan Books, n.d.); Martin Nicolaus, *Restoration of Capitalism in the USSR*, (Chicago: Liberator Press, 1975); Revolutionary Union, *How Capitalism Has Been Restored in the Soviet Union and What This Means for the World Struggle*, (Chicago: The Revolutionary Union, 1974).
2. For the Soviets' own position, see for example: M. Perfilyev, *Soviet Democracy and Bourgeois Sovietology*, (Moscow: Progress, n.d.); Progress Publishers, *The Soviet Form of Popular Government*, (Moscow: Progress, 1972); G. Shahnazarov, *Socialist Democracy*, (Moscow: Progress, 1974); Victor Torovtsev, *People's Control in Socialist Society*, (Moscow: Progress, 1973).
3. Progress Publishers, *The Soviet Union Today*, (Moscow: Progress, 1975).
4. Ronald J. Hill, 'The CPSU in a Soviet Election Campaign', *Soviet Studies*, XXVIII No.4, (October 1976).
5. D. Richard Little, 'Soviet Parliamentary Committees after Khrushchev', *Soviet Studies*, 24:1, (July 1972); Jerry Hough, 'Political Participation in the Soviet Union', *Soviet Studies*, 28:1, (January 1976); Jerry Hough, 'The Soviet System: Petrification or Pluralism', *Problems of Communism*, March-April 1975; H. Gordon Skilling, 'Groups in Soviet Politics', in H. Gordon Skilling and Franklyn Griffiths, *Interest Groups in Soviet Politics*, (Princeton: Princeton University Press, 1971); Shugo Minagua, 'The Function of the Supreme Soviet Organs and Problems of Their Institutional Development', *Soviet Studies*, 27:1, (January 1975).
6. See Ronald Hill, *Soviet Political Elites*, (London: Martin Robertson, 1977), Chs. 5 and 6.
7. Mark Hopkins, *Mass Media in the Soviet Union*, (New York: Pegasus, 1970), Chs. 1 and 8; and Skilling, *op. cit.*
8. Hopkins, *op. cit.*, Ch.1.
9. Hough, 'The Soviet System', *op. cit.*, and Hough, 'The Brezhnev Era: The Man and the System', *Problems of Communism*, November-December 1974.
10. Hough, 'The Soviet System', *op. cit.*
11. Franklyn Griffiths, 'A Tendency Analysis of Soviet Decision Making', in Skilling and Griffiths, *op. cit.*
12. Skilling, *op. cit.*
13. Hopkins, *op. cit.*, Ch.1.
14. Robert Osborn, *Soviet Social Policies*, (Homewood, Ill.: The Dorsey Press, 1970), pp.13-15.
15. Skilling, *op. cit.*, pp.43-4.
16. *Ibid.*, p.44; Hopkins, *op. cit.*, pp.302-11.
17. *Ibid.*, pp.303-4.
18. *Ibid.*, Chs. 1 and 8.
19. *Ibid.*, p.298.

20. *Ibid.*, p.306.
21. For discussions of the public debate on the relation of the C.P. to the military, see, Roman Kolkowicz, 'The Military', pp.151-66, in Skilling and Griffiths, *op. cit.*; for the public debate on proletarianizing higher education, see Osborn, *op. cit.*, Ch.4; for the public debate on writers and artists, see Ernest Simmons, 'The Writers', in Skilling and Griffiths, *op. cit.*, and for the public debate on economic reforms, see Paul Gregory and Robert Stuart, *Soviet Economic Performance*, (New York: Harper & Row, 1974), Ch. 10, and Howard Sherman, *The Soviet Economy*, (Boston: Little Brown, 1969), Ch.11. For discussion of the environmental debate, see Donald R. Kelley, 'Environmental Policy-Making in the USSR', *Soviet Studies*, XXVIII, No.4, October 1976. See Murray Yanowitch, *Social and Economic Inequality in the Soviet Union*, (White Plains, N.Y.: M.E. Sharpe, 1977), for a good discussion of many of the public debates of the mid 1970s in the U.S.S.R., especially on the questions of privileged access to higher education of children of the intelligentsia, the problem of low birth rates and the role of women, the election of managers and the question of enterprise democracy and payment systems.
22. Donald Barry and Harold Berman, 'The Jurists', in Skilling and Griffiths, *op. cit.*, p.323ff.
23. Skilling, *op. cit.*, and Richard Judy, 'The Economists', and Barry and Berman, *op. cit.*, both in Skilling and Griffiths, *op. cit.*
24. Skilling, *op. cit.*, pp.33-8.
25. Turovtsev, *op. cit.*, p.156.
26. H. Gordon Skilling, 'Groups in Soviet Politics'; and H. Gordon Skilling, 'Group Conflict in Soviet Politics', in Skilling and Griffiths, *op. cit.*
27. Frank Parkin, *Class Inequality and Political Order*, (New York: Praeger, 1971), pp.175-6. See the discussion of the Czech events in Chapter 7.
28. Turovtsev, *op. cit.*, pp.21-2; David Brodersen, *The Soviet Worker*, (New York: Random House, 1966), p.143; and Vladimir Voinovich, 'Oh, for a Room of My Own', *New York Times Magazine*, 20 June 1976.
29. Turovtsev, *op. cit.*, Ch.3.
30. Hough, 'The Man and the System', *op. cit.*, p.10.
31. Progress Publishers, *The Soviet Union Today*, *op. cit.*, Ch.2; and Hough, 'The Man and the System', *op. cit.*, p.10.
32. Hough, 'Political Participation in the Soviet Union', *op. cit.*, p.11.
33. *Ibid.*; and Hopkins, *op. cit.*, Chs. 1 and 8.
34. Alec Nove, 'Is There a Ruling Class in the USSR?', *Soviet Studies*, 27:4, (October 1975); Steven White, 'Contradiction and Change in State Socialism', *Soviet Studies*, 26:1, (January 1974).
35. *Ibid.*, p.51; and David Lane, *The Socialist Industrial State*, (London: George Allen and Unwin, 1976), p.115.
36. For figures on Soviet social structure, see Murray Yanowitch, *Social and Economic Inequality in the Soviet Union*, (White Plans, N.Y.: M.E. Shape, 1977), p.111.
37. T.H. Rigby, *Communist Party Membership in the U.S.S.R.*, (Princeton: Princeton University Press, 1963), p.306.
38. White, *op. cit.*, p.53; and *Current Digest of the Soviet Press*, 29 September 1976, p.1; T.H. Rigby, 'Soviet Party Membership Under Brezhnev',

Soviet Studies, XXVIII, (July 1976), Table 6.
39. M. Matthews, *Class and Society in Soviet Russia*, (New York: Walker and Co., 1972), p.223.
40. See *Current Digest of the Soviet Press*, 29 September 1976, p.3.
41. Perfilyev, *op. cit.*, p.121.
42. Progress Publishers, *The Soviet Union Today, op. cit.*, p.48.
43. Jeremy Azrael, *Managerial Power and Soviet Politics*, (Cambridge: Harvard University Press,1966), Ch.5.
44. M. Fainsod, p.174.
45. *Ibid.*, p.211.
46. Brodersen, *op. cit.*, p.228.
47. David Lane, *The End of Inequality?* (Baltimore: Penguin, 1971), p.122.
48. Fainsod, *op. cit.*, p.212.
49. Hough, 'The Soviet System', *op. cit.*, p.32; and Gregory Grossman, 'An Economy of Middle Age', in *Problems of Communism*, Vol.25, (November-December 1974), p.32.
50. Perfilyev, *op. cit.*, p.132.
51. Hough, 'Political Participation in the Soviet Union', *op. cit.*, p.9.
52. Fainsod, *op. cit.*, and Perfilyev, *op. cit.*, Ch.3.
53. Lane, *op. cit.*, p.122.
54. *Ibid.*, p.123.
55. D. Granick, *The Red Executive*, (Garden City, N.Y.: Doubleday, 1961), pp.274-5.
56. Lane, *op. cit.*, pp.124-5.
57. T.H. Rigby, 'The Soviet Politburo', *Soviet Studies*, 24:1, (July 1972).
58. Lane, *op. cit.*, p.127.
59. *Ibid.*, pp.124-5.
60. *Ibid.*
61. *Ibid.*, p.128.
62. *Ibid.*, p.126; and Azrael, *op. cit.*, pp.157-72.
63. O.I. Shkaratan, 'Social Ties and Social Mobility', in Murray Yanowitch and Wesley Fisher, (eds.), *Social Stratification and Mobility in the USSR*, (White Plains, N.Y.: International Arts and Sciences Press, 1973).
64. Granick, *op. cit.*, Ch.3; and John Hardt and Theodore Frankel, 'The Industrial Managers', in Skilling and Griffiths, *op. cit.*, p.180.
65. Granick, *op. cit.*, p.273; and S. White, 'Contradiction and Change in State Socialism', *Soviet Studies*, 26:1, (January 1974).
66. Hardt and Frankel, *op. cit.*, p.193.
67. Granick, *op. cit.*, Chs. 4 and 5.
68. Hardt and Frankel, *op. cit.*, p.194.
69. Granick, *op. cit.*, Ch.12; and Azrael, *op. cit.*, pp.128-9.
70. *Ibid.*, pp.157-62.
71. Hardt and Frankel, *op. cit.*, p.186.
72. Azrael, *op. cit.*, pp.131-9.
73. *Ibid.*, pp.137-47.
74. *Ibid.*, pp.147-51, Ch.6; and Gregory and Stuart, *op. cit.*, pp.179-93.
75. Azrael, *op. cit.*, pp.167-73.
76. See Barrington Moore, *Soviet Politics: The Dilemma of Power*, (Cambridge: Harvard University Press, 1950); and Herbert Marcuse, *Soviet Marxism*, (New York, Columbia University Press, 1958), for

this argument. Moore's, Marcuse's and my own argument on the role
of legitimization parallel the argument developed by Nicos Poulantzas
in his *Political Power and Social Classes,* (New York: Humanities, 1975);
and the *Kapitalistate Collective:* see 'Recent Developments in Marxist
Theories of the Capitalist State', David Gold, Clarence Y. H. Lo, Erik
Olin Wright, *Monthly Review,* 27:5 & 6, October-November, 1975.
These latter authors argue that the state in capitalist society has a
'relative autonomy' from direct capitalist class control in order to
guarantee its legitimacy in the eyes of the masses. Likewise, it can be
maintained that the Soviet state has a 'relative autonomy' from being
controlled by the Soviet 'power elite' or intelligentsia for the same reason.

6. Soviet Foreign Relations: The Logic of Trade and the Uses of the Military

The Chinese and their supporters around the world accuse the Soviet Union of being a 'social imperialist superpower'. By this they mean that there is no essential difference between either the causes or the effects of the Soviet Union's international economic, political and military relations and those of the leading capitalist countries of the West (especially the U.S.). The Chinese since 1967 have been arguing that the Soviet Union is essentially a monopoly capitalist economy ('of the Nazi type'), and thus that all the basic laws of monopoly capitalism, including the logic of imperialism as outlined by Lenin in his book *Imperialism: The Highest Stage of Capitalism,* operate.[1] In this chapter we will begin to examine the validity of this aspect of the Chinese claim.

Definitions

By imperialism is meant the political domination of one nation by the ruling group in another in order to exploit economically the dominated nation. Imperialism then has two basic components: (1) economic exploitation through trade, investments, plunder, migration, etc; and (2) political domination by military occupation or threat thereof, support of local ruling groups, cultural hegemony, etc. Imperialism can be associated with any type of social formation — class society or non-class society, capitalist or pre-capitalist.

In some Marxist circles the term 'imperialism' is used in a different sense. Inspired by the title of Lenin's book *Imperialism: The Highest Stage of Capitalism,* 'imperialism' is referred to synonymously with 'advanced capitalism', 'state monopoly capitalism' or 'late capitalism'. Such usage of the term is based on a misreading of Lenin who gave his book the title he did in order to underline the valid point that advanced capitalism necessarily generates imperialism (i.e. that imperialism is an organic outgrowth of advanced capitalism and not a policy). In *Imperialism: The Highest Stage of Capitalism* Lenin talks about 'capitalistic imperialism'. He does not use the term as many of his followers today do as synonymous with 'late capitalism'. For example he argues: 'Colonial policy and imperialism existed before the latest stage of capitalism and even before capitalism. Rome, founded on slavery, pursued a colonial policy and achieved imperialism' (*Imperialism:* Chapter 4, Paragraph 13). In this book the term 'imperialism' is used the way Lenin used it.

In the Marxist-Leninist tradition the use of the adjective 'social' before a noun indicates that, although a socialist ideology is being used to justify a course of action, the objective results of that action are the same as achieved by the unqualified noun, e.g. the communist parties of the world referred to the Social Democrats as 'social fascists' from 1928 to 1935. Thus the Chinese use of 'social imperialism' means that, although the Soviet Union justifies its international relations with a Marxist ideology, objectively it behaves just like the U.S.A. (and for the same reasons). The Chinese, following Lenin's analysis, claim that both the U.S. and the U.S.S.R. (like all monopoly capitalist economies) are driven to imperialism by the need to export capital and to secure raw materials.

Class societies are imperialistic because of their inherent economic logic. If a socialist society were imperialist, however, it would be so because of the *policies* followed by its leading forces, not because of any inherent logic. Thus a socialist society is less likely to be imperialist than a class society. However, a socialist imperialism cannot be ruled out *a priori*.

According to Lenin, capitalism in its monopoly stage is necessarily imperialistic because of the impossibility of the masses being able to purchase the rapidly growing output of industry and the consequently limited chance for profitable investment opportunities. The only real possibility for profits to be successfully reinvested therefore lies in the less developed countries where non-monopolized markets continue to exist, wages are low and the rate of profit is higher. Colonialism and neo-colonialism are then required in order to protect these investments in the poorer countries, and to guarantee against intrusion by other imperialist powers. The motive force behind imperialism is thus the endemic tendency to underconsumption inherent in monopoly capitalism (Lenin, *Imperialism,* Chapter 4).

Some Marxists argue that the motive force behind imperialism is the tendency for the rate of profit to decline in the advanced capitalist countries due to the rising organic composition of capital. In this argument capital would flow to the low organic composition areas of the world that were still unindustrialized and where wages were low. Colonialism and neo-colonialism would be required for the same reasons as in the underconsumption argument.

Neither logic of imperialism is a part of the Soviet economic system. We have already seen in Chapter Three that there is no tendency for the rate of profit to decline in the Soviet economy. We have also seen that, far from stagnation, the Soviet economy suffers from endemic shortages of labour and producer goods (the opposite of market economies that have a surplus of both workers and productive plant). Thus, far from having a capital surplus which seeks investment overseas, the Soviet economy has a shortage. Because it is guided by a plan, resources are allocated by rational and planned criteria, i.e. wages are set at a level to clear the market for consumer goods thereby ensuring that all of them are bought (i.e. making sure there is no tendency for underconsumption of consumer goods). Likewise, capital goods are allocated in such a manner that they are all used. (In fact there is always a demand for capital goods greater than the supply.) Further, there is no tendency for the rate of investment to slow down because of inadequate profit opportunities. In fact, the Soviets maintain a very high rate of capital investment which consistently averages twice that of the U.S. Thus there is no inherent economic logic requiring overseas investment in order to counteract either a tendency for profits to decline, or underconsumption.[2]

It should also be noted that the Soviet Union has the richest and most complete assortment of raw materials of any country in the world and so has no inherent requirement for dominating other areas for the sake of providing itself with secure and cheap raw materials.

Since there is no inherent imperialist logic within the Soviet economy, the Soviet Union could only be 'social imperialist' as a matter of *policy*. Because its economy really does operate according to an economic plan rather than by the impersonal logic of market forces, whether its foreign relations are aggressive and expansionist is a matter of choice (i.e. they are policies), not a matter of structural compulsion as they would be if Lenin's argument applied. Although the Soviet system is not necessarily imperialist, it could nevertheless still be imperialistic. That is, Soviet foreign relations could: (1) politically dominate other nations (in the process subordinating working-class and progressive forces and securing military advantages for the Soviets); and (2) secure special economic gains through market manipulation, control of raw materials and control over local production. To prove that the Soviet Union is social imperialist, both elements must be demonstrated. If political domination only, but not economic exploitation, is demonstrated, then all that is shown is that the U.S.S.R. is hegemonic.

The question of whether the Soviet Union can be regarded as a social imperialist superpower or is hegemonic is examined throughout the next four chapters: this chapter on trade and the military, Chapter Seven on Soviet relations with Eastern Europe, Chapter Eight on Soviet relations with the non-socialist countries of the Third World and Chapter Nine on Soviet relations with China and Cuba.

In this Chapter I will examine the nature of Soviet foreign trade — its linkages with its domestic economy, the dynamic of the balance of trade, the composition of imports and exports, and the terms of trade. Parallels and differences with the trading patterns and structures of Western capitalist countries will be focused on. This chapter will also examine the nature of the Soviet military and the principles behind both its composition and deployment. Again, the focus will be on similarities and differences with the armed forces of the advanced capitalist countries of the West. Here we will thus be concerned with basic processes which could be the dynamic, as well as a manifestation, of Soviet social imperialism in general. The subsequent chapters will focus on specific relations with three different categories of countries: the more or less industrial socialist states of Eastern Europe, the poorer non-socialist countries of the Third World and the socialist Third World countries (China and Cuba).

Soviet Foreign Trade

All foreign trade of the Soviet Union is carried on by state trading corporations (in the late 1960s there were about 30 of them), each specializing in a different type of commodity over which it has a monopoly. These corporations have the exclusive right to buy locally produced goods for export and to purchase foreign goods for import. The Ministry of Foreign Trade maintains tight control over them through detailed plans which specify how the trading corporations shall operate re volume, assortment, prices and transport of commodities.[3]

Profitability plays no role in the behaviour of the trading corporations. They purchase Soviet goods at the prevailing domestic prices and sell them overseas at the prevailing world market price. The difference between the domestic and external prices goes to the general foreign exchange reserves of the Soviet state. The Soviet domestic industrial enterprises have neither knowledge of nor interest in the price or disposition of export goods. As for imports from abroad, the state trading corporations purchase these at world market prices utilizing funds from the general Soviet state reserves. They then sell the imported commodities to the domestic consuming enterprise at the prevailing internal price. If the latter is less than the world market price, the enterprise is thus subsidized by the state; if more, the enterprise subsidizes the general state treasury. Since the Soviet productive enterprises have no economic involvement in foreign trade (although of course they are affected by imports of technology), fluctuations in world prices have no impact on their output plans, which are determined by the requirements of the overall economic plan. Generally the Soviets tend to buy and sell in the international market well below their domestic prices. This implies a subsidy for export oriented industries and a tax on import oriented industries.[4]

The Soviet economy is isolated from world market (i.e. capitalist) forces by the system of trade planning and centralized prices. Domestic enterprises are thereby shielded from fluctuations in world market conditions. The lack of correspondence between domestic Soviet prices and world market prices more or less requires bilateralism in trade relations, i.e. agreements to trade a certain set of commodities for a certain other set of commodities because there is no common scale of value that might serve to measure trade volume. This problem is especially acute in trade relations among socialist countries, none of whose domestic prices are governed by the law of value. Socialist countries thus tend to exchange goods among themselves at the world market price since deviations from the world market price are regarded by one or another party as evidence that they are losing from the trade. If they are not being paid as much as they could get in the West for their exports or if they could get more in imports for less outlay in the West, they feel exploited. The Comecon countries of Eastern Europe make, however, certain negotiated adjustments in world prices to try and rid them of erratic fluctuations, monopolistic elements and the effect of transport costs. But once a set of prices is negotiated among the Comecon countries, they usually stay in effect for approximately a five year period.[5]

It is interesting to note that in the ten years or so after World War II trade relations between the Soviet Union and Eastern Europe were not governed by the above principles. Trade was instead determined by a combination of the labour theory of value and the explicit demand that the former Axis countries should subsidize the reconstruction of the Soviet Union. Raw materials produced in Eastern Europe, Polish coal being the most notorious case, were paid for by the Soviet Union on the basis of the labour time it took to produce them, with no regard for what the world price happened to be or the need to take into account the depletion of scarce resources. The resentment produced by the application of the labour theory of value to the terms of international trade between socialist countries (because of the considerable divergence of prices from those on the world market) resulted, in the mid-1950s, in the scrapping of this basis for establishing the terms of trade, and its replacement by a system which caused much less resentment.

The state plan for foreign trade, in terms of which the state trading corporations operate, is geared to material balances (i.e. a given quantity of trade by volume) and especially to ensuring appropriate imports.[6] The plan starts with an estimate of how much of which kinds of goods are needed over and above what will be produced domestically. The planners then figure out the quantity of exports that will be necessary to pay for the required imports at prevailing world prices. They then examine domestic production to locate those commodities that are either likely to be produced in excess of domestic requirements or can easily be expanded to provide goods for export. Because the Soviet trade plan is geared to securing a set level of imports and to exporting only enough to ensure these imports, the resultant East-West trade level is relatively insensitive to world prices.[7]

The Soviet Union is the most self-sufficient industrial economy in the world. Total imports totalled only 4.7 per cent of its net material product in 1973. The U.S., the only other industrial country which approaches the Soviet Union in actual self-sufficiency, had imports constituting 5.4 per cent of its gross national product in 1973.[8] Since the Soviet concept, net material product, excludes services, it is considerably smaller than the equivalent Western concept of gross national product. The U.S.A.'s dependence on imports is therefore about one and a half times greater than the Soviet Union's. The Soviet Union's lack of dependence on imports is both because it has the richest raw material endowment of any country in the world (see the U.S. Department of Interior *Minerals Yearbook*), and because of its tendency to plan for minimizing its dependence on imports so as to isolate itself from pressures that can be put on it by capitalist countries. Conscious planning for autarchy was especially pronounced from the 1930s through to the mid-1950s. During these years trade was engaged in almost exclusively to obtain the materials and sophisticated machinery needed for the rapid industrialization of the country. By 1959 the Soviet Union was in a position to supply virtually all the industrial ingredients necessary for its growth without engaging in any trade at all. It had an abundance of coal and petroleum and virtually all the minerals necessary for an advanced industrial economy. When it did engage in foreign trade, it was because: (a) it could obtain certain materials or manufactured goods more cheaply or quickly through trade than it could produce them domestically; (b) it wanted to import technologically sophisticated equipment from the West to accelerate its economic growth; (c) it wanted, for political reasons, to support other socialist or the Third World countries; and (d) it needed a buffer for imbalances in the plan or to compensate for crop failures (thereby sparing the people emergency belt-tightening measures and assuring the economy of smoother growth). In general, then, the U.S.S.R. engages in trade primarily to organize more efficiently its domestic production and consumption and secondarily to lend economic support to other countries. It does not engage in trade because its economy could not operate successfully without such trade.[9]

All Soviet foreign trade is geared towards imports rather than exports, which is pretty much the opposite of capitalist countries' trade that focuses on exports and maintaining an export surplus. The capitalist economies have to focus on expanding exports for two reasons. Firstly, profits are to be made for individual enterprises by securing overseas markets. Secondly, maintaining overall economic prosperity and the capital accumulation process require finding export markets for the system as a whole, to counter the inherent tendency to underconsumption (which is promoted by workers not being paid enough to buy back everything that they produce). In contrast, exports for a planned economy like that of the Soviet Union are merely a necessary evil required in order to secure imports needed for more rapid economic growth. This is the opposite of the case of a capitalist economy whose *imports* tend to be the necessary evil generated by the money paid for exports. Here, of course, the greater the level of imports, the less the effect of exports in alleviating the surplus production problem and therefore the less the effect these exports have on promoting the continuation of the capital accumulation process, since the creation of new markets overseas (i.e. new outlets for surplus production) are negated by the sales of foreign produced goods imported into the capitalist economy (which thus deprives the country's corporations of their previous home markets).

Because the U.S.S.R.'s overall economy and foreign trade are governed by a plan, and because trade prices are not governed by the law of value, the Soviet Union prefers simple bilateral trade agreements with other governments or chambers of commerce. This is different from the practice of capitalist market economies where individual enterprises sell commodities overseas for money, money which has been generated through the sale of foreign produced commodities in the enterprises' own countries. In this system there need be no relation between the amount of imports and exports between any two given market economies since any deficit in one country's trade with a given country can be made up through multilateral trading with other countries. Because of the multilateral and unplanned nature of trade among market economies, foreign exchange or money markets become key in clearing international markets of goods. i.e. If an importer in country A wants to import goods from country B, he will purchase country B's currency on the international money market. The currency of the typical market capitalist countries is thus convertible and each currency has a price in terms of others.

The non-market socialist countries do not have convertible currencies. Their currencies cannot generally be bought and sold by Western importers and exporters. Those interested in importing Soviet goods must enter into a trade agreement stipulating both the imports desired and the exports to be exchanged with the appropriate Soviet trading corporations. Inconvertibility of currency, the corollary of bilateralism and state planning of trade, facilitates the integration of foreign trade into the overall economic plan.[10]

Bilateral trade agreements with countries typically cover two to six year periods. These agreements normally specify the total value of trade, the broad classes of goods to be traded, the mechanics of payment, methods of transport etc. General trade agreements are later filled out in detail with specific contracts stipulating exactly what will be exchanged under exactly what conditions of delivery.[11]

In market capitalist countries chronic trade deficits result in inflation, unemployment, declining growth rates, falling standards of living and often economic chaos because local industries lose out in their competitive struggle with foreign enterprises. Market mechanisms aided by the state attempt to lower costs (mostly domestic wages) and increase prices of imports (with a secondary effect of increasing all prices) in order to stimulate the economy and so counter the trade deficit. No such process occurs in non-market socialist economies for two reasons: (1) bilateral trade agreements generally ensure a relative balance of imports and exports, and (2) the insulation of domestic production and markets from the international market by virtue of the monopoly over trade of the foreign trading corporations prevents any trade deficit that might occur from having a significant effect on domestic pricing, wages, etc. (factors which are determined by the central plan).

If, as the Chinese claim, the system in the Soviet Union is one of monopoly capitalism and behaves according to the logic laid out in Lenin's *Imperialism: The Highest Stage of Capitalism,* we would expect that the U.S.S.R. would normally have a favourable balance of trade (a surplus of exports over imports), and that this would represent a significant proportion of capital formation. Since, according to Lenin's model, profitable domestic investment outlets would be blocked, the two major channels for allowing capital accumulation to continue would be foreign investment (perhaps in the form of foreign aid) and a surplus of exports over imports (more selling than buying overseas). In the following chapters Soviet foreign aid, the most likely channel for anything like overseas investments, is examined. Here it is shown that Soviet exports are unable to provide a significant channel for capital formation.

The ratio of the Soviet trade surplus to its fixed capital formation in the period 1970 to 1974 was only 0.8 per cent, which is slightly lower than in the 1950 to 1957 period when the average was 1.0 per cent. Clearly there is no tendency for the development of the mechanisms suggested by Lenin (the development of monopoly and the increased importance of a trade surplus). Moreover if the ratio between total exports and fixed capital formation is examined, it is seen to be virtually the same in 1950 to 1957 (16.6 per cent) as it was in 1970 to 1974 (16.0 per cent).[12] Clearly, exports could play only a tiny role in facilitating the formation of capital in the Soviet Union. No support for the thesis that the Soviet Union is run on the basis of capitalist imperialism of the type described by Lenin can be found in these statistics.

The ratio of raw material imports (excluding food) to net material product (N.M.P.) decreased considerably from the 1950s to the 1970s. While in the 1950s this ratio stood at approximately 1.5 per cent, in the 1970s it averaged only 0.6 per cent (see Table 6.1). Thus the Soviets have actually reduced their proportional reliance on imported raw materials to 40 per cent of what it had been 20 years before. If foodstuffs are included with other raw materials, a similar although not so sharp trend is seen. During the 1950s total raw material imports (including food) were 1.9 per cent of the Soviet net material product, while in the 1970-75 period they were 1.5 per cent. This trend of decreasing dependence on raw material imports is hardly what would be expected from a country which was transforming itself from socialism to social imperialism. It should be noted, however, that the ratio of total imports to N.M.P. has increased significantly from the 1950s to the 1970s. While in the first period it averaged around 3.2 per cent during the second it averaged around five per cent. The increasing reliance on imports in general thus makes the decreasing role of raw material imports all the more impressive. These opposite movements suggest that the Soviets are now engaging in foreign trade much more because it is convenient and advantageous to do so, rather than because it can obtain the necessary inputs for its economy in no other way (as would seem to have been much more the case in earlier periods).

The single biggest category of Soviet imports (see Table 6.2) is industrial equipment and machinery (35.5 per cent of the total in 1966-69). Fuels and raw materials (excluding food) are second at 24.8 per cent, followed by manufactured consumer goods (18.6 per cent) and foodstuffs (15.2 per cent). The trend over time has been a consistent increase in the percentage of industrial machinery and equipment in total imports and a reduction in the percentage of fuels and other raw materials while foodstuffs have stayed more or less constant. Again this would not be the pattern to be expected from a typical imperialist country of the advanced capitalist type (which we might expect to be importing principally and increasingly raw materials).

Turning to Soviet exports, over half are fuels and raw materials (51.2 per cent of the total in the period 1966 to 1969) and only 21.6 per cent industrial equipment and machinery (see Table 6.2). Since the early 1950s the percentage of fuels and raw materials in total exports has increased, as has the percentage of industrial equipment and machinery (while the share of foodstuffs has gone down). Again this pattern of exports differs from the typically capitalist imperialist country which tends to export principally manufactured goods.

Soviet trade with the non-socialist, less developed, capitalist countries is

Table 6.1
Soviet Imports in Relation to Net Material Product, 1950-1975

	Raw Material Including Food	Imports as %age of N.M.P. Excluding Food	Total Imports as %age of N.M.P.
1950-53	2.0%	1.6%	3.3%
1954-57	1.9	1.4	3.1
1958-61	1.8	1.3	3.3
1962-65	1.7	1.1	3.7
1966-69	1.4	0.9	3.5
1970-72	0.9	0.4	4.3
1973-75	2.0	0.9	5.8

Source: Paul Marer, *Soviet and East European Foreign Trade, 1946-69*, (Bloomington, Indiana: Indiana University Press, 1972), p.44; United Nations, *Yearbook of National Account Statistics 1976*, Vol.II, Table 2B; United Nations, *Yearbook of International Trade Statistics, 1975*, pp.984,985; and United Nations, *Statistical Yearbook, 1976*, Table 148; and earlier years' volumes from the same sources.

Table 6.2
Soviet Imports and Exports, 1950-1969

	Industrial Machinery		Fuels and Raw Materials (ex. foods)		Foods		Manufactured Consumer Goods	
	Imports (As %age of total)	Exports	Imports (As %age of total)	Exports	Imports (As %age of total)	Exports	Imports (As %age of total)	Exports
1950-53	23.2%	15.6%	48.5%	39.7%	16.5%	20.0%	6.9%	2.9%
1954-57	27.1	16.4	44.4	49.7	17.2	14.1	8.2	2.9
1958-61	27.9	19.2	40.0	53.3	13.2	13.6	16.7	3.0
1962-65	34.4	19.4	30.4	53.7	16.4	10.4	16.3	2.5
1966-69	35.5	21.6	24.8	51.2	15.2	10.4	18.6	2.4

Source: Paul Marer, *Soviet and East European Foreign Trade, 1946-1969*, pp.44, 53.

not characterized by the exploitation of these states. The terms of trade between Third World countries and the Soviet Union are generally considerably better (i.e. in favour of the Third World countries) than the terms of trade between the advanced capitalist countries and the Third World. In other words the Soviets tend to pay more for the exports of Third World countries and charge them less for their imports from the U.S.S.R. than do the advanced capitalist countries. This is documented in the detailed analyses of Soviet trade with India (see Chapter Eight) and Cuba (see Chapter Nine).

Finally, we should consider how significant is the fact that the socialist countries use approximations to world prices as the measure of value in trade among themselves. World prices of raw material exports are kept artificially low and prices of industrial products artificially high by the monopoly power of the transnational corporations and the imperialist policies of the advanced capitalist countries over the less developed raw material exporters. This means that the net raw material exporters among the socialist countries will suffer (be 'exploited') in their trade with the net exporters of industrial goods. But it is the Soviet Union that is the major supplier of raw materials to the East European countries which provide industrial products in return. The Soviet Union is a net raw material exporter and a net industrial good importer, and as such it suffers the same type of discrimination borne by the Third World countries which specialize in raw material exports. And it is the Eastern European countries who benefit from this situation.

It should be stressed that this method of pricing, considered together with the composition of trade between Eastern Europe and the U.S.S.R., means that the consequences of arguments, such as those of Arghiri Emmanuel, about unequal exchange between raw material producers and industrial exporters, work in reverse in the case of the Eastern European socialist countries. The unequal exchange between the Soviet Union and Eastern Europe operates to accelerate the growth of the smaller COMECON countries while slowing down the growth of the Soviet Union because of the 'inequitable' transfer of value from the latter to the former.

In summary, no evidence can be found in the structure, dynamic and patterns of Soviet foreign trade that either drive the Soviet Union to, or are instances of, social imperialism. The isolation of Soviet enterprises from the international capitalist market, the structural scarcity of domestic capital, the existence of perpetual excess demand, the logic of the balance of trade which is oriented towards importing rather than exporting, the rich natural resource endowment of the U.S.S.R. and the terms of trade which favour the Soviet Union's trading partners, all provide strong evidence against the thesis that the dynamic of Soviet trade is similar to that of capitalist countries.

The Soviet Military

In this section I will look both at Soviet military philosophy and, more importantly, at the actual strengths of the Soviet armed forces in order to examine whether they are in fact, as the Chinese as well as pro-NATO forces in the West claim, primarily oriented to aggressive and expansionist purposes or, as the Soviets themselves maintain, oriented to the defence of the Soviet Union.[13]

The Soviet analysis is that Western capitalism in general and U.S. capitalism in particular is inherently imperialist by nature and has consistently looked for in the past, and will continue to do so in the future, ways to undermine, and if possible destroy, the Soviet system as well as all socialist and progressive movements around the world. The official Soviet position is that only total disarmament, or at least the absolute prohibition and elimination of all nuclear weapons, will bring real security to the U.S.S.R. and the other socialist countries. But, in the absence of such disarmament, the greatest security for the Soviet Union lies in its not only having the nuclear capacity to deter an atomic attack from the U.S., but also to wage any nuclear war the U.S. initiates. The Soviets consider it quite possible that a U.S., faced with the decline of its international military and economic position, might act in an irrational and foolhardy way and attack the Soviet Union; or, alternatively, that a local conflict might escalate into a nuclear war that neither side anticipated or really wanted (e.g. another Cuban missile crisis or an Israeli-Arab conflict into which the U.S. and the U.S.S.R. could be drawn).

The Soviets view their military capacity, and their nuclear arsenal in particular, as the means by which the U.S. is constrained from attempting to roll back the advance of socialism around the world and is forced to respect the Soviet Union. In 1973 Brezhnev said:

> Together with our allies in the defensive Warsaw Pact we had to create a defensive strength that would make the leaders of the bourgeois states understand that we cannot be spoken to in the language of threats; that one must talk with us on equal terms, so to speak, in the language of reason, realism and mutual advantage.[14]

An authoritative article published by a member of the Central Committee of the C.P.S.U. in 1972 argued:

> The increased might of the U.S.S.R. and of the socialist community and the intensified anti-imperialist struggle have become prime factors for averting another world war and compelling imperialist states to display certain caution and restraint in international affairs and give most serious considerations to Soviet positions on international questions.[15]

In the Soviet view only superior military force can effectively compel the imperialist countries to restrain their aggression. Soviet Major General Ye. Sulimov argues:

> The reactionary circles of imperialism can only be forced into peaceful coexistence by making them renounce violent, armed methods of struggle. No considerations of morals, religion or international law and no

consideration based on reason can halt the aggressive desires of the reactionary imperialist circles and the military-industrial complex if they sense their impunity and their superiority in strength.[16]

Brezhnev argued in Havana in January 1974 that 'Finally the capitalist world had to face the truth. It had to recognize the impossibility of solving militarily the historical differences between capitalism and socialism.'[17]

In addition to preserving world peace and preventing either an attack on the Soviet Union or the other Socialist countries, the Soviet Union sees the fact of its military strength as a means to aid the national liberation and socialist movements around the world. General A. Yepishev, the head of the Main Political Administration of the Soviet Army and Navy, has argued that the nuclear-based strength of the Soviet Union is a 'mighty factor for preserving peace and security of the peoples, a factor which objectively promotes the development of world revolutionary forces'. The Soviet nuclear arsenal is looked on by the Soviets as providing a shield for revolutionary forces around the world which puts limits on imperialist counter-revolution.[18]

The Soviet conception of the role of their military has in recent years expanded beyond the traditional one of merely defending the Soviet Union, to encompass the prevention of imperialist attempts to export counter-revolution, i.e. deterrence of Western imperialist policies and activities that stand in the way of national liberation movements. General Yepishev, writing in 1972, argued:

> The army of the Soviet socialist state represents part of the international revolutionary-liberation forces . . . Today the defence of the socialist fatherland is closely tied to giving comprehensive assistance to national liberation movements, progressive regimes, and new states who are fighting against imperialist domination.[19]

Just because Soviet military philosophy and publicly enunciated strategy (both that announced to the West and that presented in military journals inside the Soviet Union) maintains that the Soviet military establishment is geared to deter aggression, does not make it so. The public statements of the U.S. military also stress the purely defensive nature of its military machine (e.g. the Department of War was renamed the Defense Department in 1947). To determine whether the Soviet military machine and strategy, unlike that of the Americans, is essentially defensive, it is necessary to examine concretely the composition and deployment of Soviet armed strength.

Virtually every major advance in modern military weaponry since World War II has been introduced by the United States and subsequently imitated by the Soviet Union. She has done so in order to protect herself against the possibility of intimidation and even destruction made real by the U.S.'s exclusive possession of advanced military technology. The atom bomb was first developed by the U.S.A. in 1945 and was used to intimidate the Soviet Union until the Soviets exploded their own bomb in 1949. Before this, there was serious talk in the West of a pre-emptive strike against the Soviet Union in order to destroy the socialist system. The U.S. exploded the world's first hydrogen bomb in 1952. Again the Soviets (in 1953) were forced to follow suit or suffer intimidation and possible destruction. The use of guided missiles to deliver atom and hydrogen bombs was developed by the U.S. and later copied by the U.S.S.R. The first submarine-launched, rocket-delivered atom and hydrogen bombs were developed and deployed by the U.S., followed a few years later by the U.S.S.R. The first multi-warhead and independently targetable nuclear missiles were both developed by the U.S., again forcing the Soviets to follow suit. In the late 1970s the two most advanced weapons systems: the neutron bomb (which kills people with minimum damage to property) and the Cruise missile (a cheap drone-delivered hydrogen bomb which flies under Soviet radar) are both being initiated by the U.S. Once again the Soviets will be forced to duplicate American efforts and develop their own neutron bombs and Cruise missiles in order to deter the U.S. from credibly threatening their use. Except for the first intercontinental range-guided missiles (which because of their bases surrounding the U.S.S.R., the U.S. didn't need), in no case have the Soviets introduced a major new weapons system ahead of the U.S. These facts are thus thoroughly consistent with the Soviet claim to have developed only a defensive armoury designed to deter attack and intimidation from the U.S.

The Soviet military goal, as expressed publicly both at home and abroad, is for essential parity with the U.S. It wants freedom from fear of intimidation or destruction as a result of a decisively superior U.S. military capacity. But it was not until 1972 that the U.S., at the Moscow Summit meetings, grudgingly conceded the legitimacy of essential nuclear parity between themselves and the U.S.S.R. And the U.S. military still remains qualitatively superior and more advanced in almost every area to their Soviet counterpart. This is so much the case that there is always a possibility of the U.S. making a successful first strike against the Soviet military establishment. While the opposite has never remotely been possible. The Soviet military machine is designed for land war in Eurasia, both in defence of Soviet territory against attacks like those launched by Germany in 1915 and 1941, and in pre-emptive strikes against the NATO countries in the event of war becoming inevitable and the Soviet Union being forced to strike first in order to avoid a surprise attack (again, like that by Germany in 1941). The memory of 1941 and the two subsequent years of devastating defensive warfare is very real for the Soviet Union. A total of over 20 million Soviet citizens were killed by the Germans in World War II.

The mission of the Soviet military is reflected in the relative sizes of its three services. In 1976 the Soviet Army had 1,825,000 soldiers compared to 782,000 for the U.S. But the Soviet Navy had 450,000 sailors compared to 720,600 for the U.S. and the Soviet Air Force 450,000 compared to 584,100 in the U.S.A.F. The smaller but technically more proficient U.S. Army together with the larger and far more technically advanced U.S. Air Force and navy, are decisively superior to the Soviet military. The reason the Soviets maintain such a large army is precisely because of their acknowledged technical inferiority. The Soviets learned in World War II that their ability to survive and defeat an invasion lay in their superior numbers (as well as in guerrilla warfare) and that the technically superior Nazi armies could be beaten by using this advantage. Soviet military literature is full of discussions which uphold the importance of superior troop ratios (a lesson drawn largely from World War II battles) as the key to military success.[20]

In mid 1976 the U.S. strategic arsenal of independently targetable nuclear warheads deliverable by bombers, submarine-launched missiles and land-based strategic missiles, was 8,530 compared to the Soviets' 3,250 (an advantage of 2.6 times for the U.S.). While there is a parity between the land-based I.C.B.M.s possessed by both sides, the U.S. has 5,120 submarine-based warheads compared to only 785 for the Soviet Union (an advantage of 6.5 times for the U.S.). These figures reflect the emphasis placed by the U.S. on submarine-deliverable weapons compared to the Soviets' outdated continuing reliance on land-based missiles (which are far more easily destroyed in a first strike than the hard-to-find nuclear submarines). In addition, U.S. bombers in 1976 were capable of delivering 1,256 nuclear bombs to the Soviet Union compared to the Soviets' ability to deliver 270 to the U.S. (an advantage of 4.7 times for the U.S.).

In sharp contrast to the U.S., the ability of the U.S.S.R. to project its military strength beyond its immediate frontiers is severely constrained by the limited strategic mobility of the Soviet military. It is simply not designed to carry on warfare beyond its immediate borders (unlike the U.S. whose military is oriented to fighting wars anywhere in the world).

The contrast between the Soviet and U.S. navies underlines this essential difference in the missions of the two militaries. The U.S. Navy has twice the tonnage of the Soviet Navy, its ships are more modern, its equipment more advanced in most areas and it is designed to transport military forces anywhere in the world (while the Soviet Navy is designed mainly to protect the U.S.S.R. and its merchant shipping from attack). The U.S.A. has 13 operational aircraft carriers with a total of 1,200 combat airplanes stationed on them. These floating military bases can project U.S. military presence into any area of the world. In contrast the U.S.S.R. has no full-size aircraft carriers. Only in the 1970s did the Soviet Union build even miniature carriers. As of 1976 the U.S.S.R. had one miniature carrier, the Kiev, capable of handling 25 airplanes or 36 helicopters, and two helicopter carriers (each capable of carrying 25 helicopters). These three miniature Soviet carriers are designed for anti-submarine warfare, specifically to try and locate and if necessary destroy U.S. nuclear missile submarines, thereby preventing them from launching their missiles against the U.S.S.R. The Soviet Navy, unlike the U.S. Navy, has very limited amphibious capacities, i.e. it is not designed to deliver and support troops in coastal areas. The U.S. Navy meanwhile continues to be geared to putting down wars of national liberation anywhere in the world.

The Soviet strategic airlift capability is also very limited, especially compared with that of the U.S. The heavy armour that Soviet motorized and tank divisions are equipped with make them ill-suited for airlift. The heaviest Soviet air transports (of which there are only 30) can carry just two medium tanks. In summary, it is clear that the Soviet Air Force and Navy are not designed to project Soviet military power around the world, but are rather intended for the defence of the integrity of the U.S.S.R.

Much is often said about the superiority of Soviet tank divisions. The Soviets (with huge land borders) in fact have about 40,000 battle tanks compared to 10,000 for the U.S.A. However, the North American tanks are superior, as is their anti-tank technology. A Soviet tank offensive would in all likelihood be easily defeated by the use of the highly sophistically arsenal of U.S. anti-tank weapons, even without the neutron bomb — a most effective anti-tank weapon. Probably the most serious technological lag of the Soviet military lies in precision-guided munitions (precisely the strength of anti-tank warfare). Television and laser guided projectiles (missiles and artillery shells, both with conventional and tactical nuclear weapons) are specialities of the U.S. Army (its so-called 'smart-bombs'). In 1975 the Pentagon announced the successful development of a laser guided artillery shell. Such shells, employed in 155 millimetre and eight inch howitzers, will transform the U.S. artillery from an indiscriminate area fire weapon into a precise instrument with the capacity to destroy individual mobile targets, such as tanks, thereby wiping out any Soviet advantage in armour.

Furthermore, the U.S. main battle tanks of the 1970s are qualitatively superior to those of the Soviets in almost all respects. They have a more rapid rate of fire, bigger ammunition storage capacity, greater long range accuracy, greater armour protection and better shielded fuel tanks. The inferiority of Soviet compared to U.S. armour was decisively demonstrated in the 1973 War between Egypt and Israel. Further the U.S., beginning in 1980, is introducing a new and superior main battle tank, the XM-1, while the Soviets only have plans for a slightly improved model of their 1970s main battle tank, the T-62. The XM-1 is said to possess a spectacular new type of armour capable of withstanding the impact of any contemporary gun or anti-tank missile.

The general inferiority of Soviet military equipment to that of the U.S. was spectacularly revealed in 1977 when a defecting Soviet pilot brought his MIG-25 (the most advanced Soviet fighter plane) to Japan. The C.I.A. itself described this plane as a generation or two behind U.S. fighter technology and conceded that it was primarily a defensive weapon designed to intercept enemy bombers.

The new U.S. Cruise missile is, according to *Jane's Fighting Ships* (the world's most authoritative appraiser of naval strength), 'altering the naval equation beyond recognition' because of the ability it gives the U.S. Navy, using these relatively inexpensive but highly accurate self-guided missiles, to destroy any target it chooses.

The U.S.S.R. simply doesn't have anything even approximately as sophisticated as the U.S. technological military arsenal. Few question the latter country's demonstrable lead in such areas as sophisticated avionics, precision guidance and fire control systems. U.S. superiority in most military

technologies, especially its overwhelming superiority in independently targetable warheads based on hard to locate (and thus hard to destroy) nuclear
submarines, together with the Soviet inability to project its military power
beyond its borders, gives it a considerable military advantage over the Soviet
Union, even while the Soviet Union has sufficient nuclear capacity to deter
the U.S. from attacking it or too aggressively pushing it or other socialist
countries and national liberation movements around. The danger is ever present
that a new technological breakthrough by the U.S. would make its lead over
the Soviets sufficient once again to use nuclear blackmail against the U.S.S.R.
or even to launch a successful first strike.

Western media have made much of the expanding Soviet naval presence
throughout the world and the supposed Soviet bases that such a world-wide
naval presence entails. Unlike the U.S. Navy, whose prime functions are to
put U.S. military power ashore anywhere in the world and to carry the major
strategic nuclear capacity of the U.S., the primary function of the Soviet
Navy is to deter or cripple a nuclear attack on the U.S.S.R. The stated purpose
of the world-wide Soviet naval presence is to maintain a presence wherever U.S.
naval units are deployed in order to carry out 'an immediate counter-attack'
should war break out. Just as the U.S. Navy expects continuously to track
down all Soviet missile-carrying submarines and immediately destroy them in
the event of war, the Soviets too hope eventually to be able to do the same in
order to prevent the possible launching of thousands of hydrogen bomb
warheads by the U.S. submarine fleet.

The expanded world-wide Soviet naval presence has coincided exactly with
the expanding range of U.S. missile-launched submarines. This was obviously
necessary if the Soviets were to have any chance of neutralizing the threat of
Polaris submarine launched I.C.B.M.s. In June 1962 the Polaris A-2, with a
range of 1,600 miles, became operational. Its deployment in the Mediterranean
put the Ukraine and Baku oil fields within striking distance. As a consequence,
in 1963 the Soviet Navy began to have an active and permanent presence in the
Mediterranean. In September 1964 the longer range A-3 Polaris missile became
operational; this could hit any part of the Soviet Union from Leningrad to
Eastern Siberia (including virtually all the Soviet's major industrial areas)
from the north-western corner of the Indian Ocean. As a consequence, the
Soviets in December 1964 proposed to the U.N. that the Indian Ocean
become a nuclear-free zone in which nuclear missile submarines would be
prohibited from operating. Failing this, the Soviets were forced permanently
to deploy their navy in the Indian Ocean to track U.S. Polaris submarines. A
similar process has occurred in all the seas of the world where U.S. missile-
carrying submarines have been deployed. For the Soviets to follow any other
policy could well amount to suicide. In no way can the expanded world-wide
Soviet naval presence then be taken to mean that the U.S.S.R. is primarily
interested in projecting its power ashore or attempting to intimidate other
countries (as is the case with the U.S.).[21]

Much has also been made of the alleged Soviet bases around the world,
especially the so-called Soviet base (since removed) in Berbera, Somalia. The

term 'base' as applied to the Soviet Union is much abused. Traditionally the
term meant a sanctuary which provided guaranteed physical security, storage
for ammunition, spare parts, stores and fuel and often overhaul facilities,
together with political guarantees that it would not be withheld during a
political crisis. The U.S. for example has such facilities in a great many
countries all over the world including many on the borders of the Soviet
Union. The U.S.S.R., on the other hand, has no such facilities anywhere
outside its own country and the Eastern European countries of the Warsaw
Pact (and probably Mongolia). What U.S. propaganda describes as Soviet
bases are almost exclusively berthing stations (a fancy term for mooring buoys).
Such was the case with the highly publicized Soviet Somali base. The Soviet
Navy's basic requirements, in the Mediterranean or Indian Oceans (as well as
elsewhere), for stores, water and fuel are in fact supplied by accompanying
supply ships based in Soviet ports. The Soviet Union has nowhere in the world
(outside of the Eastern European countries) anything remotely resembling the
massive U.S. naval and air bases that the U.S. possesses around the U.S.S.R.
and scattered all over the world, e.g. Canada, Greenland, Iceland, Cuba
(Guantanamo Bay), Panama, Turkey, Diego Garcia, the Philippines, Korea,
Australia, Taiwan, Japan, Guam, Hawaii, Germany, Spain, The United
Kingdom, etc.

In sum, there is nothing in the evidence of either the Soviet arsenal or the
deployment of the Soviet military that suggests imperialist motivation or
behaviour. This contrasts sharply with the constellation and deployment of
U.S. weapons. The evidence clearly points to a purely defensive role for the
Soviet military. There is no evidence that the Soviet military is designed or
used as an instrument of imperialism.

In this chapter it has been demonstrated that both Soviet trade relations
and the nature of the Soviet military are qualitatively different from those of
the advanced capitalist countries such as the United States. In the next three
chapters we will look at the concrete relations, both economic and political,
between the U.S.S.R. and the countries of Eastern Europe and the non-
socialist and socialist countries of the Third World. In each case we will
attempt carefully to screen the evidence in search of support for the thesis
that the U.S.S.R. acts like a 'social imperialist superpower'.

References

1.   For the Chinese position see, for example, 'How the Soviet Revisionists
     Carry out All-Round Restoration of Capitalism in the USSR', (Peking:
     Foreign Languages Publishing House, 1968) and 'Down with the New
     Tsars!', (Peking: Foreign Languages Publishing House, 1969). Perhaps
     the two most thorough arguments in support of the Chinese thesis
     generally available in English in the U.S.A. are Martin Nicolaus, *The
     Restoration of Capitalism in the USSR*, (Chicago: Liberator Press,

1975); and The Revolutionary Union, *How Capitalism has been Restored in the Soviet Union and What this Means for the World Struggle,* (Chicago: The Revolutionary Union, 1974). This latter booklet contains one of the most systematic and lengthy presentations of the Chinese argument about Soviet foreign relations.

2. See especially Paul Gregory and Robert Stuart, *Soviet Economic Structure and Performance* (New York: Harper and Row, 1974); Josef Wilczynski, *The Economics of Socialism,* (Chicago: Aldine Publishing Co., 1970), as well as the other authors cited in Chapter Three.

3. Gregory and Stuart, *Soviet Economic Structure and Performance, op. cit.,* Chapter 8; J. Wilczynski, *The Economics of Socialism, op. cit.,* Chapter 13; Howard Sherman, *The Soviet Economy,* (Boston: Little, Brown, 1969), Chapter 8.

4. Gregory and Stuart, Chapter 8; Sherman, Chapter 8.

5. *Ibid.,* Wilczynski, *op. cit.,* Chapter 13; Guy Gilbert, 'Socialism and Dependency', *Latin American Perspectives.* 1:1, (Spring 1974).

6. Franklyn Holzman, *Foreign Trade Under Central Planning,* (Cambridge, Mass: Harvard University Press, 1974), pp.53-56; Lawrence J. Brainard, 'Soviet Foreign Trade Planning', U.S. Congress, Joint Economic Committee, 94th Congress, 2nd session, *Soviet Economy in a New Perspective,* p.698.

7. Sherman, *op. cit.,* Chapter 8; Holzman, *op. cit.,* Chapter 10.

8. See the United Nations, *Yearbook of National Account Statistics,* (1975); and the United Nations, *Yearbook of International Trade Statistics,* (1975).

9. Holzman, *op. cit.,* Chapter 2; Wilczynski, *op. cit.,* Chapter 13.

10. *Ibid.,* Chapter 13; Sherman, *op. cit.,* Chapter 8.

11. Wilczynski, *op. cit.,* Chapter 13.

12. See Paul Marer, *Soviet and East European Foreign Trade,* (Bloomington, Indiana: Indiana University Press, 1972), Vol.III, p.34; United Nations, *Yearbook of National Account Statistics,* (1975), Table 2B; and United Nations, *Yearbook of International Trade Statistics,* (1974), p.926.

13. The discussion of the Soviet military's main purpose relies heavily on the following sources: Center for Strategic and International Studies, *Soviet Sea Power,* (Washington D.C.: Georgetown University, 1969); Joseph Coffey, *Deterrence in the 1970's,* (Denver: University of Denver, 1971); Leon Goure, Foy Kohler and Mose Harvey, *The Role of Nuclear Forces in Current Soviet Strategy,* (Center for Advanced International Studies, University of Miami, 1974); David Jones, *Soviet Armed Forces Review,* (Annual), (Academic-International Press, 1977); William Kinter and Harriet Scott, (eds.), *The Nuclear Revolution in Soviet Military Affairs,* (Norman: University of Oklahoma Press, 1968).

14. Leon Goure *et al., op. cit.,* p.44.

15. *Ibid.,* p.44.

16. *Ibid.,* p.27.

17. *Ibid.,* p.28.

18. *Ibid.,* p.33.

19. *Ibid.,* p.6.

20. The statistics on the strength of the Soviet and American militaries are taken from the International Institute for Strategic Studies, *The Military*

Balance, 1976-77, (London, 1976).
21. The discussion of Soviet naval deployment relies heavily on The Center for Strategic and International Studies, *Soviet Sea Power;* and Christopher Stevens, *The Soviet Union and Black Africa,* (New York: Holmes and Meier, 1976).

7. Soviet Relations with Eastern Europe

Those who accuse the Soviet Union of imperialism typically argue that the six COMECON countries of Eastern Europe (Bulgaria, Czechoslovakia, East Germany, Hungary, Poland and Romania) are essentially neo-colonies of the U.S.S.R. in a sense similar to the relationship between, for example, the U.S. or Britain and much of the Third World. These 'satellites' are supposed to be both politically dominated and economically exploited by the U.S.S.R. in much the same way as the Western powers dominate the Third World. Let us then examine the concrete relations between the U.S.S.R. and Eastern Europe in order to determine whether these six countries can in fact be considered *de facto* colonies of the U.S.S.R. I will first examine the contemporary economic relations between the two, looking at the composition, significance and terms of trade; the possible uses by the Soviet Union of trade as a political weapon; economic assistance; regional economic co-ordination; joint enterprises; and the effect which Eastern Europe's economic relations with the U.S.S.R. have on the economic growth and sectoral structure of their economies. I will also analyse the historical development of the political relations between Eastern Europe and the U.S.S.R. in the post World War II period, focusing on the transformations in economic relations that occurred around 1956, and on the Soviet interventions in Yugoslavia, Hungary and Czechoslovakia.

Trade Relations

In the period 1970 to 1972, 37.2 per cent of all exports of the Council of Mutual Economic Assistance (C.M.E.A. or COMECON) countries of Eastern Europe went to the Soviet Union. This represented a slight decline from the 1960s when exports to the Soviet Union averaged 41 per cent of all exports. In 1970-72 total COMECON imports from the Soviet Union totalled 35.5 per cent of all imports, down slightly from an average of 37 per cent in the 1960s.[1] Thus, slightly over one-third of all East European trade is with the Soviet Union.

In the period 1969-73 about two-thirds of all the exports from the six East European COMECON countries (plus Yugoslavia) went to COMECON

countries (including the Soviet Union) (plus Yugoslavia), one-seventh went
to the advanced capitalist economies and about ten per cent went to the less
developed market economies. This contrasts with the miniscule percentage of
Latin American (excluding Cuban), African, Middle Eastern and Asian
countries' exports that go to the COMECON countries; about three-quarters
of the exports of these areas are to the advanced capitalist countries. (see
Table 7.1). Thus comparing the less developed market economies (most of
which are satellites of the advanced capitalist countries) to the COMECON
countries, we see that the COMECON countries are much less trade dependent on the U.S.S.R. than are the Third World countries on the advanced
capitalist countries: only one-third of exports for the COMECON countries
versus three-quarters of exports for the Third World. While COMECON
countries have alternative export markets in the capitalist countries (over a
quarter of total exports), the non-socialist Third World countries have only a
tiny alternative export market in the COMECON countries (about one
twenty-fifth of total exports).

Table 7.1
Exports of Comecon and Third World Countries Compared,1969-1973

	To Advanced Capitalist Countries	To Less Developed Non-Socialist Third World Countries	To Soviet Union six COMECON countries plus Yugoslavia
The Six COMECON countries plus Yugoslavia	15.0%	11.7%	64.2%
Latin America	74.5	19.4	3.6
Middle East	75.7	19.8	2.2
Africa	81.1	11.0	6.1
Asia	66.5	28.3	4.2

Source: United Nations, *Yearbook of International Trade Statistics,* 1974,
Table B.

It is interesting to note that 65.5 per cent of Canada's exports go to the U.S.
and 76 per cent of its imports come from there. Canada, a country of comparable location, population and economic development in relation to
the U.S., as the six COMECON countries are to the U.S.S.R., is twice as trade
dependent on the U.S. as the COMECON countries are on the Soviet Union.[2]
Yet Canada, while its economy is closely integrated with that of the U.S., is
generally regarded not as a dependency of the latter, but as a country whose
ruling class simply has the same interests as the U.S. If Canada can remain
politically independent of the U.S., the COMECON countries of Eastern
Europe, which are far less trade dependent on the U.S.S.R. than Canada is on

121

the U.S., should be even more capable of remaining independent.

The 35 per cent of imports that the six East European countries take from the U.S.S.R. compares as follows with the percentage of imports that selected Third World countries, often regarded as dependencies of the U.S., take (circa 1973) from the U.S.: Colombia 39.6 per cent, Dominican Republic 47.2 per cent, Guatemala 31.9 per cent, Honduras 44 per cent, Mexico 62.9 per cent, Nicaragua 34.3 per cent, Panama 35.3 per cent and Venezuela 45 per cent. Turning to exports, the 37 per cent of the COMECON countries' exports that go to the Soviet Union compares as follows to the percentage of total exports of selected Third World countries to the U.S.: Colombia 37.4 per cent, the Dominican Republic 73.3 per cent, Guatemala 29.3 per cent, Honduras 56.5 per cent, Mexico 68.8 per cent, Nicaragua 33.3 per cent, Panama 44.7 per cent, and Venezuela 39.7 per cent.[3] The trade dependence of the U.S.A.'s Caribbean satellites is greater than the trade dependence of the East European countries on the Soviet Union, although the difference between the two sets of countries is not all that great.

In the period 1970 to 1972, the balance of trade between the Soviet Union and the six East European countries was slightly in the latters' favour — the COMECON countries exported to the Soviet Union about four per cent more than they imported from it. During the 1960s total exports and imports between the Soviet Union and the COMECON countries almost exactly balanced, while in the previous decade exports of Eastern Europe exceeded imports by about two per cent.[4] Clearly, then, there is no significant imbalance in trade which might reflect a permanent net flow of resources to the Soviet Union from Eastern Europe. This leaves open the possibility, however, of Soviet exports being overvalued and East European exports undervalued. Such a situation would result in trade exploitation of Eastern Europe by the Soviet Union.

The six East European COMECON countries primarily export industrial machinery and equipment to the Soviet Union and import raw materials and fuels in exchange. In 1966-68 48.2 per cent of all East European exports to the Soviet Union were industrial machinery and equipment and only 26.1 per cent were raw materials, fuels or food. During the same period 62.8 per cent of Soviet exports to Eastern Europe were raw materials and another 10.7 per cent was food, and only 24.4 per cent was industrial machinery and equipment (and a negligible 2.1 per cent manufactured consumer goods). The proportion of East European exports made up of industrial machinery and equipment has risen slightly over time, while the proportion that consists of raw materials and fuel has decreased drastically (it stood at 43.7 per cent in 1950-53). The proportion of East European exports in the shape of manufactured consumer goods has risen significantly since the 1950s. (See Table 7.2). The proportion of Soviet exports in the form of raw materials and fuel has stayed about the same since the 1950s. The Soviet Union is the principal supplier of these two elements for Eastern Europe, while Eastern Europe is a major supplier of capital goods and manufactured consumer goods for the Soviet Union. This is of course exactly the reverse of the pattern of trade observable between the advanced capitalist countries (which specialize in capital goods and manufactured exports) and the less developed countries of the Third World (which specialise in raw material and food exports).

Table 7.2
Soviet Trade with Eastern Europe, 1950-1968

	Industrial Machinery and Equip-ment		Fuels and Raw Material (exclud-ing food)		Foodstuffs		Manufactured Consumer Goods (excluding food)	
	Exports (% of total)	Imports	Exports (% age of total)	Imports	Exports (% age of total)	Imports	Exports (% age of total)	Imports
1950-53	22.0%	39.2%	51.7%	43.7%	25.2%	7.2%	1.1%	9.9%
1954-57	15.5	46.8	60.7	37.1	21.6	5.8	2.3	10.3
1958-61	13.9	45.8	64.4	27.0	18.6	7.6	3.0	19.6
1962-65	19.7	49.8	65.9	20.5	12.2	7.9	2.2	21.9
1966-68	24.4	48.2	62.8	16.9	10.7	9.2	2.1	25.7

Source: Paul Marer, *Soviet and East European Foreign Trade, 1946-1969*, pp.87, 111.

In comparison to the 26 per cent of total East European exports to the Soviet Union which comprise raw materials, fuels or food, the percentages of total exports of such commodities from countries often regarded as dependencies of the U.S. to the U.S. are considerably greater, e.g. (circa 1973) Colombia 88.9 per cent, Dominican Republic 98 per cent, Guatemala 84.4 per cent, Honduras 97.9 per cent, Mexico 54.3 per cent, Nicaragua 82 per cent, Panama 73.5 per cent, the Philippines 95.6 per cent and Venezuela 98.8 per cent. There is thus a qualitative difference in the trade patterns of the COMECON countries of Eastern Europe with the Soviet Union, compared with the trade patterns of the U.S.'s Third World dependencies with the U.S. The latter almost universally specialize in the export of raw materials to the U.S. (primarily in exchange for manufactured goods), while the East European countries export manufactured goods, especially capital equipment, to the U.S.S.R. in exchange for raw materials. Unless the terms of trade between the Soviet Union and Eastern Europe were highly imbalanced in favour of the U.S.S.R. (which, being based on world prices, they are not), it would be very difficult to interpret the trade relationship as imperialist.

As previously noted, the prices of commodities exchanged between East European socialist countries and the Soviet Union are approximations of prices in the world capitalist market. Because the law of value is not the essential determinant of prices in the planned economies of these countries, domestic prices of commodities are in good part arbitrary (i.e. not based on the value contained in a commodity). Different countries might thus price the same commodity at very different levels because of various political or long-term economic considerations. Because of the arbitrary nature of domestic pricing, these prices cannot be used in inter-socialist trade without one or other party complaining of exploitation, this exploitation becoming apparent if an export is offered at a higher price than the equivalent price on the world capitalist market.[5] COMECON regulations therefore specify that all prices of raw materials are based on adjusted world market prices in the previous five year period.

As is well known, a few advanced capitalist countries have a monopoly on manufacturing technologically advanced producer goods. This allows them to sell these goods to the Third World at monopoly prices. In return, except for petroleum, overproduction, competition and foreign ownership in the raw material and food producing Third World countries depresses (albeit erratically) the world prices of their exports. As a result, a real transfer of value occurs from the raw material and food producing countries (except for the oil exporters) to the advanced capitalist countries. The Third World raw material suppliers are in this sense exploited. But the socialist countries are utilizing world prices for capital goods and raw materials. The result is that the exports of the raw material exporters, namely the Soviet Union, tend to be undervalued and the exports of the capital goods exporters, most of the countries of Eastern Europe, tend to be overvalued. In this respect the Soviet Union is being exploited in its trade with Eastern Europe in the same way that the Third World raw material exporters are exploited by the advanced capitalist countries.

A further point needs to be made. Although the rule is that exports are exchanged at approximately world prices, the Soviet Union has, since the mid-1950s, been supplying crucial raw materials, especially petroleum products, to Eastern Europe at considerably below the world market price. For example, the price charged to the East Europeans for Soviet oil in 1974 was approximately one-fifth the world market price. Even after a substantial increase in the price of Soviet oil in 1975, the cost to COMECON countries in 1976 was still about one-third less than the world market price.[6]

Detailed empirical studies show that the East European socialist countries are not discriminated against or exploited in their trade relations with the U.S.S.R. One careful study of prices for Bulgarian and Polish exports to, and imports from, the Soviet Union (i.e. their terms of trade) shows that they tend to be significantly better than those obtainable with the advanced countries. In 1959, of 32 leading categories of Bulgarian exports, the prices paid by the Soviet Union were higher than those obtainable in Western Europe for 24 and lower for eight. In the case of Poland, the Soviet prices were higher in 20 out of 28 categories and lower in seven. In the case of Soviet exports to Bulgaria, the prices charged Bulgaria in 1959 were lower than those of West European equivalent commodities for 18 of the 32 basic categories and higher for 12, while for Poland the Soviet prices were lower for 11 categories of commodities and higher for six.[7]

Since it is logically possible that the few goods the Soviets trade to their advantage could represent the majority of goods traded, or that an advantage on a few goods could be so great as to outweigh a slight disadvantage on most goods and thus that the Soviets could secure a net gain from trade, it is important to look at measures of trade advantage which incorporate quantity as well as price. The same study cited above found that overall Polish exports (measured by unit value, a concept which includes both price and volume) to the Soviet Union were purchased at 1.45 times the prevailing prices for similar goods on the West European market and Bulgarian goods at 1.32 times those prices. It was also found that overall Soviet exports to Poland were purchased by Poland at 81 per cent of the prices similar goods were available at in Western Europe, and Soviet exports to Bulgaria at 69 per cent.[8] Thus the net barter terms of trade (a concept which incorporates both price and volume) between Poland and the Soviet Union in 1959 were 1.8 times better for Poland (and worse for the Soviet Union) than Poland could have obtained in trade with the West. The terms of trade for Bulgaria were 1.9 times better. Substantially identical results were found for 1960, indicating that 1959 was not a fluke year. Thus, even though the prices of commodities traded among the non-market socialist economies officially approximate world market prices, the East European countries gain at the expense of the Soviet Union in this trade. Part of their advantage may be a result of the different commodity mix, especially of different qualities of goods within the basic commodity categories employed in this study. Hence the general difference in favour of the East European countries may not typically be as large as found in this study. But these data at least make clear that, if there is any systematic deviation from world market prices in trade between Eastern Europe and the Soviet Union, it is not in favour of the Soviet Union.

In addition to complaining about the subsidy they give Eastern Europe through supplying petroleum at significantly less than the world market price, the Soviets have also been complaining of an exploitation effect caused by their having to undertake all the heavy investment expenditures of developing and producing oil in the Soviet Union. It was estimated that in the late 1960s the capital intensity of the basic raw materials and fuels exported by the U.S.S.R. to the COMECON countries was 3 to 3.5 times higher than that of the machinery supplied by them to the U.S.S.R., i.e. the value of materiál investment (machinery and fixed facilities such as pipelines and other transport) per worker was considerably higher in raw material production than in the machine producing sectors. The Soviets have therefore begun fostering integration in the production and distribution of raw materials and fuel so that the Eastern European countries share more equitably in the costs of acquiring their own raw materials. Beginning in the early 1970s, the COMECON countries have begun to finance projects jointly to produce fuel and raw materials mostly in the U.S.S.R. In return for these capital investments in raw material production enterprises, the investing countries (mostly East European) are repaid in raw materials.[9]

Since the mid 1950s, there is no evidence that the Soviet Union obtains unrequited goods from Eastern Europe. In fact it costs the Soviet Union considerably more to trade with Eastern Europe than with the West, while Eastern Europe disproportionately benefits from trade with the Soviet Union. i.e. If anyone is being exploited it is the Soviet Union. Moreover, the terms of trade of the COMECON countries with the Soviet Union have shifted considerably in favour of Eastern Europe and against the Soviet Union since the mid 1950s.[10]

The East European countries depend very heavily on their raw material imports from the Soviets. Around 1970 the Soviets provided 100 per cent of Czechoslovakia's oil imports (about 97 per cent of its consumption), 85 per cent of its iron ore imports (about 75 per cent of its consumption), 92 per cent of its aluminium and 76 per cent of its copper. During the same period the U.S.S.R. supplied about 90 per cent of East Germany's oil, 60 per cent of its iron ore and 70 per cent of its aluminium and lead. Hungary imports most of its oil, iron ore, phosphates and electric power from the Soviet Union, and so on.[11] Because it is the main supplier of raw materials to Eastern Europe the Soviet Union is in a potential position to exploit them economically. That it does not take advantage of its position is indicative of the lack of a typical imperialist relation between the two areas. No wonder, Vietnam decided after liberation to join COMECON.

Things were not always so advantageous for Eastern Europe. Before the mid 1950s the terms of trade, essentially dictated by the Soviet Union, were overwhelmingly in favour of the Soviets. Soviet trade with the East European countries during the immediate post World War II period was primarily a mechanism to reconstruct the war devastated Soviet economy. The former Axis countries (East Germany, Hungary, Romania and Bulgaria) were especially badly treated; but Poland, Czechoslovakia and Yugoslavia were treated little better. One of the clearest examples of the exploitation of Eastern Europe through unequal exchange before the mid 1950s was the export of coal from Poland to the Soviet Union. Until November 1953 Poland was supplying coal to the Soviet Union at approximately one-tenth of the world price. In 1956 the Soviets acknowledged that there had been exploitation of Poland in the coal trade and cancelled the $626 million in debts owed by Poland to the U.S.S.R. This was in compensation for the coal subsidy supplied the U.S.S.R. by Poland from 1946 to 1953.[12]

Although the Soviet Union has clearly not exploited Eastern Europe through trade relations since 1956, it has, both before and after 1956, used trade as a weapon against recalcitrant socialist countries (in Eastern Europe and elsewhere) in attempts to get them to follow its leadership.

The first time the U.S.S.R. used the trade weapon was against Yugoslavia which was cut off from trade relations with both the Soviet Union and all the other socialist countries in 1948. This trade embargo was imposed in an attempt to get the Yugoslavs to accept Soviet hegemony. China and Albania in 1960-61 were the next socialist countries to suffer from Soviet economic pressure. Economic and technical advisers, with their plans, were withdrawn from these countries and trade with Albania embargoed. While trade with China has never been suspended, it was considerably reduced. Again, in 1962-64, when North Korea was leaning toward the Chinese position in the Sino-Soviet dispute, the Soviets refused to sell advanced military equipment or jet fuel to that country. As soon as the Koreans renounced their position of support for China, Soviet supplies were resumed. The cutting off of trade is an especially strong weapon since both the industry and armed forces of the socialist countries are typically highly dependent on spare parts from the Soviets. The Soviets have also used the technique of delaying delivery as a weapon of control over bloc members who become too critical of the Soviet Union, e.g. against Romania in 1967.[13]

Thus, although there is no evidence in the post 1956 period that the Soviet Union exploits the other socialist countries through trade, there is evidence that the Soviet Union has striven for political hegemony over the other socialist countries by using trade as a weapon to get them to follow policies approved by her.

It should also be noted, however, that China has behaved in essentially the same way as the Soviet Union towards those smaller and more vulnerable Socialist countries of which she disapproves, namely Vietnam and Albania in 1978. The Chinese thus find themselves in the ironic situation of doing to others exactly what the U.S.S.R. did to them — withdrawing advisers, ending assistance and reducing trade in order to pressure countries they are having differences with. It is difficult to see any difference between the Soviet Union's and China's behaviour in these questions, other than that the Soviet Union has become more gentle and tolerant of differences in recent years while the Chinese as reflected in their recent behaviour towards Vietnam and Albania have not.

Economic Assistance

The Soviets extended some economic assistance to Eastern Europe in the immediate post-war period (1946-52), mainly to relieve especially troubled situations and to persuade the East European countries to reject the U.S.A.'s Marshall Plan aid, e.g. a proferred $450 million loan to Poland in 1947-48. The most generous period of Soviet aid to Eastern Europe however was · 1953-58, following the rebellions and riots in East Germany, Poland and Hungary which were in good part directed against the exploitive relationship the East European countries found themselves in regarding the Soviet Union. The most comprehensive aid programme took place in the 1956-58 period when the U.S.S.R. extended $3.6 billion in aid ($1.5 billion in loans, $1 billion in debt cancellations, and $1 billion in free transfers of jointly owned enterprises to the East European countries). Generous export credits were also granted to these countries during this period.[14] The year 1956 marks a watershed in the economic relations between Eastern Europe and the U.S.S.R.; the remaining joint stock companies were handed over to the local countries, much of their debt was cancelled, terms of trade favourable to the East European countries established, and generous aid extended. The total value of Soviet aid to Eastern Europe (including debt cancellations, handing over of enterprises, loans and credits) was of the same order as that of the Marshall Plan to Western Europe, approximately $14 billion dollars.[15] The Soviet Union, at least since the mid 1950s, has thus played a central role in accelerating the economic growth and all round development of the East European economies. This is hardly a phenomenon to be expected from an imperialist-type relation such as exists between the United States and Western Europe on the one hand and most of the countries of the Third World on the other.

In the period 1954 to 1964 the majority of Soviet loans and grants to socialist countries went to the COMECON countries of Eastern Europe — 53 per cent of all Soviet aid. But in the period 1965 to 1972, only 21 per cent of all loans and grants were to the East European countries. In the 1954-64 period, East Germany and Bulgaria were the principal recipients of Soviet aid in Eastern Europe, while China, Mongolia and Cuba were the principal recipients among Third World socialist countries. In the 1965-72 period, Poland and Bulgaria (two of the least developed COMECON countries) became the principal recipients in Eastern Europe while Cuba, North Vietnam and Mongolia (in that order) were the principal beneficiaries of Soviet aid amongst the Third World socialist countries.[16]

Co-ordinated Planning

During the first decade of the C.M.E.A., the co-ordination of the COMECON countries' economies was limited to planning trade among themselves. Since 1958, however, there has been a gradual increase in overall economic integration and co-ordination of production plans among the COMECON countries. While the ideal is the eventual total integration of the various economies as nation states wither away, all parties are extremely jealous of maintaining their economic independence and all-round development. So the process advances very slowly. The procedures of economic integration adopted in 1971 after many years of struggle and compromises stipulated that:

> . . . further intensification and improvement and the development of the socialist economic integration of C.M.E.A. member nations will be carried out in accordance with the principles of socialist internationalism and on the basis of respect for national sovereignty, independence and national interests, of nonintervention in the internal affairs of nations, and of total equality, mutual advantage, and comradely reciprocal aid. . . . socialist economic integration is carried out on an entirely voluntary basis and is not accompanied by the creation of supranational organs, nor does it affect matters pertaining to internal planning or the financial, and cost-calculating activities of organizations.[17]

No supra-national planning authorities exist which can dictate to any member state what to produce or how to distribute their production. Instead, voluntary agencies have been set up to co-ordinate joint efforts and integration. A Committee for Co-operation in Planning exists to promote co-ordination of five year plans and exchanges of information. Discussions are held among the COMECON countries in the process of each constructing their operative plans. The primary concerns of the Committee for Co-operation appear to be systematically developing adequate raw material and energy supplies throughout the COMECON countries, promoting the most advanced technological processes by allowing economies of scale, and developing integrated transportation networks. COMECON also continues to promote co-ordination of production for purposes of planning trade among the COMECON countries. This mostly means the development of intra-industry specialization, e.g. Czechoslovakia specializes in metal pipe, East Germany in steel for bearings, Poland in thin rolled steel and Hungary in fine bore tubing. Each country decides whether or not to participate in a given integration project (of which there are many) on the basis of what it thinks it would gain from participation. COMECON rules, deferring to the interests of the less developed COMECON countries, especially Romania, specify that one of the goals of COMECON is to eliminate differences in the levels of development of the member countries. Concretely this takes the form of the less developed countries being given preference in developing new lines of industrial production (providing the new products are of sufficiently high quality) and the granting of economic assistance to the less developed by the most developed COMECON countries.[18]

While economic integration of the socialist countries has for a long time been an ideal, little real progress was made in co-ordinating economic plans until the late 1960s, when the advantages of economic co-ordination became clear to all participants. The Soviets had long pushed for integration, with the East European countries, led by Romania, resisting out of fear of losing their economic independence. The major force pressing them to move towards co-ordinating their economies was the need to overcome technological backwardness. None of the small East European countries could develop an all-round technologically advanced economy on their own. They were increasingly forced to participate in a regional exchange of scientific and technological knowledge, and to engage in specialization in order to accelerate technological advance. The small East European countries, with limited internal markets, were also increasingly unable efficiently to produce all the advanced goods they needed. Efficient production of advanced industrial goods required international markets to make economies of scale possible, as well as to promote research and development in specialized areas. The economic advantages of co-operation accruing to each country became more and more difficult to resist as the potential gains became greater and greater. It seems that the pressures from the East European countries have resulted in institutions which represent an internationally unified system increasingly autonomous of the U.S.S.R.[19]

There is a bias among the COMECON countries against inter-industry specialization along the lines of broad economic sectors. Instead, economic integration tends to take the form of intra-industry specialization (e.g. one country manufacturing one kind of truck; another some other kind, and so on). It does not take the form of one country building all the trucks and another making all the shoes, etc. All the COMECON countries are determined to possess balanced industrial economies encompassing all branches of production.[20]   As a result, their economies are far more balanced, especially in the industrial sector, than the economies of capitalist countries of similar size and per capita wealth. This gives these East European countries a sound base for political independence.

Joint Enterprises Today

Economic co-operation among the COMECON countries of Eastern Europe (including the U.S.S.R.) takes a number of specific forms: (1) technological co-operation including exchange of blueprints and knowledge about processes and the results of scientific research, as well as training of scientists and specialists in each other's countries; (2) standardization of products and parts; (3) development and co-ordination of transport and communications, including a common freight car pool and canal and river networks; and, (4) joint undertakings in which the capital, know-how and personnel of several COMECON countries are pooled.

These joint enterprises are mostly concentrated in the extractive sector, e.g. bauxite, cellulose, coal, copper, iron ore, lead, phosphates, potash, sulphur and zinc. The more famous ones include the Kingisep potash works in the U.S.S.R. (jointly developed by Bulgaria, Czechoslovakia, East Germany, Hungary, Poland and the U.S.S.R.), the Friendship Pipeline linking the Urals with Eastern Europe, the Peace electrical power transmission grid linking all the East European countries, and Intermetal, an iron and steel association developed by Czechoslovakia, Hungary and Poland.[21]

Increasingly, the COMECON countries have been resorting to joint enterprises after a 10 to 15 year hiatus in this organizational form. While the earlier joint-stock companies were dominated by the Soviet Union and pretty much exploited Eastern Europe to the advantage of the Soviets, the new enterprises seem to be truly joint operations functioning to mutual advantage. As the principal supplier of raw materials to the other COMECON countries, the Soviets have been encouraging the formation of these joint enterprises to exploit natural resources *in the Soviet Union*. General agreements among the various participants in a project establish its broad outlines, then bilateral agreements between the U.S.S.R. and each participating COMECON country specify the precise contribution (financing, equipment, construction workers) and product accruing to each country.

Another form of COMECON co-operation involves leasing of land in one country to another. Bulgaria and the Soviet Union have an arrangement where

Bulgaria leases forest land in the Soviet Union for purposes of building and operating a forestry enterprise for lumber exports to Bulgaria. In return for providing building materials, land, technical advice, equipment and transportation, as well as the trees, the Soviets get a share of the Bulgarian enterprise's output proportionate to U.S.S.R.'s contribution to the project. The key element the Bulgarians provide is the lumberworkers. This is an example of incipient labour mobility among COMECON countries from areas of relative labour surplus to areas of relative labour shortages. Another example is Polish workers working in the Czechoslovak construction industry.[22]

Economic Growth

The radical literature on the less developed countries focuses a lot on how capitalist imperialism underdevelops, or blocks, the development of the Third World satellites of U.S. and European imperialism. It is therefore important, in an examination of whether the Soviet Union's relations with Eastern Europe are essentially equivalent to the advanced capitalist countries' relations with the Third World, to determine whether Soviet economic links with Eastern Europe hinder or promote the latter's economic development and industrialization.

If the relationship between the U.S.S.R. and Eastern Europe is of the kind that the dependency literature (e.g. Gunder Frank, Baran, Magdoff, Samir Amin, Dos Santos, etc.) describe as existing between the U.S. or Western Europe and the Third World, then we would expect the rates of economic growth and industrialization of Eastern Europe and the Third World non-socialist countries to be comparable. We would also expect these rates to be much lower than in the U.S.S.R. Yet this is not the case, as Table 7.3 shows.

The average rate of growth in *per capita* Net Material Product (the socialist equivalent of Gross National Product, which excludes the service sector) in the six COMECON countries of Eastern Europe in the 1960-73 period was almost double that of Latin America in the Third World. It was also almost double the rates of growth in the U.S.A. and the Common Market, the heartlands of advanced capitalism. Further it was virtually identical to the rate of growth of the Soviet Union, the most mature of the socialist economies. Eastern Europe's average rate of growth of industry in the same 1960-73 period also compares favourably with the rates for Latin America (that part of the Third World most comparable to Eastern Europe), and the U.S.A., the Common Market and the Soviet Union.

The economies of the East European countries also differ from the economies of Third World countries in their overall level of development and their sectoral composition. Fifty-five per cent of the net material product of Eastern Europe originates in the industrial sector, compared to around 30 per cent of the G.N.P. of the major countries of Latin America (which are among the more developed, and most influenced by the U.S., countries of the Third World).[23] The East European figure is also slightly higher than that of

Table 7.3
Economic Growth Rates of European COMECON Countries and Others,
1960-1973

	Rate of Growth (N.M.P. or G.D.P.)	Rate of Growth per capita (N.M.P. or G.D.P.)	Rate of Growth in Industry
Bulgaria	8.1%	7.3%	11.0%
Czechoslovakia	4.7	4.1	4.9
German Democratic Republic	4.8	4.8	5.3
Hungary	5.7	5.3	6.8
Poland	6.6	5.6	3.5
Romania	8.8	7.7	12.8
Average of Six East European COMECON Countries	6.5	5.8	8.2
U.S.S.R.	7.1	5.9	9.1
U.S.A.	4.3	3.1	4.8
E.E.C.	4.6	3.8	5.1
Latin America	5.9	3.0	7.0

Source: United Nations, *Yearbook of National Account Statistics,* (1975),
Tables 4A, 4B.

the Soviet Union (51 per cent.) Granted these figures must be reduced somewhat because of the exclusion of the service sector from the concept 'net
material product', but the figures for Latin America must also be reduced
because of the extremely low level of monetary income in the rural sector
and hence under-evaluation of the product of that sector.

The percentage of the economically active population engaged in manufacturing in the six COMECON countries of Eastern Europe ranges from
36.9 per cent for the German Democratic Republic through 34.7 per cent for
Czechoslovakia, to 30.9 per cent for Hungary, 25.7 per cent for Bulgaria,
24.0 per cent for Romania and 23.6 for Poland. This compares with 25.2 per
cent for the Soviet Union, 26.1 for the U.S., and only 10.2 for Chile, 8.6
for Venezuela and 8.4 per cent for Brazil and Colombia.[24] The average
of 29.3 per cent for the six Eastern European COMECON countries
is actually higher than the comparable figure for the Soviet Union. It is
the exact reverse of the relation between these indicators of economic
development for the U.S. (or other advanced capitalist countries) and the

non-socialist countries of the Third World. In keeping with these figures, in 1964 personal consumption *per capita* in the German Democratic Republic was 156 per cent (or one and a half times) that of the Soviet Union, Czechoslovakia was 150 per cent, Hungary 117 per cent, Poland 103 per cent, Bulgaria 100 per cent and Romania 86 per cent.[25] In general the level of economic development and the standard of living are both generally higher in most of the COMECON countries of Eastern Europe than they are in the Soviet Union.

That the period of socialist construction in Eastern Europe has resulted in the rapid industrialization and economic development of these formerly agricultural, underdeveloped countries can be seen by comparing them now to what they were in the 1930s. In 1937 Czechoslovakia had 17 per cent of its economically active population working in manufacturing, Hungary 7.3 per cent, Poland 6.2 per cent, Bulgaria 5.9 per cent and Romania 2.7 per cent. These figures are generally lower than for most Latin American countries of comparable size in the 1970s. The gross domestic product *per capita* of these countries in 1937 (in 1973 U.S. dollars) was $440 for Czechoslovakia, $428 for Hungary, $300 for Poland and $271 for Bulgaria. These figures are again comparable with or lower than many Third World countries today. For example in 1973, the G.D.P. *per capita* of Colombia was $400, the Dominican Republic $480, Guatemala $402, Chile $579, and Egypt (in the Middle East) only $245.[26] In comparison, the 1937 G.N.P. *per capita* (in 1973 dollars) of the United Kingdom was $1,676 and of Italy $503. In 1974 the *per capita* income of the East European countries was $3,599 for East Germany, $2,505 for Czechoslovakia, $1,812 for Romania, $1,812 for Poland, $1,520 for Hungary and $1,002 for Bulgaria (the Soviet figure was $1,880). These figures compare well with the less affluent countries of Western Europe in 1974, e.g. Spain $1,991, Ireland $2,021, Italy $2,442 and the United Kingdom $3,016.[27]

Eastern Europe was truly a poor and backward area in the pre-socialist period, fully comparable to the middle level underdeveloped countries of Asia, Africa and Latin America today. It is the past 30 years of planned socialist development policies since 1948 that have modernized these economies and greatly increased the standard of living, especially of the working and peasant classes.

In summary, we see that nothing like the processes described by dependency theory operate between the Soviet Union and Eastern Europe. The Soviet Union does not grow rich at the expense of East European countries, neither does it develop a specialization in industrial production while the latter specialize in raw materials. In large part it has been the economic ties between Eastern Europe and the U.S.S.R. which have been responsible for the rapid economic growth and industrialization of the former region. In fact, Eastern Europe has consistently had the highest rates of economic growth and industrialization of any region in the world.

Economic Relations Before and After the mid 1950s

It is claimed by the Chinese that there was a qualitative change in the way in which the Soviet Union related to other socialist countries in the mid 1950s. They see Soviet Social Imperialism as a phenomenon of the 1960s and 1970s, while under the leadership of Stalin there were comradely relations among socialist countries. In examining this claim, it is essential to study the changes in the relationships between the Soviet Union and the other socialist countries before and after the mid-1950s.

There was indeed a major change in the economic relations between these countries after 1956, but it was in exactly the opposite direction from that which the thesis of social imperialism predicts. The vastly one-sided trade policies and joint stock companies (beneficial to the Soviet Union) were ended in the period 1953-56 and considerable economic assistance was granted by the Soviets to Eastern Europe which had previously not been available. While prior to 1956 Soviet relations with Eastern Europe were exploitative (a basic, but not the sole, characteristic of imperialism), this has not been the case since 1956. Economic co-operation between COMECON countries and the Soviet Union before 1956 was largely dictated by the latter and designed to serve its interests. But since 1956 economic co-operation has been voluntary and projects participated in only when all parties independently agreed that it was in their interests.

A leading example of the transformation in economic relations between Eastern Europe and the U.S.S.R. which occurred in the 1953-56 period was the liquidation of the inequitable joint stock companies which had been established in Eastern Europe in the aftermath of the Second World War. In these enterprises the bloc partners contributed labour and most of the material inputs, while the Soviets contributed the assets which were almost always former German owned properties and equipment expropriated by the Soviet Union in Eastern Europe. In good part German reparations took the form of equipment and factories formerly German owned (both in Germany and throughout Eastern Europe) staying in place but run by the Soviets usually in co-operative arrangements with the locals. Much of the industrial output of such enterprises was exported to the Soviet Union. When the economies of the East European countries were nationalized in the late 1940s, normally the only exceptions to the nationalization decree were the Soviet owned joint enterprises.

From the 400 formerly German enterprises in Romania, 16 joint stock companies were formed in such key sectors as oil, civil aviation, river transport, banking, and lumber. In 1948-49 eight new companies were formed in chemicals, tractor manufacturing, natural gas, coal metallurgy, construction, films and insurance. In Bulgaria there were five joint stock companies (plus some wholly Soviet owned power stations) in non-ferrous mining, construction, shipbuilding, civil aviation and uranium ore. In Hungary the Soviets incorporated at least 69 former German enterprises into joint stock companies.

Most of the joint enterprises created were in countries formerly part of or allied with Nazi Germany (Bulgaria, Romania, Hungary, East Germany and Austria). But joint stock companies were also formed in Yugoslavia with the voluntary agreement of the Yugoslavs. The agreements signed in 1946 and 1947 between the Soviets and the Yugoslavs stipulated that these companies were to promote the economic development of Yugoslavia and to serve as mechanisms by which the Soviets would channel capital goods and technical assistance to Yugoslavia. Two companies were formed, one in civil transport-ation and the other in Danubian shipping. In both cases they came to domin-ate their respective sectors, driving out purely Yugoslav enterprises. The Soviet managing of these enterprises to the advantage of the U.S.S.R. became an important issue in the split between the Yugoslavs and the Soviet Union in 1948.[28]

The joint stock companies typically were granted concessions not available to purely locally owned enterprises. They often had special property and legal rights, and were normally free from taxation, customs duties and most foreign exchange restrictions. These privileges virtually amounted to extra-territoriality and gave them a strong competitive advantage over local state enterprises.

The joint stock company was first developed with Mongolia, the world's second socialist country, and with the Republic of China, both in the mid 1920s. Among the first to be established were those in wool and leather procurement and export (trading companies) and the Chinese Eastern Railway, both initiated in 1924. In the course of the pre-World War II period, numer-ous other joint stock enterprises were established in all fields of trade, trans-port and banking. After the War joint enterprises were set up in mining and processing of oil and minerals. The mutually endorsed purposes of the numerous Mongolian-Soviet joint stock companies were to force out Chinese, Japanese, British and American capitalist interests and to aid the economic development of Mongolia.[29]

Following the outbreak of overt opposition to Soviet domination in Eastern Germany in 1953, the Soviets rapidly began to liquidate their various joint stock enterprises. They turned all assets over to the local countries and in the process recognized the disproportionate and unjust benefit the Soviet Union had been gaining from their operation. The earliest liquidations were partly in the form of outright gifts to the countries concerned and partly as sales to be paid off gradually. After the Polish and Hungarian events óf 1956, which also indicated considerable resentment against Soviet domination of Eastern Europe, all remaining joint stock companies (in both Eastern Europe and Mongolia) were turned over without compensation and almost all of the debt inherited from the earlier liquidation of joint stock companies was cancelled. By 1957 all but a single joint enterprise with Bulgaria (main-tained at Bulgaria's insistence) had been liquidated and all assets turned over (almost always without charge) to the Eastern European governments.[30]

It is of some interest to note that after the liberation of China in 1949 joint Soviet-Chinese stock companies were set up in oil, uranium prospecting, civil aviation and shipbuilding. But unlike in the cases of Mongolia and

Eastern Europe, when these joint enterprises were liquidated in 1954 the Soviets insisted on full payment (which was collected), making China unique among the socialist countries in this regard. The Manchurian railway, which had been joint Soviet-Chinese property before being taken over by Japan in the 1930s (the Soviets sold their interests to Manchukuo) and which reverted to Soviet control in 1945, was turned over to China in 1952.[31]

The voluntary liquidation of the inequitable joint stock companies of the 1945-53 period, and the turning over of their assets to the various socialist countries without compensation (China excepted) is a phenomenon unknown to a capitalist imperialist country. The only known cases of amicable liquidations of imperialist owned enterprises (e.g. Arabian or Venezuelan oil holdings) occur on the basis of sale at prices acceptable to the imperialist owned transnational corporations. The Soviet Union's mid 1950s massive liquidation of joint stock companies without compensation, at the very time when the Chinese and their supporters now argue capitalism was being restored and the Soviet Union was becoming social imperialist, is a strong argument against the Chinese thesis. The revival of the joint enterprise in recent years, on terms mutually agreeable to both the Soviets and the COMECON countries, must be considered a qualitatively different phenomenon from the old East European enterprises in the ex-Axis countries in the 1945-53 period. Rather than being set up and run primarily in order to aid the reconstruction of the Soviet Union (as a form of reparations), the current joint enterprises are entered into voluntarily by the various countries by mutual agreement and with benefit to all parties. Another key difference is that most of these present enterprises are located in the Soviet Union rather than in Eastern Europe, and are geared to the production and export of raw materials from the Soviet Union to the other COMECON countries (whereas the earlier joint stock companies were geared to exporting machinery and raw materials from Eastern Europe to the Soviet Union). The reality that the COMECON countries of Eastern Europe fare much better with the new joint enterprises than with the old joint stock companies directly contradicts the thesis that the Soviet Union has evolved in the direction of capitalism and social imperialism since 1953. The qualitative change in economic relations between the East European countries and the U.S.S.R. after the mid 1950s (in terms of joint enterprises and also trade relations) refutes the Chinese notion of the development of social imperialism during this period. The evidence clearly shows that either the Soviet Union was social imperialist from at least 1945 and is becoming substantially less social imperialist over time, or that it is not social imperialist at all. The evidence is clearly incompatible with the notion that social imperialism has arisen since 1953.

It might be added, out of fairness to the Soviets, that their exploitation of Eastern Europe in the post-World War II decade was historically justified by the fact that the Soviet Union had suffered so grievously to defeat fascism and liberate Eastern Europe. Thus all of Eastern Europe owed the Soviet Union a debt that could justly be repaid by aiding in the reconstruction of the devastated Soviet economy. Further it could be claimed that since the Red Army provided the decisive ingredient in allowing local communist parties to assume leadership of their societies, the 'motherland of socialism' was in the best position to decide for the newly born socialist countries what policies they ought to adopt. Whether one accepts these arguments as legitimate or not, the reality is that the Soviet Union did insist on guiding all the world's communist parties and all the new socialist states during this period. The Soviet Union for good or ill was hegemonic in Eastern Europe at this time.

This hegemony over socialist countries has declined considerably since 1953-56. Considerable deviations from Soviet positions are increasingly, if reluctantly, tolerated, that would not have been before 1956. Romania's long-term and successful defiance is a leading example: she refused to participate in the intervention in Czechoslovakia in 1968, consistently drags her feet on COMECON integration, maintains neutrality in the Sino-Soviet dispute, is a member of the International Monetary Fund, etc. So is the independence from Soviet leadership of most of the West European communist parties which has emerged since the mid 1960s. And Vietnam (until 1978) and the Democratic People's Republic of Korea have both kept clear of the Sino-Soviet dispute. Yet the Soviet Union continues as a hegemonic force (albeit decreasingly successfully) as the intervention in Czechoslovakia in 1968 showed.

That the Soviets were considerably more active in interfering in the domestic affairs of the East European countries before 1956 than after, is illustrated by the drastic sanctions taken against Yugoslavia in 1948 and the military intervention in Hungary in 1956. The advice and supervision provided by the Soviets in every sphere of activity were all pervasive in determining the course of government and party policies in Eastern Europe before 1956.

It is instructive to look at the actions taken by the Soviet Union against Yugoslavia in 1948 and Hungary in 1956 in comparison with the actions taken against China in 1960, Albania in 1961 and Czechoslovakia in 1968. If these interventions differed qualitatively, with the latter being manifestations of social imperialism, but not the former, we would have some support for the Chinese position.

The Break with Yugoslavia

Yugoslavia had, more than any other country in Eastern Europe, won its own revolution independently of Soviet assistance. Its base among the people had been won during the course of partisan warfare against the Germans and much of the country had been liberated without the aid of the Red Army. It had a long tradition of autonomy and militancy. It was Serbia that defied the demands of Austria-Hungary in 1914, setting off World War I. It was the Yugoslav resistance that most effectively defied Hitler in World War II. It was Yugoslavia that in 1946 shot down a U.S. plane which had strayed over its territory, this incident precipitating the Cold War. And it was Yugoslavia that was the first among all the communist parties and socialist countries successfully to resist Soviet hegemony.

Although Yugoslavia had not collaborated with the Nazis in World War II, the Soviet Union adopted economic policies towards her which benefited mainly the Soviets. As we noted earlier, two joint Yugoslav-Soviet stock companies were set up in 1946, one of which came to have a virtual monopoly of Danube shipping, the other of internal air traffic. Most of the modern equipment formerly owned by the Yugoslavs was taken over by these companies. They paid no taxes or customs. For the purposes of allocating profits, the Yugoslav asset contributions were valued at 1938 prices, while the Soviet contributions were valued at the considerably inflated prices of 1946-47 (thereby giving the Soviets a disproportionate share of the profits). The Yugoslavs also had to pay 52 per cent higher rates than the Soviets for the use of river transport.[32]

After these two companies were set up, the Soviets began negotiations to set up joint companies in oil, non-ferrous metals, coal, iron and steel. In these negotiations the Soviets were insisting on special concessions. For example, the Yugoslav contribution to the oil company, for the purpose of allocating profits, would not be considered to include the land or oil in the ground, but only labour and equipment; the Soviets would be given priority access to the oil produced, and the joint stock companies would not have to grant welfare benefits to Yugoslav workers comparable to those given by solely Yugoslav enterprises. The Yugoslavs refused to conclude such agreements and began expressing resentment, both over the operation of the two existing companies and over the new Soviet demands. As for the Soviets, they were disturbed by the Yugoslavs' general independent role in the Balkans and wanted to bring them to heel. Two leading issues in this respect were Yugoslav support for the Greek insurgents and her attempt to dominate Albania.

The actual break between Yugoslavia and the U.S.S.R. occurred over the Soviet demand in February 1948 that Bulgaria and Yugoslavia form a federation. The Yugoslavs rejected this demand and as a result the Soviets, in March 1948, began taking strong sanctions against Yugoslavia. On March 18 all Soviet military advisers were withdrawn, and on March 19 all economic advisers. An embargo was placed on trade with Yugoslavia by the Soviet Union and all the other socialist countries. This threatened the collapse of the Yugoslav economy which was heavily dependent on trade with the East European countries because of the West's hostility to recent Yugoslav nationalizations and the friendly relations since 1945 among the East European countries. The Yugoslav Communist Party was expelled from the world communist movement and its leaders compared to fascists. Leading communists were put on trial throughout Eastern Europe and charged with treason for being Titoists. The Soviets also tried to overthrow Tito's leadership inside his own country by supporting alternative leadership within the Yugoslav Party. Although never carried out, the Soviets also made threats of military intervention against Yugoslavia.

In response to these sudden and drastic sanctions imposed by the Soviet Union for defying its requests on the questions of joint stock companies, federation with Bulgaria and policies in Albania and Greece, the Yugoslavs were forced to resort to desperate actions to mobilize domestic support and international aid to preserve their regime. In order to cement peasant support, they reduced pressures on the peasantry and reversed collectivization. To further consolidate enthusiasm in the working class, they adopted the system of workers' councils which came to make basic policies for enterprises, thereby undercutting the economic plan and in good part restoring market principles to the Yugoslav economy with all the problems of unemployment, inflation, inequality, commercialism and all-round economic irrationality that this implies. Internationally the Yugoslavs were forced to turn to those who had previously been their arch enemies, the Americans, for economic assistance to prevent the collapse of their economy. The cost of Yugoslavia's successful resistance to Soviet hegemonism in 1948 has been the degeneration of the most militant socialist country in Eastern Europe — the country which had the most enthusiastic support of its people — into a market socialist economy well on its way to restoring capitalism (in a joint state capitalist private capitalist form).

Soviet sanctions against Yugoslavia were both more sudden and more drastic than the similar sanctions taken against China 12 years later. They were taken with less provocation and had considerably greater effects. The Soviet actions against China and Yugoslavia were, however, similar in that they were taken against two of the most militant and independent minded socialist regimes, regimes whose defiance of Soviet hegemony had the greatest chance of succeeding and thus of undermining Soviet hegemony all around the world. In no reasonable sense can Soviet action against Yugoslavia be considered justifiable, while the action against China is regarded as social imperialism. Yugoslavia's tendencies to degenerate occurred after and because of Soviet sanctions. Yugoslavia's fault was to defy Soviet hegemony, precisely the same thing that China began doing in 1957. Both interventions are equally examples of Soviet hegemonism.

Intervention in Czechoslovakia

The most cited and apparently clearest example of Soviet social imperialism was the intervention of the Soviet army, along with the armies of Poland, Hungary, Bulgaria and East Germany in Czechoslovakia in 1968, in order to reverse the course of Czech 'liberalization'. The majority of Czechs would have preferred the Soviet army not to have intervened. But to prove social imperialism, it must be shown that the U.S.S.R. gained economic advantages (or at least that such was the intention) and that the intervention was against the more progressive forces and classes in the Czechoslovak struggle. In the case of U.S. imperialism, or other capitalist interventions, such elements can always be found. Capitalist imperialist intervention always overthrows popular regimes, like that of Goulart in Brazil, Arbenz in Guatemala, Mossadegh in Iran, Bosch in the Dominican Republic or Sihanouk in Cambodia, in order to instal right wing military regimes in their place. The governments so installed then remove the restrictions on imperialist investment, encourage economic exploitation of their countries by transnational corporations, and typically become closely allied militarily with the U.S., granting the U.S. bases and other military assistance (including interventions in favour of the U.S. in third countries) when desired. If it cannot be shown that the Soviet intervention in Czechoslovakia was more or less equivalent to U.S. interventions in these respects, it cannot be cited as a case of social imperialism, however improper or hegemonic it may be judged.

In judging whether the Czech intervention was a case of social imperialism, it is also instructive to examine other cases of military intervention by socialist countries, e.g. the Soviet intervention in Hungary in November 1956 and the Chinese ending of Tibetan autonomy in 1959. If it be granted that some interventions are legitimate, e.g. Hungary and Tibet, in order to counter rightist regimes, and that such interventions are not manifestations of social imperialism, then of course merely proving that a socialist country militarily intervenes in another is not proof of social imperialism. It must in addition be shown that the intervention was self-serving, that it reversed a progressive course and hindered the advance of socialism. Whether the Chinese are correct or not, they have consistently defended both the Soviet military intervention in Hungary and their own in Tibet, on the grounds that they were none of these things, that instead they were motivated by a desire to advance the interests of the working class and peasants in the countries intervened against. They argue these interventions were not self-serving, but rather effectively countered reactionary forces which were pushing these countries to the right. They argue further that they set or reset the intervened in country on the road to socialism, and that the world movement was spared a demoralizing reverse at the same time as the forces of imperialism were denied an important propaganda victory which might have undermined the solidarity, resolve and military position of the remaining socialist countries. If it can be shown that the intervention in Czechoslovakia was equivalent to the ones in Tibet and Hungary, rather than being similar, for example, to the U.S. intervention in 1965 in the Dominican Republic, then the Chinese case for the Soviets being social imperialist in this instance cannot stand.

As we shall see below the reforms which occurred in Czechoslovakia in 1966-68 were led by and served the interests of the class of professionals and technocrats (the professional intelligentsia). These reforms neither had the support of the Czech working class nor were they in this class's interest. They reflected a clear shift in power within Czech society from the working class to the new petty bourgeoisie of technicians and professionals who increasingly came to dominate Czech society in their own class interest. Their ideology of liberalism, which had such a great attraction in the West, served the interest of these intellectuals who wanted to be free of control by a working-class party, and of the industrial managers and state bureaucrats who wanted both more income and other privileges, and greater freedom to run enterprises and the economy without interference by the working class. If ever there was a clear case of a socialist country going revisionist and moving rapidly towards restoring capitalism through using legal forms (rather than through extra-legal action as in Hungary in 1956), it was Czechoslovakia in the 1966-68 period.

In the 1961-68 period the real wages of Czech workers grew at one of the slowest rates of any country (capitalist or socialist) in Europe. This was, however, not true of the salaries of managerial and technical personnel. As a result the latter gained significantly in relation to the working class in the pre-1968 period. From 1961 to 1967 engineering and technical personnel increased their salaries some 42 per cent more than manual workers.[33]

The essence of the Czech reforms of 1968 were economic. They included: (1) the granting of managerial autonomy to industrial enterprise managers; (2) increasing the income of the new petty bourgeoisie at the expense of the workers; (3) the expansion of the use of material incentives, including incentive pay systems, for the workers; and (4) the reduction in trade union control over enterprises.[34]

The draft enterprise bill of 1968 called for three types of enterprise: (1) social enterprises which would be 'autonomous units', managed exclusively by their own directors within the broad framework of the government's general economic policies and solely responsible for their own business transactions and obligations, receiving no subsidies from the state and relating to one another and the public basically through the market; (2) privately owned co-operatives in the service, handicraft and other sectors which were to be entirely independent bodies; and (3) state owned organizations in certain basic services such as railways, water and roads which would be neither autonomous nor self-supporting.[35] The managers of the autonomous enterprises were to be appointed by the state and made responsible for the effective management of their enterprises without interference from the state or trade unions.[36]

The reforms merely proposed *pro forma* workers' advisory organs to the management's indivisible authority. The reformers' fear of giving workers any say in enterprise management was based in their belief that the workers, if allowed to vote in such matters, would work for their own short-sighted economic interests and ignore economic viability.[37] Workers' participation was dismissed as 'so-called direct democratism' − this being considered dangerous to the economy. Considerable anti-working class elitism permeated the proposals, discussions and plans of the Czech technocratic reformers. Not only did the wide ranging enterprise management reforms not include any real mechanism for workers' participation in decision making, but the formal powers of the trade unions were also considerably cut back, so as to 'improve management efficiency' and 'create a freer flow of labour'. The unions' control over recruitment and specific questions in relation to hours, wages, and disciplinary actions were eliminated, making all decisions in these crucial fields the exclusive prerogative of management.[38]

Wages were to be determined by each enterprise. A significant part of them were to depend on the worker's output, i.e. piece work was increased. Direct penalties for poor quality work were to be instituted. And the abolition of any restraints on firing workers meant that many would lose their jobs, yet no provisions were initially made to cover unemployment. (After strong opposition from workers, a 60 per cent rate of unemployment compensation was proposed.) The technocrats insisted that there wouldn't really be any significant unemployment,[39] but when a number of plants were closed for reasons of inefficiency, many jobs were lost.[40]

Those with greater 'responsibility' in production (managers and foremen) were to receive special remuneration as well as considerable bonuses dependent on the results of their efforts.[41] The creation of a much wider wage spread, allegedly intended to increase productivity through the use of material incentives, was a keystone of the whole reform. This 'delevelling' of wages was consistently defended by Dubcek as a means of combatting the 'all destroying mediocracy'.[42]

After considerable working-class opposition to the enterprise reform was expressed, the idea of setting up workers' councils with very limited authority was reluctantly introduced. These councils, far less influential than those in Yugoslavia, were to be mainly advisory bodies to management with a number of members being appointed as experts. Only in the most basic questions, where workers' wages could be jeopardized, would the councils have a veto over managerial prerogatives. Throughout the revised proposal on workers' councils, it was stressed that the managers must still run the enterprise, determine the programme of development and control personnel policy. It was stipulated that the managers could be dismissed by the councils only in the most extreme and specified conditions.[43]

The Czech working class not only had nothing to do with formulating these liberal reforms, there was active working class opposition to them. There was particular resentment over the imposed reforms which involved economic penalties for poor work, the threat of unemployment, the linking of salaries to enterprise income, the closing of inefficient plants and the removal of wage equalization policies.[44] Most workers were opposed to the whole package of economic reforms, understanding that they would operate against their interests. They saw them as an attack on their wages and economic security.[45] A public opinion poll administered in the spring of 1968 reported that 36 per cent of all people expected their economic situation to get worse in the immediate future and that another 37 per cent were uncertain about their future economic situation.[46]

Numerous strikes, slow downs, refusals to pay union dues and protests on the part of workers in opposition to the technocratic liberal reforms occurred, beginning in 1966 and continuing through 1968. Some of the workers' strike actions were spontaneous protests against reorganization of production lines or plant closures and similar issues, while others were offensive actions to demand changes in the workers' favour in the running of enterprises. Large numbers of letters were received by Czech newspapers from workers protesting against the reforms.[47] In January and February 1968 Novotny, the ex-party secretary who had been deposed by the liberal technocratic reformers, began to agitate among industrial workers against the economic reforms. At one Prague factory he received enthusiastic applause when he declared: 'If to be a conservative means to oppose the lowering of the workers' standard of living, I am proud to be a conservative.'[48]

In 1969 — a year after the intervention — there was an active rank and file movement within the Czech Communist Party (branded 'ultraconservatives' by the Western press) which grew impatient at the slowness of the reversal of the liberalization measures, and which mounted an active (and in good part successful) campaign against liberals in the Party. The Soviets were apparently fearful of this rank and file movement, worrying that it might adopt a pro-Chinese, anti-bureaucratic, militant, anti-revisionist form.[49] This widespread and influential movement indicates considerable ongoing working-class opposition to liberalization.

During the late 1960s, the role of the Communist Party in Czech society was in the process of being very much constricted and weakened.[50] In the summer of 1968 there was a debate on amendments to the Party constitution to allow minorities within the Party to voice public disagreements with the majority, and to permit the organization of factions within the Party. The Soviets argued that this would have transformed the party 'into a debating club'.[51]

Beginning in 1965 and 1966, North American programmes began to appear on Czech T.V. Jackie Gleason, Dinah Shore, Dr. Kildare and the 97th Precinct became regular features.[52] In June 1968 direct control of the content of the mass media by state agencies was abolished. The intellectuals took full advantage of this change to call increasingly into question more and more of the socialist institutions of Czech society.[53] In the course of 1968 there was also a mushrooming of political clubs and other organizations and an increase in the demand to restore some of the old non-Communist political parties.[54]

In the realm of foreign policy, the Czechs cut back their military assistance to Egypt and Nigeria (Egypt's defeat at the hands of the Zionists had just taken place and the war against Biafra's secession was going on at the time). Favourable public discussion of the Israeli and Biafran positions began to appear. There was increasing discussion of an 'independent' foreign policy for Czechoslovakia, improved relations with West Germany, and all-round improved relations with Western Europe.[55] The rapid development of events — especially the growing Czechoslovak coolness to participation in the Warsaw Pact and support of Third World struggles, and a warming towards NATO countries especially West Germany — caused considerable anxiety among the other participants in the Warsaw Pact. East Germany, Poland and the Soviet Union all have very real reasons to fear NATO, and especially West Germany, given the history of the 20th century.

The increase in unfriendly comments about the Soviet Union appearing in the mass media was also a cause of alarm in the U.S.S.R., always most sensitive about maintaining a solid front of Warsaw Pact countries against possible invasion from the West.[56]

The Soviets during 1968 expressed increasing concern to the Czechs, about both the course of their domestic and their foreign policies. They argued that socialism was being undermined in Czechoslovakia, and that the Warsaw Treaty's front against possible Western attack was being undermined. The Soviets expressed their concern about the course of domestic events to the Czechs as follows:

> The developments of events in your country causes us deep apprehension. The offensive by the reaction supported by imperialism against your party and the foundations of the social regime in the Czechoslovak Socialist Republic threatens, we are deeply convinced, to push your country away from the socialist path, and consequently, threatens the interests of the whole socialist system ... Anti-socialist and revisionist forces have taken the press, radio, and television into their own hands and have transformed them into a tribune for the attacks on the Communist Party, for the disorientation of the working class and all working people, for an unbridled anti-socialist demagogy, and for undermining friendly relations between the USSR and the other socialist countries ... In this atmosphere attacks are being carried out against the socialist foreign policy of the USSR and against alliance and friendship with the socialist countries. One hears voices which demand the re-examination of our joint and agreed policy toward the Federal Republic of Germany regardless of the fact that the West German government follows without change a policy hostile to the interest of the security of our countries. Attempts by the government of the FRG and the revanchists to engage in a flirtation find echoes in the leading circles of your country ... The leading circles of the FRG display particular activity; they intend to make use of events in Czechoslovakia in order to plant the seeds of disagreements among the socialist countries, to isolate the GDR, and to carry out their revanchist plans ... Do you not see that the counterrevolution deprives you of one position after another, and that the party is losing control over the course of events and is retreating more and more under the pressure of anti-Communist forces? ... It is our conviction that a situation has been created where the threat to the socialist foundations of Czechoslovakia menaces the common vital interests of the remaining socialist countries. The peoples of our countries would never forgive us for indifference and carelessness in the face of that danger ... Our parties and peoples bear the historic responsibility for not allowing the loss of the revolutionary gains already obtained ... This is why we consider that a resolute rebuff to the anti-Communist forces and a resolute struggle for the preservation of the socialist regime in Czechoslovakia are not only your task but also our task.[57]

The Soviets, together with the four other Warsaw Pact states which were shortly to intervene in Czechoslovakia, issued a letter to the Czech Party on July 15 1968 which very explicitly expressed their fears and intentions:

> We cannot accept that the hostile forces push your country away from the socialist path and create the threat of pulling Czechoslovakia out of the socialist commonwealth. This is not only your problem. This is the common problem of all Communist and Workers' parties and of all states united by alliance, co-operation, and friendship. This is a matter of common concern for the countries which have joined together in the Warsaw Treaty in order

to ensure their independence as well as peace and security in Europe and to erect an unsurpassable barrier against attempts by imperialist forces of aggression and revanche . . . The borders of the socialist world were pushed into the centre of Europe up to the Elbe and the Shumar Mountains. We shall never assent to the prospect of a threat to these historic achievements of socialism as well as to the independence and security of our peoples. We shall never assent to the prospect that imperialism might peacefully or not, from the outside or the inside, make a breach in the socialist system and change the balance of power in Europe to its advantage.[58]

The doctrine, invoked when the five countries sent their troops (unopposed) into Czechoslovakia, reflected the principles contained in the above two statements. To what extent the intervention was in fact motivated by these ideals can only be evaluated in the light of the evidence for this model versus the evidence for a social imperialist type intervention. It is a fact that the Soviets and four other countries sent troops into Czechoslovakia to reverse the liberal reforms. It is also a fact that this intervention was not generally welcomed by the Czech people, even though the Czech working class was opposed to the economic reforms. It is equally a substantial fact that the liberal reforms were a product of the new petty bourgeoisie of professionals and technocrats, were instituted against the working class, served the interests of the class which proposed and implemented them, and at least the economic reforms,which were the heart of the entire programme, were often actively fought by the working class. The Soviet intervention, even though it was not called for by the Czech working class, was nevertheless decisively on their side in the internal class conflict which Czech society was undergoing around the question of liberalizing the economy to the advantage of the managerial class. Furthermore, the subsequent measures forced on the regime by the Soviets had considerable support in the Czech working class. The intervention, unlike any by a capitalist imperialist country, overthrew the rule of a privileged elite that was consolidating itself; and restored a regime much more favourable to the interests of the lower classes. This alone would make the accusation of social imperialism questionable.

In addition, it must be pointed out that no special Soviet economic advantage was gained through the intervention. As we have already shown, the economic relationship between Eastern Europe and the Soviet Union today is fully equitable and most beneficial to countries like Czechoslovakia. No investment opportunities, special trading rights or other economic concessions were granted the Soviets as a result of their intervention. This, too, sharply distinguishes it from interventions by capitalist imperialist countries.

The Soviet and other Warsaw Pact countries' arguments about maintaining military security also reflected a very real concern. Eastern Europe had been invaded and conquered twice in the previous 53 years by the Germans. The Soviets alone, as previously mentioned, had suffered the loss of 20 million lives only 25 years before. They are militarily inferior to the U.S./NATO countries, especially in nuclear weapons. Whether realistically or not, they are extremely afraid of another attack by West Germany and the U.S., and are thus insistent on maintaining the integrity of the Warsaw Pact as long as NATO exists. While the wishes of one or another East European people to be neutral in the dispute between East and West may get trampled on by the Soviets, to call their insistence that the Warsaw Pact stay solid 'social imperialist', which implies domination in the self-serving economic interest of the Soviet Union, is a considerable distortion.

Hungary, 1956

Clearly, at least in the eyes of the Chinese and their followers, military intervention is not sufficient to categorize a country or action as social imperialist since China (and Yugoslavia) at the time supported, and has continued to support, the Soviet intervention in Hungary in November 1956. China argues this was justified by the need to prevent the complete overturn of the socialist system there and its replacement by capitalism. Let us examine the differences and similarities between the 1956 intervention in Hungary and the 1968 intervention in Czechoslovakia.[59]

Because of serious bureaucratic distortions and forced industrialization in the previous seven years, there was considerable unrest amongst the Hungarian population, including the industrial working class, which manifested itself in spontaneous riots and rebellions in October 1956 after a period of liberalization. During the course of two weeks, the Hungarian Workers' Party (the Communists) virtually fell apart and ceased to function. There were numerous acts of terror against Communists. The old pre-socialist political parties were reorganized and started to function again. Openly anti-socialist propaganda and agitation became common and foreign supported rightist groups began to operate. In two weeks the situation in Hungary degenerated a lot more than its equivalent in Czechoslovakia in 1968, where the Communist Party continued to function and criticism of the socialist system remained much less vociferous. On the other hand, the Hungarian working class, unlike the Czech, was actively involved in the process. Hungarian workers formed workers' councils which tended to be pro-socialist but anti-party, while the Czech workers in 1968 were hostile to the basic liberalization reforms and split on the question of Soviet intervention. Had the Soviets not intervened in November 1956, it is likely that within a short time a Western type of parliamentary regime, not under the leadership of a communist or socialist party, would have come to power and undone most of the socialist reforms of the previous ten years. As in the case of Czechoslovakia, the Soviets were mainly interested in preserving the Warsaw Pact as a defensive screen against Western invasion. They saw the Hungarian withdrawal from the Pact and adherence to neutrality (steps the Czechs never took) as a major threat to their defences. In short, except that the Hungarian working class (unlike the Czech) gave active support to the liberalization process, the Hungarian events represented a greater immediate threat to both socialist institutions and Soviet defence than did the Czechoslovak events.

Both the Yugoslavs and the Chinese argue that the intervention in Hungary was an act of 'proletarian internationalism' while the intervention in Czechoslovakia was not. However, to make this argument, one must analyse both the motives of the intervening power and the conditions in the countries intervened against, and not just refer to the act of intervention. To make a credible case that the Czech intervention, but not the Hungarian, was a manifestation of social imperialism, it must be shown that the Soviets were pursuing their own economic interests in the former case, (i.e. that they gained economically from the Czech intervention), but not from the Hungarian. It would probably also be necessary to establish that pro-working class forces were supported in the Hungarian intervention, but anti-working class forces were supported in the Czech. Neither of these two points can be substantiated. The Soviets did not gain economically from either intervention (although their defence structure was preserved in both cases). Further, they actively opposed the workers' council movement among the Hungarian workers while essentially siding with the Czech working class in 1968. In sum both the Czech and the Hungarian events must be categorized as instances of Soviet *hegemonism*, albeit hegemonism exercised by and large in the interests of the preservation and advance of socialism. Neither of these actions can legitimately be considered manifestations of social imperialism since both are lacking the essential characteristics of the interventions by the advanced capitalist countries in the affairs of Third World nations.

The Autonomy of Eastern Europe Today

The consistent independence of Romania is clear proof that the East European COMECON countries today exercise great autonomy from the Soviet Union and cannot be categorized as satellites, either in the sense of being economically exploited by, or politically subordinate to, the Soviet Union. The interests of the COMECON countries seem pretty much to coincide. The economic relationships among them are mutually beneficial, although probably somewhat less so for the Soviet Union. Their military alliance is mutually advantageous since they all fear a U.S./West German sponsored revanche, invasion or support of local reactionary forces. The fact that the COMECON countries freely choose whether to participate in joint projects (often declining a specific invitation) is further proof that they are not co-ordinated by some central decision making bureau operating out of the Soviet Union. There are considerable differences in economic organization amongst them (e.g. between Hungary and East Germany), degree of liberalization (e.g. Bulgaria and Hungary), degree of collectivization (Poland versus the rest of Eastern Europe), worker participation in industrial management (Poland versus Hungary), involvement with world capitalist economic institutions such as the I.M.F. (Romania is a member), economic relations with the U.S. (Poland accepts U.S. foreign aid), relations with other socialist countries

(Romania is on good terms with China), etc. Before 1956 the U.S.S.R. was clearly the hegemonic power in Eastern Europe and used its position to its own economic advantage. Although the Soviet Union continues to insist on the integrity of the Warsaw Pact and vows to prevent the total disintegration of socialism in any of the COMECON countries, it can no longer be said that the COMECON countries are exploited by, or subordinate to, the Soviet Union in anything like the way many Third World countries are subordinate to the U.S. and other advanced capitalist countries.

The Soviet Union within rather broad parameters is still hegemonic in most of Eastern Europe, but does not use its superior position in its own economic interests as it would if it were a social imperialist superpower. The countries of Eastern Europe by and large control their own affairs provided only that the basic socialist organization of their society is preserved, and continued participation in the Warsaw Pact is ensured. The economies of the COMECON countries are co-ordinated in the genuine interests of all participants and the beneficial trade and aid relations with the U.S.S.R. have greatly helped the industrialization of the six Eastern European countries since 1956. To sum up, while the U.S.S.R. is hegemonic in Eastern Europe, in no sense can it be considered to be social imperialist.

References

1. Paul Marer, *Soviet and East European Foreign Trade, 1946-1969,* (Bloomington: Indiana University Press, 1972), pp.33, 43; and United Nations, *Yearbook of International Trade Statistics,* (1974), p.926.
2. *Ibid.,* Special Table B.
3. *Ibid.*
4. Paul Marer, *op. cit.,* pp.33, 43; and United Nations, *op. cit.,* p.932.
5. John Kramer, 'The Energy Gap in Eastern Europe', *Survey,* 21:1-2 (Winter-Spring 1975).
6. *Ibid.,* p.71.
7. Franklin Holtzman, *Foreign Trade Under Central Planning,* (Cambridge, Mass.: Harvard University Press, 1971).
8. *Ibid.*
9. Z.M. Fallenbuchl, 'COMECON Integration', in Morris Bornstein and Daniel Fusfeld (eds.), *The Soviet Economy,* (Homewood, Ill.: Richard Irwin Inc., 1974), pp.401-2.
10. Paul Marer, 'The Political Economy of Soviet Relations with Eastern Europe', in Steven Rosen and James Kurth (eds.), *Testing Theories of Economic Imperialism,* (Lexington, Mass.: D.C. Heath and Co., 1974).
11. Ellen Mickiewicz, *Handbook of Soviet Social Science Data,* (New York: The Free Press, 1973), p.215; *Current Digest of the Soviet Press,* 'Fuel and Raw Materials for CMEA Lands', 28:33 (7 July 1976), pp.12-13.
12. Marshall Goldman, *Soviet Foreign Aid,* (New York: Praeger, 1967), p.7.
13. For a good discussion of the Soviets' use of trade as a weapon, see

Robert Owen Freedman, *Economic Warfare in the Communist Bloc,* (New York, Praeger, 1970).
14. Marer, 'The Political Economy of Soviet Relations with Eastern Europe', *op. cit.,* Goldman, *op. cit.,* pp.34-7; and Howard Sherman, *The Soviet Economy,* (Boston: Little Brown and Co., 1969), p.194.
15. Marer, *op. cit.*
16. Leo Tansky, *Soviet Foreign Aid: Scope, Direction and Trends* in Morris Bornstein and David Fusfeld (eds.), *The Soviet Economy,* (Homewood, Illinois: Richard Irwin Inc., 1974).
17. Fallenbuchl, *op. cit.,* p.403.
18. L. Brainard, 'Soviet Foreign Trade Planning' in U.S. Congress Joint Economic Committee, 94th Congress, 2nd Session, 1976, *The Soviet Economy in a New Perspective;* Fallenbuchl, *op. cit.,* Wilczynski, pp.195-203; Goldman, *op. cit.,* pp.51-59; Gregory, pp.276-8.
19. Fallenbuchl, *op. cit.;* Jan Triska and David Finley, *Soviet Foreign Policy,* (New York: Macmillan, 1968), pp.223-9.
20. Fallenbuchl, *op. cit.;* Sherman, *op. cit.,* pp.192-8; and Wilczynski, *op.. cit.,* p.198.
21. Wilczynski, pp.196-7; Triska and Finley, pp.219-220; and *Current Digest of the Soviet Press* (July 7 1976), p.13.
22. Fallenbuchl, pp.404-5; *Current Digest of the Soviet Press* (July 7 1976), p.13.
23. U.N. *Yearbook of National Account Statistics,* Vol.III, 1975.
24. U.N. *Statistical Yearbook,* 1975.
25. Ellen Mickiewicz, *Handbook of Soviet Social Science Data,* (New York: The Free Press, 1973), p.209.
26. U.N. *Yearbook of National Account Statistics,* Vol.III Table 11A, 1975.
27. Business International Corporation, *Investing, Licensing and Trading Conditions Abroad,* June 1976.
28. Marer, 'The Political Economy of Soviet Relations with Eastern Europe'; Goldman, Ch.1.
29. Goldman, Ch.1.
30. Goldman, Ch.1.; Marer, 'The Political Economy of Soviet Relations with Eastern Europe'.
31. Goldman, pp.20-21.
32. The information for this discussion of the Yugoslav-Soviet confrontation is taken from the following sources: Robert Owen Freedman, *Economic Warfare in the Communist Bloc.,* (New York: Praeger, 1970); Vladimir Dedijer, *The Battle Stalin Lost,* (New York: Viking, 1971).
33. Frank Parkin, *Class Inequality and Political Order,* (New York: Praeger, 1971), p.178. Galia Golan, *The Czechoslovak Reform Movement,* (Cambridge, England: The Cambridge University Press, 1971), p.78.
34. Golan, Ch.21.
35. *Idem.*
36. *Ibid.,* Ch. 5.
37. Golan, pp.97-98; Alex Pravda, 'Some Aspects of the Czechoslovak Economic Reforms on the Working Class in 1968,' *Soviet Studies,* July 1973, 25:1, pp. 115-79.
38. Golan, pp.96-100.

39. Golan, pp.67, 231.
40. Pravda, p.106.
41. Golan, p.67.
42. Pravda, pp.106-9.
43. Pravda, p.119.
44. Golan, pp.76, .231, 276.
45. Pravda, p.107; Golan, pp.230-231.
46. Pravda, p.110.
47. Pravda, p.113; Parkin, p.176; Golan, pp.76, 230-231.
48. Pravda, p.104.
49. The *New York Times,* December 10, 1969, 2:4.
50. Golan, pp.300-303.
51. W.W. Kulski, *The Soviet Union in World Affairs,* Syracuse, New York: Syracuse University Press, 1973.
52. Golan, Pravda,
53. Golan, p.138.
54. Golan, p.295.
55. Golan, pp.312-315.
56. Golan, Ch.24.
57. Kulski, pp.326-7.
58. *Ibid.,* pp.320-321.
59. The discussion of the Hungarian events of 1956 draws primarily on Herbert Aptheker, *The Truth about Hungary,* (New York: Mainstream Publishers, 1957); Paul Kecskemeti, *The Unexpected Revolution,* (Stanford, California: Stanford University Press, 1961); and Paul Zimmer, *Revolution in Hungary,* (New York: Columbia University Press, 1962).

8. Soviet Relations with the Non-socialist Third World

In this chapter we will examine Soviet economic and political relations with the non-socialist countries of Africa, Asia and Latin America in order to determine whether its relations with them are imperialistic, or hegemonic, or truly supportive of progressive and revolutionary movements in ways which offer no special advantage (other than the weakening of Western imperialism). We will examine Soviet economic assistance, military aid and anything that could be considered analogous to Soviet investments. Through looking at the case of one of the U.S.S.R.'s main trading partners in the Third World — India — the nature of Soviet export and import trade with the Third World will also be examined. In considering these economic relations, careful attention is paid to the question of whether Soviet assistance and trade are essentially analogous to that of the leading Western capitalist countries. Can the Soviet Union be said to exploit the countries of Africa, Asia and Latin America, to hinder their economic development and to make them subservient to Soviet interests? This chapter also examines whether the Soviet Union intervenes politically in Third World countries against the interests of progressive and revolutionary movements in order to advance its own narrow self-interest. In this examination, the countries and situations which China and her supporters most often cite as manifestations of Soviet social imperialism are looked at in turn : India, Bangladesh, Cambodia, Angola and the Horn of Africa.

Economic Assistance

The foreign assistance of a typical capitalist imperialist country such as the United States is designed to: (1) facilitate the exports of the major domestic corporations to the Third World (assistance is almost exclusively in the form of export credits which must be used on designated products of the donor's major corporations); (2) pressure the recipient countries to follow policies favourable to the transnational corporations based in the donor country, (e.g. no restrictions on the repatriation of profits, no protection of locally owned businesses, low wages, etc.); and (3) very often, result in a profit for the treasury of the donor nation which normally requires repayment with interest in hard currency.[1] In this section Soviet foreign assistance is examined to determine whether it possesses similar characteristics.

Before the mid 1950s the Soviet Union did not provide economic or military assistance to non-socialist countries. It was not until ten years after the end of World War II and some years after the beginning of the programme of U.S. assistance that the Soviets began their foreign assistance programme. The total amount of Soviet foreign assistance to the less developed capitalist countries of the Third World has fairly consistently averaged only about 10 per cent of U.S. aid in the period 1954 to 1974. In the period 1954 to 1965 Soviet aid averaged 8 per cent of U.S. aid, while in the period 1967 to 1974 it averaged 10 per cent, a slight but not very impressive growth.

Over three-quarters of all Soviet aid to the Third World is to the Near East and South Asia. In the period 1954-74, the largest recipients of Soviet aid were: India ($1,943 million), Egypt ($1,300 million), Afghanistan ($826 million), Iran ($750 million), Pakistan ($652 million), Iraq ($549 million), Turkey ($530 million), Algeria ($425 million), and Syria ($417 million). Priorities in aid for these countries were basically the same in the periods 1954-66 and 1967-74, with the exception that aid to Turkey and Pakistan has been concentrated in the post 1966 period (most of Pakistan's aid has been granted *since* the restoration of civilian rule in 1971 and before the overthrow of Bhutto). In the post 1966 period, Chile, (prior to Allende's overthrow in 1973), Bangladesh, Argentina (during the neo-Peronist period) and Guinea have also been major recipients of Soviet aid.[2] An examination of the countries favoured by Soviet aid reveals two factors motivating its distribution: (1) Soviet strategic interests around its southern borders, e.g. Turkey, Iran, India, Pakistan and Afghanistan, which seems to dictate aid independent of the nature of the regimes; and (2) support of progressive anti-imperialist forces, e.g. Iraq, Algeria, Egypt (during the pre Sadat period), Syria, Argentina (during the neo-Peronist period), Chile (during the Allende years), Guinea and Pakistan (during the Bhutto era).

In terms of the total amount of aid received, the two factors appear equally important. India, a mildly progressive regime somewhat antagonistic to U.S. imperialism and to the Chinese, and fitting to some extent into both categories, has been the major recipient of aid. Regimes like in Chile, Algeria, Guinea and Argentina seem to have received it for purely political reasons. And regimes, such as in Iran (the fourth biggest recipient of Soviet aid) and Turkey, seem to have received it for purely strategic reasons. We should note that, since the independence of Bangladesh in 1971, the Soviets have been even handed in their aid to India and Bangladesh on the one side and to Pakistan on the other. Since the 1971 War Pakistan has received $496 million, India $350 million, and Bangladesh $299 million.[3]

Only in the Near East and South Asia is Soviet aid more than a quarter of that of the U.S. In the post 1967 period it was only greater than American aid in Guinea, Mali, the Sudan, Argentina, Afghanistan, Egypt, Iraq and Syria. In this period U.S. economic aid to India was ten times greater than Soviet aid ($3,552 million for the U.S. compared to $350 million for the Soviets), and four times greater for Bangladesh than Soviet aid.

About 95 per cent of Soviet aid to non-socialist countries is in the form of export credits, i.e. promises to deliver Soviet products in return for eventual repayment. As a rule these credits call for repayment over a 12 year period from one year after completion of a project, generally in goods and at 2½ to 3 per cent interest. In the event of the country having difficulty in meeting its repayments, the U.S.S.R. often extends the repayment terms, frequently after long periods of grace. Sometimes it even cancels outstanding debts altogether. The interest rate on U.S. loans is now the same as on Soviet loans, but the form of repayment is very different. Repayment to the Soviets is in the form of locally produced goods, very often the goods produced by enterprises developed with Soviet assistance, thus ensuring that these enterprises are making a net addition to the local economy and not depriving it of either foreign exchange or the products of other enterprises. Repayment in local goods rather than in foreign currency distinguishes Soviet aid from U.S. and most West European aid. The latter requires payment in dollars or their equivalent, an undesirable and difficult task for Third World countries, since to pay back a loan in dollars or any other 'hard' currency requires an increase in exports, meaning emphasis on developing the export sector, (in contrast, to pay back in local currencies or goods does not.) Increasing exports to make repayments often entails forcing down the world market price for raw materials so that the labour necessary for repayment is greater than would be the case if the donor took local goods or currency. Further, the Western insistence on repayment in 'hard' currency means that the international division of labour between advanced industrial exporters and backward raw material exporters is aggravated. This is because the country being aided must gear its economy to expanding raw material exports. Again in contrast, repayment in local goods or currencies (especially, as is the case with Soviet aid, in manufactured goods produced from the industries financed by the assistance) facilitates industrialization and undermines the international division of labour. In comparison to U.S. aid, Third World states find the Soviet method of repayment a most agreeable aspect of her assistance.[4]

Repayment in goods produced by the enterprises constructed with Soviet aid has the additional benefit of providing a market for an industrial enterprise which might otherwise have difficulty selling its output. This is likely to be the case where a project, essential for all-round and rapid economic growth, is built before there is sufficient domestic demand. For example, a technologically efficient steel mill might have to produce, say, one million tons of steel a year to be run efficiently, but local demand might only be 500,000 tons, not enough to justify building a local mill. However, if a local steel mill existed, it would greatly facilitate economic growth such that in a few years local demand for steel might well be one million tons. By accepting payment in locally produced industrial goods, the Soviets thus accelerate the rate of industrialization of a country by allowing it to increase its industrial capacity (and hence its ability to accelerate its all-round economic growth) more rapidly than local demand would allow. By 1971 about 20 per cent of all Soviet imports from the less developed non-socialist economies were industrial goods. For example, tractors, industrial machinery, aluminum products, rolled steel, wire, automobile stampings, clothing, fabrics, footwear, furniture and other consumer goods. Iran, Iraq and Afghanistan repay much of Soviet aid with natural gas and petroleum (from projects in good part developed with Soviet aid).[5]

An additional aspect of the Soviet practice of accepting repayment in goods produced by projects built with their own aid is that this gives them a special interest in ensuring both the high quality of the goods produced with their assistance and the smooth running of these enterprises. It should also be remembered from our earlier discussion that the Soviet Union is virtually self-sufficient in raw materials and actually a net exporter of petroleum, natural gas and almost all metals. So it cannot be considered to be driven to acquiring otherwise unobtainable raw materials through foreign aid.

Soviet aid generally has few strings attached. It is efficient and allows for considerable flexibility. In the mid and late 1950s, when the Soviet Union first began granting foreign assistance to non-socialist, less developed countries, it tended to specialize in highly visible projects such as the Aswan dam, a major steel mill in India, or sports stadiums. However, this is no longer the case. Since the 1960s Soviet aid has focused on promoting sustained and balanced economic development, rather than on a few large projects. Soviet aid projects receive priority treatment — the best Soviet engineers and designers, and the best resources available. Emphasis is given to training local technicians (both on site and in the Soviet Union) and turning the operation of projects over to them.[6]

Soviet aid does result in expanding the U.S.S.R.'s relations with Third World countries. On the one hand, once a project is completed, the U.S.S.R. is in a position to provide spare parts and to sell equivalent goods to those who have become used to dealing with it. On the other hand, the local countries must export locally produced goods to the Soviet Union in repayment. Once such a trade pattern is established, it is likely that it will continue after repayment is completed. It is important to note that the Soviet Union does not have ownership rights in the enterprises established through its assistance. Ownership rights remain with locals, almost always with the state sector. However, it should be noted that, for the first time, in 1970, an agreement (with India) for the establishment of jointly conducted productive enterprises on the Eastern European model was approved.[7]

Soviet aid goes almost exclusively to the state sector. This allows the local government to establish an economic basis independent of private enterprise, as well as free of ties to foreign corporations. The Soviets also emphasize industrial projects. From 1955 to 1965, about 55 per cent of its aid went into them. This emphasis has become even more pronounced since the mid 1960s. Since then, up to the mid 1970s, about 65 per cent of Soviet aid has been for industry. About 20 per cent of all Soviet aid since 1954 has been for the construction of steel plants.[8] In both its almost exclusive aid to the state sector and in its great emphasis on industrialization, Soviet aid differs radically from U.S. aid. The latter emphasizes the private sector, both directly and in terms of the conditions which require the local government to promote private enterprise, especially U.S. corporations' investments. U.S. aid also almost never assists industrial development (almost all U.S. aid is for development of raw material production or infrastructure that facilitates raw material exports). Needless to say, Soviet aid encourages all-round development, economic independence and the strengthening of the state sector, while discouraging dependence on foreign owned corporations and U.S. and European imperialism. U.S. assistance encourages specialization in raw material exports, and facilitates the investments of U.S. corporations and general dependence on the U.S.

One of the major accomplishments of Soviet aid has been that it has stimulated the amount given by capitalist countries. It has even increased the latters' willingness to give aid to the state sector and industrial projects, and led them to improve their terms by reducing the interest rates to the 2.5 per cent level offered by the Soviets and attaching fewer conditions to loans.[9]

The Soviets provide extensive technical assistance to the Third World in the form of training in modern skills. In 1975 there were about 18,000 technicians in the Soviet Union from the less developed countries. By that year, the Soviets had also trained about 23,000 local technicians in the U.S.S.R. and 450,000 on the job in the Third World.[10] They provide elaborate training projects which are far superior to those provided for locals by the West's transnational corporations. The Soviets train locals for positions of responsibility at all levels of the operation since it is they who will be running the enterprises. Locals are also very often integrated into the designing of projects.[11] Such technical assistance is considered part of the costs of project construction and so must be eventually reimbursed by the local government.

By the end of 1972 an estimated $1.4 billion had been repaid on more than $4 billion in actual Soviet aid distributed to the less developed non-socialist countries. Repayments reached $260 million in 1972.[12] Repayments in locally produced goods in 1973-74 accounted for about 10 per cent of total Soviet imports from the less developed non-socialist countries. Because of a reduction in Soviet economic aid to India and Egypt in recent years, plus the fact that so much assistance was granted to these countries in the 1950s and 1960s, the value of the goods exported to the Soviet Union in repayment for past aid has exceeded the value of new assistance in the mid-1970s.[13] It should also be noted that, because the Soviet Union often agrees to take repayment in goods it does not really need, it sometimes resells these goods on the world market.

Soviet foreign assistance is a real burden on the Soviet economy because, as a planned economy, it has full employment and no surplus production capacity or workers. Everything produced in the Soviet Union has an immediate domestic use. In a capitalist economy, on the other hand, there is a perpetual spare capacity which can be brought into production via aid-subsidized exports to the less developed countries. With the U.S., foreign assistance actually takes the form of the American government paying its corporations to ship goods to the Third World, i.e. subsidizing private enterprise to increase production and profits. Without such a state subsidy to private enterprise, the goods exported would never have been produced and the profits made never have been gained. In this way foreign assistance does not reduce total consumption in a capitalist economy. But it does reduce the total amount of goods available to a socialist economy.[14] Thus, although the less developed countries have to pay a two and a half to three per cent interest rate on the credits they get from the Soviet Union, a considerable subsidy component is contained in these loans. For if she did not export advanced equipment to the less developed countries on credit for local industrial projects, but instead utilized such equipment at home, its contribution to Soviet economic growth would be far higher (since the Soviet rate of growth averages 7 per cent) than the tiny rate of interest she gets on foreign assistance.

Suggestions that the Soviet Union is an imperialist country, driven by the same economic logic as a monopoly capitalist country, are also not substantiated by the data on the role of foreign assistance in the Soviet economy. The value of Soviet foreign assistance totals only 0.23 per cent of the Soviet net material product (compared to 0.54 per cent of the U.S.'s G.N.P.); 0.57 per cent of the value of total fixed capital investment (compared to 4.0 per cent of the U.S.'s); and 4.1 per cent of total Soviet exports (compared to 12.2 per cent of the U.S.'s). In Lenin's model of the motive force of imperialism, foreign investment serves as the primary mechanism by which the capital accumulation process can continue. Quite clearly nothing like the process laid out by Lenin could possibly be operating in the Soviet Union where domestic capital investment is 200 times larger than foreign aid. We must also take into account that there has been a slight *decrease* in the ratio of Soviet foreign assistance to domestic fixed capital formation from the period 1955-66 to the period 1967-74. This shows that there is no tendency to need overseas capital outlets to maintain the rate of capital accumulation inside the U.S.S.R.

It is interesting to contrast Soviet assistance to that from the People's Republic of China. An examination of the leading recipients of Chinese aid reveals that its motive does not appear to be very different from that of Soviet aid. Both countries seem to combine support of progressive regimes, e.g. Tanzania and Indonesia (before 1965), with strategic considerations, e.g. Pakistan, Zaire and Zambia.[15] In the Chinese case, strategic considerations primarily imply winning friends against the Soviet Union and hence supporting regimes which tend to be hostile to the Soviets. For the Soviets, strategic interests mainly imply an attempt to neutralize U.S. influence (e.g. in Iran, Turkey and the Middle East in general), but also secondarily Chinese influence (e.g. supporting the only mildly progressive Indian regime against China, and attempting to neutralize Chinese influence in Pakistan).

Chinese assistance terms are more generous than Soviet, and dollar for dollar it is probably more effective in winning friends and encouraging local development. However, the differences between the two are not sufficient to call the first truly altruistic and the second a form of imperialism. Soviet assistance is far more beneficial to the less developed countries than American aid (dollar for dollar), and results in making them less dependent on imperialism.

It promotes industrialization and helps the containment of private industry (local and international) without generating significant dependence on the Soviet Union (other than that implicit in securing spare parts).

Economic Assistance: The Case of India

As one of the two leading recipients of Soviet aid in the Third World, it is instructive to examine the case of India. Although since 1954 India has been the principal recipient of Soviet economic assistance in the non-socialist world, most of this was received in the 1950s and during the first part of the 1960s when India was leader of the non-aligned movement in the Third World. Generous Soviet aid was given during this period in order to encourage similar policies in both India and other countries, as well as to encourage the advance of progressive domestic policies within India. When India's role as a major progressive force in the Third World declined (its domestic policies also showing less progressive promise), Soviet assistance declined. In the period 1967-74 India has received only one credit from the Soviet Union (for $350 million in 1973).[16]

By far and away the major supplier of economic assistance to India in both the 1954-66 and the 1967-74 periods has been the U.S. It has supplied 4.3 times more assistance than the Soviet Union to India in the period 1954-74 as a whole and 10 times as much in the most recent period (1967-74). It is clear that not only does the U.S. dominate foreign assistance to India, but it is also dwarfing the Soviets more and more in this respect.

India, along with Egypt, were in the mid 1950s the first non-socialist countries to receive Soviet economic assistance. The generous terms of repayment offered by the Soviets (two and a half per cent rate of interest and repayment in local goods for the most part not saleable for hard currency in the world market, or in goods actually produced in factories built with Soviet assistance) forced the U.S. and other capitalist countries to offer economic assistance on much better terms to India in order to keep up with the Soviets.

The capitalist countries traditionally charged more or less commercial rates of interest and repayment for the most part had to be in hard currencies earned by Indian exports on the world market. Soviet assistance to the Indians had the major secondary benefit to India of forcing the capitalist countries to provide much better terms.[17] The U.S. government reduced the rate of interest on loans to India to the same level as the Soviets, extended the repayment period beyond theirs, and expanded the proportion of assistance repayable in Indian currency (but the U.S. still required the repayment of a large proportion of its economic assistance in dollars).

In the period 1951-66 India paid back to the Soviet Union 24.9 per cent of the value of all economic credits utilized by India during that period. This figure has risen during the 1970s because only $350 million of new credits have been extended to India since 1967 and the average term of Soviet loans is only 12 years. Naturally in all years since 1967, except 1973 when the

$350 million credit was extended, repayments to the Soviet Union for past loans have exceeded the value of new Soviet credits. In the case of U.S. aid, in the period 1951 to 1966, the ratio of repayment for past loans to total credit utilized by India was 47.1 per cent. Because a great deal of American economic aid to India comes in the form of grants and surplus agricultural commodities which are sold for rupees which are then re-lent in India, the ratio of repayment to total gross assistance utilized from the U.S. is much lower, only 7.8 per cent in 1966.[18]

Between two and three per cent of total Indian exports in the early 1970s were going to the Soviet Union in repayment for previous Soviet credits (both military and economic).[19] A U.N. study found that only 20 to 25 per cent of the commodities shipped by India to the Soviet Union in repayment for past credits could have been sold in the world market to earn hard currency.[20] Thus it is clear that Indian repayment on past credits is no real burden on India. For example, even if all Soviet military and economic assistance had been a grant instead of a loan, India's foreign exchange earnings would have been increased by between 0.5 and 1.0 per cent of her total export earnings. This is far less than the added export capacity developed, thanks to Soviet assistance, in manufacturing. The fact that so few of the goods received in payment by the Soviet Union are saleable on the world market, indicates a significant grant-like component in Soviet assistance (the U.S.S.R. taking relatively undesirable local products not wanted by the advanced capitalist countries).

Unlike American aid, Soviet economic assistance to India has been heavily concentrated in the industrial sector and designed to help the country modernize her economy.[21] And of course, unlike American aid, Soviet assistance is given almost exclusively to state agencies and not to private enterprise, thereby facilitating the development of the state sector. Soviet aid has included modern steel mills, heavy machinery plants, coal-mining machinery plants, glass factories, power stations, precision instrument plants, oil refineries, hydro-electric power stations, petroleum exploration, pump and compressor construction plants, high pressure boiler plants, heavy equipment plants, machine tool factories, and foundries.[22]

The beginning of Soviet economic assistance to India's state owned industrial sector, in the mid-1950s, had the important effect of allowing her to break the domination of her industrial economy, exercised by Western transnational corporations.[23] The famous Soviet aided Bhilai steel mill (announced on 2 February 1955) had major repercussions on both Indian industrial development and her treatment by the Western capitalist countries. The Bhilai project prompted the British and West Germans, who had been engaged in prolonged (and until then fruitless) negotiations about the construction of two other steel mills, to reach favourable agreements with the Indians. The Soviets, by giving top priority to the project, completed the Bhilai steel mill before either the British or West Germans finished theirs. Moreover, the Soviet rate of interest (2.5 per cent) payable in locally produced goods, was much better than the 4.5 per cent and 6.3 per cent payable

in hard currency charged by the West Europeans. In 1964 the Soviets offered
to build a second steel mill at Bokaro after another long fruitless negotiation
between India and the U.S. to build the project. This again provided the
Indians with a major source of leverage in their dealings with the capitalist
countries.[24]

Soviet assistance has never been offered to or withdrawn from India (as it
has in the case of China and some other socialist countries) as the price for
bad or good behaviour.[25] While, as we have seen, the Soviets often agreed to
accept repayment in the form of goods produced by a factory aided by
Soviet credits (so as not to place an undue burden on the Indian economy)
such export agreements cease when the period of repayment is up. There are
no Soviet investments in India, although in 1970 agreements were signed
allowing for the formation of joint Soviet/Indian enterprises on the
COMECON model. In contrast, in 1974, U.S. corporations had a total of
$345 million worth of investments in India.[26] In no sense can the state
owned factories constructed with Soviet assistance be considered as analogous
to U.S. or British transnational corporation owned industries. For these re-
patriate profits to the metropolitan country and operate under profit maximizing principles, without concern for or control by the local Third World
countries. Neither can this be said for any joint Soviet/Indian enterprises
organized on the Eastern European model as a result of the 1970 agreement.

Ownership and Control of Enterprises

Unlike the Western capitalist countries, the Soviet Union does not own productive business enterprises in Third World countries. Consequently she does
not have any interest in promoting profits and protecting the value of foreign
investments. This allows her to give support to progressive policies designed
to give locals authentic control over their economy, where the imperialist
countries must support the interests of their transnational corporations
against those of the local countries.

There are, however, Soviet economic activities in Third World countries,
which do bear at least a superficial resemblance to Western style investments.
They are often pointed to, by both Chinese and Western interests, as manifestations of Soviet social imperialism and it is important to examine them
carefully. The activities referred to are: (1) Soviet trading and shipping
companies; (2) temporary ownership of local property secured by such companies in bankruptcy proceedings; (3) enterprises jointly owned with Third
World governments; and (4) enterprises established through Soviet economic
assistance, which are paid for through the temporary export of part of their
output to the U.S.S.R.

As an outgrowth of its foreign assistance programme and to facilitate its
trade, the Soviet Union has entered into some joint ownership projects with
Third World countries in shipping and trading. Joint trading companies have
been established with Singapore, Ethiopia, Nigeria, Iran, Morocco and some

other countries. They exist under joint Soviet-local management in order to facilitate bilateral trade. The Soviets enter into such agreements (on a 50-50 basis) mostly with the local Third World governments, but occasionally (as in Morocco) where the local state is reluctant to undertake such agreements, with a consortium of private businesses.[27]

To facilitate its trade with the Third World (as well as with the advanced capitalist countries) and to avoid being exploited and dominated by Western financial institutions, the Soviet Union finances much of its trade through banks that it sets up for such purposes (banks which therefore have to have branches in many Third World countries which trade with the Soviet Union).

Occasionally, companies which such trading banks have advanced credit to, to finance imports from the U.S.S.R., fail, leaving these Soviet banks the owners of property liquidated in bankruptcy proceedings. Thus, as occurred in Singapore in 1978, the Soviets find themselves the temporary owners of productive property in Third World countries. Such properties are, however, liquidated as soon as possible in an attempt to recoup part of the losses incurred when the original owners went bankrupt. Temporary ownership of this kind, which typically represents a considerable economic loss for the Soviets (since it is only partial compensation for unpaid debts), can hardly be considered analagous to Western profit oriented investments in Third World countries.

There are a few irrigation and electric power generating projects which are jointly owned by the Soviet Union and its immediate neighbours (such as Afghanistan) which involve the damming of rivers on the borders of the U.S.S.R. The Soviets may also be entering into arrangements with friendly Third World countries of the kind that have become common with Eastern Europe for joint production by enterprises permanently under the control of two or more countries. The first agreement of this kind was signed with India in 1970.[28] If the East European model is followed (see the discussion on joint enterprises in Eastern Europe in the previous chapters), the Third World countries can expect to receive most equitable treatment from the Soviets. Joint ownership and management is not in itself evidence of imperialism. In any event, as of the mid 1970s, the Soviets have not to any appreciable extent implemented such agreements outside of the COMECON countries.

The Soviet Union also assists in the development of raw material production in some Third World countries. An agreement was signed between the Soviets and Afghanistan in 1963 for assistance in prospecting for and extracting natural gas and constructing a pipeline. Afghanistan agreed to repay the Soviets with natural gas up until 1985. The Soviets did not maintain any ownership rights in the enterprise or any rights to the product. A similar agreement was reached with Iraq in 1971 when they granted that country a loan of 200 million rubles to finance a refinery, two pipelines and several industrial projects, to be repaid over a period of years entirely in oil produced by the Iraq National Oil Company. Another example is Guinea, where they constructed a bauxite mining operation in exchange for repayment in 60 million tons of bauxite over a 30 year period. In none of these cases did the Soviets retain any ownership rights or any claims to the products of the enterprises they built, beyond the stipulated repayments.[29]

In comparison to the absence of anything resembling Soviet ownership rights in enterprises in Third World countries, the transnational corporations, based in and owned by nationals of the U.S., had total assets of $27.9 billion in the less developed countries, and another $74.1 billion in assets in the developed countries in 1973. The U.S. corporations in the same year extracted $4.9 billion in profits from their investments in the Third World (a return of 17.6 per cent) and another $4.3 billion on their investments in the advanced capitalist countries.[30] This immense economic stake by U.S. corporations provides a powerful motive behind American government policies designed to guarantee the security and profitability of these investments against the interests of the people of these countries. The absence of a Soviet equivalent to U.S. transnational investment means that the Soviets have no equivalent motive and are thus free to support national liberation movements designed to eliminate foreign economic influences, while the Americans are, of course, not.

Trade: The Case of India

The Soviets have been accused of exploiting Third World countries through trade, in a manner analogous to the advanced capitalist countries, by paying less than their value for the raw material exports of the Third World while charging more than their value for the industrial exports of the Soviet Union. It is often suggested by the Chinese that Soviet, like Western, trade propels the Third World economies into being raw material suppliers for the industrialized countries. To examine the extent to which Soviet trade with the Third World is analogous to that of the West, we will examine this trade with one of its main commercial partners in the Third World — India.

In 1972-73, 14.1 per cent of Indian exports went to the Soviet Union. There has been a steady increase over time in the percentage of Indian exports going to the U.S.S.R. (5.5 per cent in 1960-63, 10.6 per cent in 1964-67, 12.5 per cent in 1968-71). Today the Soviet Union is the second largest consumer of Indian exports in the world (the largest being the United States).[31]

Turning to imports, in 1972-73 only 4.7 per cent of Indian imports came from the Soviet Union, down from 7.7 per cent in 1968-71 and 5.5 per cent in 1964-67. This compares with 16.5 per cent of India's imports from the U.S., 11.2 per cent from Britain, 9.2 per cent from Japan, 7.9 per cent from West Germany and 5.4 per cent from Canada. The Soviet Union is thus only the sixth largest supplier of the Indians. Clearly the Soviet Union does not dominate Indian trade, nor is the overall trend in the direction of Soviet dominance. These patterns do not reflect those to be expected if India were a neo-colony or satellite of the U.S.S.R.[32]

India receives rather better terms of trade in its dealings with the Soviet Union than it does in its dealings with Britain, the U.S.A. and the rest of the capitalist world. Studies of the price of Indian exports to the Soviet Union compared to the price of comparable exports to the capitalist countries show that the Indians usually get higher prices from the Soviets. Of 12 leading export commodities studied by Datar in the period 1960-69, six (tea, coffee, black pepper, cashew nuts, iron ore and footwear) were consistently purchased by the Soviet Union at higher than their world prices. Three (skins and hides, oil cake and raw wool) were usually purchased at prices higher than those paid by the capitalist countries. Two (castor oil and jute) were purchased on a year to year basis sometimes above and sometimes below the price given by capitalist countries. Only one (unmanufactured tobacco) was sold to the Soviets at consistently below the world price (see Table 8.1). Another study, reported in a pamphlet issued by the Communist Party of India (M-L) and designed to show that the Soviet Union *was* social imperialist in relation to India, admitted that of 15 important Indian exports the Soviet Union paid less than the world price in the case of only four.[33]

All these studies are based on unit prices, calculated by dividing the total value of a category of exports (e.g. tobacco) by the total quantity of exports in that category. Consequently unit value does not take into account systematic differences in the quality of products, nor does it specify the mixture of products within the somewhat broad categories. These figures have therefore to be examined carefully. For example, the fact that the unit price paid by the Soviets for Indian tobacco is consistently less than the world price reflects the fact that the more discerning tobacco tastes of smokers in the capitalist countries dictate that only the highest quality is shipped to them while the lower quality goes to the Soviets. Consequently the Soviets pay less per kilo for the poorer quality tobacco, which the Indians would probably have great difficulty selling on the world market. Similar qualifications could be made about other Indian exports as well. But it is clear from the data that no case can be made that the Soviet Union in any way exploits India by underpaying for its exports. The evidence strongly suggests that India in fact gets higher prices for its exports to the Soviet Union than to the capitalist countries. Likewise, there is no evidence that the Soviet Union charges more than the capitalist countries for its exports to India. This is as we would expect since India is free to purchase its imports from the lowest priced supplier. Both the U.N. study by Datar and studies cited by the pro-Chinese Communist Party of India (M-L) agree on this point.[34]

The results of this analysis of Soviet trade with India indicate that it cannot be considered exploitative, compared to India's trade with the Western capitalist countries. All indications are that Soviet trade with India is typical of Soviet trade with all Third World countries, both socialist and non-socialist (see for example the discussion of Soviet trade with Cuba in the next chapter).

The evidence of both Soviet trade with India and Soviet economic assistance makes it clear that there is no evidence that India is exploited or that it can be legitimately considered a neo-colony of the U.S.S.R. North American economic influence in India is considerably greater than that of the Soviets (as measured by levels of trade, economic assistance or investment). But

Comparative Unit Values of India's Leading Exports, 1957-1969

India's Exports	Purchasing Countries	1957	1958	1959	1960/1	1961/2	1962/3	1963/4	1964/5	1965/6	1966/7	1967/8	1968/9
Raw Wool	East Europe	7.69	5.80	5.79	6.07	5.91	6.16	6.53	6.55	6.25	—	—	—
	Others	6.26	5.64	5.39	5.34	5.71	5.51	6.06	6.31	5.54	—	—	—
Raw Skins and Hides	East Europe	9.10	6.62	9.28	8.82	7.25	7.50	8.59	6.56	8.60	—	—	—
	Others	4.06	5.32	5.96	5.63	6.81	7.42	7.78	9.33	9.91	—	—	—
Tobacco	East Europe	1.52	1.29	1.77	1.59	1.40	1.98	2.50	2.36	2.56	4.03	5.29	5.86
	Others	3.53	3.20	3.64	2.54	3.68	3.99	4.11	3.94	4.19	6.19	6.44	6.32
Cashew Nuts	East Europe	3.66	3.90	3.92	5.22	4.41	3.90	4.12	5.10	5.20	9.16	7.98	9.37
	Others	4.19	3.75	3.95	3.26	4.33	3.99	4.22	5.27	5.39	9.06	8.60	9.59
Tea	East Europe	7.54	7.65	7.47	5.69	7.12	6.97	6.32	6.40	6.72	9.15	9.76	9.35
	Others	5.87	5.85	5.43	6.60	5.86	5.73	5.82	5.80	6.27	7.25	8.38	7.56
Jute	East Europe	129.6	148.2	86.2	195.3	198.4	173.2	168.2	170.0	200.0	245.5	289.7	175.9
	Others	148.0	123.0	116.2	157.1	180.1	174.6	166.7	178.3	204.7	371.6	316.5	431.7
Iron Ore	East Europe	202.0	533.4	495.2	666.4	495.0	488.7	438.3	442.6	417.3	582.9	606.2	625.9
	Others	320.9	524.3	522.4	474.2	296.2	376.5	351.4	331.0	328.2	533.8	521.7	540.6
Coffee	East Europe	6.55	5.56	5.89	4.76	3.03	3.85	3.67	4.39	5.20	5.17	5.61	6.65
	Others	5.04	4.70	3.45	3.28	3.04	3.24	3.47	4.25	4.30	7.75	5.02	4.98
Black Pepper	East Europe	2.04	2.12	1.96	5.09	3.57	3.20	3.23	3.94	4.27	5.77	5.53	5.80
	Others	1.36	1.76	3.22	4.33	3.67	3.11	2.38	3.85	4.17	5.70	4.89	9.27
Castor Oil	East Europe*	—	15.3	14.6	15.8	16.1	14.2	13.4	18.5	17.1	—	—	—
	Others**	—	14.0	13.3	18.8	15.3	13.4	12.7	13.9	20.0	—	—	—
Oil Cake	East Europe	—	—	—	—	—	—	—	—	—	408.6	624.6	607.3
	Others	—	—	—	—	—	—	—	—	—	810.5	571.7	567.0
Footwear	East Europe	—	—	—	—	—	—	—	—	—	20.8	33.8	28.4
	Others	—	—	—	—	—	—	—	—	—	4.7	4.7	5.1

Source: Asha Datar, *India's Economic Relations with the USSR and Eastern Europe, 1953 to 1969*, pp.170-172, 196-197.

* U.S.S.R. only.
** United Kingdom only.

India's trade and economic assistance arrangements with the Soviets, although smaller in quantity, are more beneficial to India than those with the West. While there is Western transnational investment, there is no Soviet investment in India. She cannot be considered to be dominated by the Soviet Union. The secondary economic position of the Soviets in India vis-a-vis the United States does not even give them an economic base to use to put pressure on India if they wanted to (although the provision of considerable military assistance does give the Soviets some important potential clout). Further, there is no evidence that the Soviets have ever put significant pressure on the Indians to tow their line. On the contrary, the Indians, on at least two major occasions, have successfully pressured the Soviets to support Indian foreign policies: in the Sino-Indian conflict of 1962-63 and the Indo-Pakistan War of 1971. The Soviets were also not initially inclined to support the secession of Bangladesh, but seem to have been pressured by India into endorsing Indian intervention in the civil war in East Pakistan.

In no sense can India be considered a neo-colony of the Soviet Union. Likewise the Soviet Union cannot be considered social imperialist in relation to India. In comparison to its relations, even with many socialist countries, Soviet economic and political relations with India have been consistently beneficial to the latter and non-demanding. India has gained considerably more than the Soviets out of their friendly relationship since 1955. Whereas she has received a lot of economic and military help which has enabled her to establish a real independence from Western imperialism, and without losing any of it to the Soviets, the latter have only gained a none too reliable friend in their struggles with China and the U.S. The U.S.S.R. has also been able to use her relations with India to point out to other Third World countries her benevolence and non-interference in internal affairs. But, as the case of Egypt showed, long-term military and economic support of a Third World country is no guarantee that that country will continue to stay friendly to the Soviet Union. If an opportunity presents itself, India may well follow in the wake of Egypt, without having to worry about suffering any serious consequences. The Indian ruling class maintains friendly relations with the Soviets, as did the Egyptians, only as long as they judge it to be in their interests. It is they who are in command of the country, not the Soviets. History may well judge that, if anything, the Soviets, far from being social imperialists, were 'patsies', i.e. were used and then discarded when no longer useful (as they were by Egypt).

Political Interventions in Third World Countries

In the preceding parts of this chapter Soviet economic relations with Third World countries were examined. We paid special attention to whether the Soviet Union was economically exploiting Third World countries and thus whether it was a social imperialist country in an economic sense (i.e. in the sense that Marxism has always insisted is fundamental to the concept of imperialism). Next we will examine the extent to which the Soviet Union intervenes politically in Third World countries; specifically, the extent to which (as the Chinese and others claim) such interventions advance Soviet interests at the expense of the peoples of the Third World; or whether, on the contrary, its interventions advance progressive and revolutionary movements. The second will be looked at in terms of whether the Soviets gain from such interventions in any way other than merely weakening the forces of Western imperialism arrayed against it.

Although it has already been shown that Soviet economic relations with Third World countries are not exploitative and thus that, in the Marxist sense, the Soviet Union cannot be social imperialist, the term may still be applied to it in a metaphorical or ideological sense — i.e. meaning it aspires to be hegemonic in pursuit of its self-interest. After briefly examining the role of Soviet military assistance to Third World countries, we will look at four cases where the Soviets are most often accused of social imperialism (or more precisely self-interested hegemonism) in the Third World.

Military Assistance

Soviet military assistance to the less developed non-socialist countries has expanded considerably during the 1970s. In the period 1955 to 1960 it averaged $214 million a year, in 1961-64 $628 million, in 1965-69 $405 million and in 1970-74 $1,238 million. In the first half of the 1970s Soviet military assistance has averaged over twice Soviet economic assistance.[35] The leading beneficiaries of Soviet arms deliveries in the period 1964 to 1974 have been Egypt ($2,305 million), India ($1,273 million), Syria ($1,153 million), Iraq ($742 million), Iran ($438 million), Algeria ($281 million), Afghanistan ($246 million), Indonesia ($144 million), Libya ($125 million), and Somalia ($ 69 million). With the obvious exceptions of Indonesia and Iran (and possibly Afghanistan and India), it is clear that the Soviets tend militarily to support the most progressive Third World countries. In the cases of Iran, Indonesia, India and Afghanistan strategic considerations, trying to neutralize North American or to a lesser extent Chinese influence, are clearly operating.[36]

It should be noted that, in the period 1965 to 1974, Soviet arms transfers to the less developed countries totalled 58 per cent of U.S. transfers (39 per cent if North Korea, Cuba and North Vietnam are excluded).

During that time the Soviet Union and Czechoslovakia were virtually the only suppliers of weapons to Egypt, Syria, India, Afghanistan, Iraq, Algeria, Somalia and Guinea. The U.S. supplied almost no military equipment to these countries. Thus the Soviet Union had a decisive impact in arming the more progressive non-socialist countries of the Third World, as well as Cuba, North Korea and Vietnam (who respectively received a total of $295, $585 and $3,245 million in military equipment from the Soviet Union during these years).[37] Soviet military supplies played a decisive role in keeping these countries independent of U.S. imperialism, but without producing any material gain for the Soviet Union.

The U.S.S.R.'s military assistance programme in the Third World, as the above cases and, most recently, Ethiopia's have shown, has broken the domination of Third World countries exercised by capitalist countries through the supply or withholding of arms. Modern military establishments can now be created by the less developed countries without automatically promoting dependency on the U.S., France or Britain.[38]

As with economic assistance, the role of Soviet military assistance is considerably greater than its total value, since by competing with U.S. military assistance it forces that country to be more liberal in who it supplies weapons to. A given Third World country is therefore in a position to bargain with both the U.S. and the U.S.S.R. for weapons, with both suppliers knowing that if the one doesn't supply the weapons, the other probably will. This means that regimes, of which one or the other country disapprove, are still able to get weapons. Most importantly, the fact that there is now competition between the U.S.S.R. and the West, as major arms suppliers, means both that revolutionary movements can be regularly supplied with arms and that the less developed countries have a real option to being dominated by Western imperialism.

Soviet military assistance to liberation movements throughout Asia and Africa in recent years has been a decisive factor in their growth and victories. It is unlikely that the Vietnamese would have defeated the U.S., and almost certain that the Angolans would not have defeated the South African invasion in 1975, without such support. Movements like the Palestine Liberation Organization, Frelimo in Mozambique, the Popular Front for the Liberation of Oman, the South-West Africa People's Organization, Z.A.P.U. and more recently Z.A.N.U. as well, have been and still are heavily reliant on weapons supplied by the Soviets and their allies. If the Soviet Union did not exist (or if it refused to supply vital military materials to liberation movements), these movements would be far less advanced in the world today than they are. The Soviet role has indeed been a key one in strengthening such movements to the point where they can succeed. There is little evidence that the price of such decisive military support is subordination to Soviet political direction, or promises of economic or military concessions. The Soviets support a wide range of liberation movements (as well as progressive states) which have well deserved reputations for jealously guarding their independence and controlling their own struggles. The Soviets have equipped movements which are even somewhat antagonistic to each other. For example, Z.A.N.U. and Z.A.P.U. (Contrary to some claims, the lack of significant Soviet military assistance to Z.A.N.U. in the early stages of the Zimbabwe struggle was not due to Soviet attempts to support less militant Z.A.P.U. policies in Zimbabwe, but was due rather to Z.A.N.U.'s refusals to accept Soviet aid — a reluctance which has since ceased.)[39] The clear differences between the Ethiopian Dergue and the P.L.O. (the latter supports the Eritrean Popular Liberation Front), both of which are heavily supplied with Soviet weapons, is another case in point. Little need be said about the Somali intervention in Soviet supported Ethiopia which occurred even though the Somali military was almost entirely equipped with Soviet supplied weapons; or the Egyptian transformation into the leading conservative force in the Arab world, in spite of its heavily reliance on Soviet weapons. It is clear that Soviet military assistance is provided to a wide range of progressive regimes and liberation movements without the Soviets coming to dominate them or securing economic or military advantage.

Bangladesh

The Soviets have been accused of social imperialism for encouraging the separation of Bangladesh from Pakistan in 1971. The facts make it difficult to accept this conclusion for, at least during October 1971, they were trying to prevent a break-up of Pakistan. During this crucial month they were publicly calling for 'respect for Pakistan's territorial integrity'. They were urging a political solution for the problems in East Pakistan on the basis of restoration of democracy in the country as a whole, the freeing of the imprisoned East Pakistani leadership and the return of refugees who had fled to India. The Soviets even sent a deputy foreign minister to Delhi in an attempt to persuade Awami League leaders to accept autonomy for Bangladesh within a united Pakistan. Unlike some Western powers, they did not suspend economic aid to Pakistan during the crisis or the war with India, Further, immediately after that war, they provided Pakistan with generous economic assistance. In fact, since the India-Pakistan war, Pakistan has received more Soviet assistance than either India or Bangladesh (in good part to support and encourage the progressive Bhutto regime).

The reason for these Soviet policies is that it preferred the restoration of parliamentary democratic forms and the continuing unity of Pakistan because this would have meant a stronger, progressive, and not especially pro-Western or pro-Chinese regime in all of Pakistan.[40]

It should be remembered that the immediate cause of the events in East Pakistan in 1971 was the victory of the Awami Party, headed by Sheik Mujibur Rahman, in the national elections of December 1970. Winning all but two seats in the more populous East Pakistan, Mujibur would have become prime minister of all Pakistan, but for a military *coup* which not only suppressed his party but also launched a military operation in East Pakistan to crush the movement for autonomy and democracy. The response to the military regime's repression was growing guerrilla warfare, engaged in both by small communist oriented groups (the most important of which was associated with the National Awami Party generally sympathetic to China) and by the much larger Mukti Bahini associated with the Mujibur's own Awami Party.[41]

When Pakistan attacked India on 3 December 1971, portraying the war as a conflict between Hindu India and Muslim Pakistan, the Soviets announced, in contradiction to Indian claims, that they regarded the principal aspect of the conflict as the uprising of the people of East Pakistan, not against West Pakistan, but against 'the West Pakistani military oligarchy'. After hostilities broke out between Pakistan and India the Soviets sympathized with the Indians and the East Pakistani insurgents. Their major contribution to the struggle in East Pakistan was directed towards diplomatic activity, aimed at keeping the super powers, specifically China and the U.S.A. , out of the conflict. They put pressure on the Indians to effect a speedy withdrawal from East Pakistan once the West Pakistani army had been defeated and not to prolong hostilities against that country in the West. The Soviets provided no significant help to either the Indian army or to the Mukti Bahini, other than diplomatic and moral support. As for the Indians, they actively intervened in support of the Mukti Bahini and the Awami Party (which had the overwhelming support of the people of East Pakistan) for their own reasons of state. They wanted to weaken Pakistan and prevent the development of a revolutionary movement in East Bengal, which might spread to West Bengal and other parts of India. They may also have wanted to secure a dependency for their own sub-continental imperial ambitions. But — whatever its motives — the Indian intervention was supported by the majority of the people in East Pakistan and did serve to install in power the party that had, a year before, won an overwhelming vote in the country. It should be stressed that the Soviet Union did not instigate the creation of Bangladesh nor did it play any significant role in its actual creation.[42] The continuing support of most of the people of Bangladesh for the Awami League was demonstrated in the elections of 1973 when 73 per cent of the vote went to this party, compared to 11 per cent for the two major pro-Chinese groups and 8 per cent to the pro-Soviet party.[43]

It should also be noted that by far the greatest amount of economic aid received by Bangladesh has come from the U.S. and the international financial institutions associated with it (by the end of 1974, direct U.S. aid totalled $560 million and I.M.F. and World Bank aid $350 million). This compares with just $138 million from the Soviet Union.[43] In conclusion Bangladesh can hardly be considered to be either a creation or satellite of the Soviet Union.

Cambodia

Some people accuse the Soviet Union of having engaged in social imperialist activities in Cambodia by supporting the Lon Nol regime instead of the government in exile of Prince Sihanouk and the Khmer Rouge during the early 1970s. Evidence for this accusation is that the Soviet Union allegedly extended diplomatic relations to the Lon Nol government, rather than to the Sihanouk government in exile. In fact the Soviet Union maintained a policy of dual recognition of both governments until only 9 October 1973, two full years before the Lon Nol regime fell. The Soviets then informed that regime that they recognized Prince Sihanouk's government in exile in Peking as the sole sovereign government of Cambodia. It should also be noted that, while the Soviets kept their embassy in Cambodia open from 1970 to 1973, they never sent an ambassador to Cambodia (precisely in order not to give moral support to the *coup* against Sihanouk). Although the Soviet Union formally broke diplomatic relations on 9 October 1973, when it was becoming apparent that a real civil war was going on and that the Sihanouk government in exile represented a real force within the country, some Soviet diplomats continued to stay in Cambodia, and vice versa. The last Lon Nol diplomats were not expelled from the Soviet Union until March 1975, two months before the collapse of the Lon Nol government.[44]

The diplomatic policies of socialist countries have, since the beginning, been directed towards establishing trade and other state-to-state relations, and not towards serving as a means of expressing political approval or disapproval of a regime. If a government has real control of its territory, socialist regimes have normally sought diplomatic relations. It has been the capitalist countries which typically have used the weapon of denying diplomatic recognition – for example, the U.S. of the U.S.S.R. til the mid 1930s, China til 1978, and Cuba right up to the present. Traditionally, the Soviet government has only denied diplomatic recognition to a capitalist (even fascist) government in periods of civil war where two real governments co-exist in the same territory, one representing the people and the other reaction (e.g. Spain in 1936-39). The Soviet policy of dual recognition of the Lon Nol and Sihanouk regimes was fully within the socialist tradition. Indeed it was more supportive of insurgent forces than has been the norm, since in the immediate years after the Lon Nol *coup*, the strength of the insurgent forces in Cambodia (in contrast to Vietnam) was not clear. The breaking of formal diplomatic relations with Lon Nol in 1973, when it was clear that there were two states now existing within the territory of Cambodia, was also in the socialist tradition.

Like Soviet diplomatic behaviour, the Chinese is just as much in the tradition of recognizing *de facto* governments created by military *coups* against popular progressive regimes. For example, after the fascist *coup* in Chile against the Allende government in 1973, China was among the first countries in the world to recognize the new junta and to expel pro-Allende diplomats from their country. Unlike the Soviets in Cambodia, however, the Chinese, did not attempt to establish dual relations with any incipient Chilean government in exile.[45]

No evidence could be found of any Soviet economic or military assistance to the Lon Nol government, or of any economic or military advantage granted by it to the Soviets. We must conclude that there was nothing in the Cambodian situation that in any way justifies the accusation of Soviet socialist imperialism.

Angola

Suggestions have been made that Soviet support to the M.P.L.A. in Angola represented an instance of social imperialism. There is in fact simply no substance either for the claim that the Soviet Union made economic or military gains out of Angola or that it now has any special control over that country. All the evidence points to the reality that the Soviet Union normally supports progressive struggles in Third World countries, that the M.P.L.A.'s struggle against the South African invasion (which began before the Portuguese had withdrawn from Angola) and against U.N.I.T.A. and F.N.L.A., was a progressive and popular struggle, and that Soviet and Cuban assistance to the M.P.L.A. allowed the progressive forces to triumph and prevented the establishment of a neo-colonial South African-U.S. dependency in Angola (similar to that set up in Zaire in the early 1960s).[46]

During the 1965-74 period, only the M.P.L.A. fought a continuous guerrilla war, only it sought to be a national rather than a regional movement and only it avoided anti-white racism and insisted instead on political, rather than racial, criteria for deciding who was a friend and who was an enemy. While support for the F.N.L.A. and U.N.I.T.A. was almost entirely tribal, support for M.P.L.A. came from intellectuals, mulattoes, the working class and urbanized population throughout the country, although it did get specially solid support from certain tribal areas too. The F.N.L.A., after 1965, built itself up in Zaire under the protection of Mobutu's conservative regime and was sustained in part by American C.I.A. money, while U.N.I.T.A. organized peacefully in South-eastern Angola with the complicity of the Portuguese (as became public knowledge when the Portuguese revolution of April 1974 released previously secret documents). When the Portuguese departure from Angola became imminent, the South African government began more and more actively supporting U.N.I.T.A. with arms and mercenaries. In October, just before Angolan independence, the South African army – acting in collusion with the C.I.A. – itself entered Southern Angola and together with U.N.I.T.A. forces began marching up the seacoast towards Luanda taking one city after another. At the same time, with the aid of arms and troops from Zaire, and considerable financial support from the U.S., the F.N.L.A. marched South out of Zaire towards Luanda. Within a few weeks it looked as if the progressive M.P.L.A. regime was about to collapse and a South African/U.S. backed neo-colonial regime installed in all of Angola. (The U.S. gave more than $32 million to U.N.I.T.A. and the F.N.L.A. during the Civil War.)

The Soviets and other East Europeans had been giving rather modest military assistance to the M.P.L.A. since the mid 1960s in the struggle for independence from Portugal. From its origins the movement had close ties with the Portuguese left. (Many M.P.L.A. leaders had become radicalized as students in Portuguese universities and had made lifelong friendships with Portuguese students who later became leaders of the left in their country.) Soviet supplies of military equipment to the M.P.L.A. were stepped up in

January 1975 (10 months before independence). Soviet military deliveries were accelerated again immediately after independence in November 1975, when the U.S./South African backed advance on Luanda looked as if it was about to succeed. The Soviets provided a lot of crucial equipment, including such heavy weapons as T34 and T54 tanks, 122mm ground to ground rockets and SAM-7 missiles which played a key role in turning back the invasion. Although there were a few Soviet technicians in Angola, no Soviet troops of any kind were ever dispatched to the country.

Other socialist countries, including Yugoslavia, Romania, Czechoslovakia, the German Democratic Republic and Cuba, had also been sending *materiel* and technicians to help the M.P.L.A. Civilian technicians from Cuba began arriving in Angola in August (three months before independence). When the rapid U.S. supported South African and Zairean advances on Luanda began, the Cubans sent, at M.P.L.A.'s urgent request, large numbers of troops to support the M.P.L.A. defenders (the total reached about 11,000 in February 1976). These Cuban troops together with the military equipment from Eastern Europe were decisive in reversing the course of events and allowing the popular government to triumph.

The M.P.L.A. was also given solid support by all the progressive regimes in Africa. The recently victorious liberation movements in Mozambique and Guinea Bissau gave unreserved support to the M.P.L.A. To quote Samora Machel, President of Mozambique:

In Angola, there are two parties in conflict: on the one side, imperialism with its allies and its puppets; on the other side, the progressive, popular forces who support the MPLA. That's the whole story. It is not Spinola, Holden [Roberto], Savimbi or anyone else who matter to us. They are only instruments of imperialism. It is imperialism that is the danger and the true menace. (Interview in *Afrique-Asie,* 20 October 1975).[47]

Other progressive regimes such as Congo-Brazzaville, Tanzania, and Algeria also gave enthusiastic support to the M.P.L.A.

About the only people in the world who did not see clearly what was at stake in Angola (i.e. which forces were working towards a neo-colonial regime which would make Angola's rich natural resources safe for exploitation by the transnational corporations, and which forces were fighting for genuine independence and popular self-determination) were the Chinese and their active supporters, mostly organized in tiny sects in the advanced capitalist countries. The Chinese since the early 1960s appear to have adopted the principle that anyone whom the Soviets support must be their enemy and that anyone who opposes the Soviet Union should be supported. The Chinese had long given some support and training to U.N.I.T.A. and F.N.L.A. forces (as well as the M.P.L.A.) while maintaining that the three organizations were equally important and progressive in the struggle against the Portuguese. This position was rejected by the M.P.L.A. as unacceptable. To the extent (which was questionable) that the F.N.L.A. and U.N.I.T.A. were seriously fighting against the Portuguese for independence, it was correct for the M.P.L.A. to join in a united front with them (which is what the M.P.L.A. tried to do). But the nature of the struggle in Angola changed qualitatively once the Portuguese became fully committed to leaving. By late 1975, the question was no longer whether Angola would be a Portuguese colony, but what was to be the nature of the post-colonial state and society there. At that time (beginning a few months before the last Portuguese had left), the primary contradiction in Angola was between the forces (domestic and international) desiring a Zaire type regime supportive of transnational exploitation, versus the forces wanting a radical Tanzania/Mozambique type, or even socialist, state which would exclude foreign domination and actively promote progressive social policies.

The Soviet Union won no military or economic advantages in Angola as a result of its support for the M.P.L.A. It gained no bases, no investment opportunities, no unequal trade treaties. The Angolan government is just as independent as those of the other recently liberated ex-Portuguese colonies, and in fact is in a much better position because of the rich natural resources it controls. The generous supplying of military equipment, and now economic aid, to Angola is clearly an example of the Soviet Union helping the growth of progressive forces in the Third World, even at the risk to itself of cooling relations with the U.S. and endangering detente (which has consistently been a keystone of Soviet foreign policy). It is ironic that the same people who in the 1960s were critical of the Soviet Union for giving insufficient support to Third World liberation struggles (these people identified with the verbally more militant line of the Chinese), in the mid 1970s accused the Soviets of social imperialism for giving support to progressive Third World movements. These people at the same time defended the Chinese who, more than just refusing to support the struggle of the M.P.L.A., launched a vicious propaganda attack on both that movement and those who made great sacrifices in its assistance (the Cubans).

The Horn of Africa

Ethiopia is the second most populous country in Africa. Before the overthrow of Haile Selassie in 1974, it was an extremely backward feudal society. It was one of the poorest countries in the world and had one of the most exploited peasantries anywhere. Ninety per cent of the population was engaged in agricultural production using techniques not involving fertilizers or mechanized equipment. About 95 per cent of the land belonged to landlords. Two-thirds was in the hands of a tiny group of noble families with a substantial portion of the remainder belonging to the Ethiopian Orthodox Church. The *per capita* income of the country was about $60 a year.[48]

The devastating famines of the early 1970s, combined with the Emperor's lack of responsiveness (manifested in continuing price increases in the face of growing poverty) precipitated spontaneous rioting and strikes in 1974 which led to the overthrow of the Emperor by progressive elements in the army. The Ethiopian masses, especially the students, intellectuals and working class, were politically aroused in 1974 and formed a wide range of leftist political organizations (almost all of them claiming to be Marxist-Leninist). After two years of promises of radical reforms and intrigues among the army officers who had seized power, The Dergue (the leadership body elected by the army) underwent two sharp struggles and consequent purges, one in 1976 and the other in 1977. These consolidated a leadership committed to rapid revolutionary transformation in Ethiopian society. The Dergue intended, in the short run, to implement this transformation using the military's own organizational structure. In 1977 the leading figure of the revolution emerged as Lieutenant-Colonel Mengistu Haile-Mariam, a member of the Galla minority in Southern Ethiopia which has been especially oppressed by the Amharic ruling class. The ascendancy of Mengistu marked the end of a period of sharp internal struggle around the question of whether to break with the United States and adopt Marxism-Leninism as the ideological commitment of the revolution.

In March 1975 the government nationalized all rural land, taking it away from the feudal landlords and Church which had controlled it for aeons (much of this land, it should be noted, had already been seized by the peasants). In July all urban property was similarly nationalized. The largest estates were transformed into state farms while the larger urban businesses also came to be run by the state. Each peasant was given the right to farm up to 10 hectares, and the use of hired labour was forbidden. In 1976 Peasant Associations in the rural areas and Urban Dwellers Associations in the towns were organized. The Peasant Associations were to be groups of peasants collectively farming units of up to 800 hectares. These units came to have broad powers of self-government including judicial powers over their own members. Former landlords were generally barred from joining these collectives. Large numbers of students were mobilized in the cities to help implement the land reform and establish the peasant associations. The Urban Dwellers Associations in the cities were also given broad powers of self-government.

The government nationalized all basic industries and banks in 1975. Medical care throughout the country became free for the needy. The schools were put under the control of the masses through a committee system whose members were drawn from the Peasant Associations and Urban Dwellers Associations as well as representatives of the teachers and students. In February 1978 Lieutenant-Colonel Mengistu Haile Mariam announced that the Dergue would build a Marxist-Leninist Workers Party which would eventually take over direction of the revolutionary process from the military.

In summary, between 1974 and 1977, the revolution under the leadership of the Dergue destroyed the political institutions of the feudal nobility and commercial classes, instituted a thorough land reform which ended feudal land tenure and put the land in the hands of the peasantry, nationalized all major industry and banking, established democratic peasant, workers and women's associations, created the mechanisms for local and regional self-government, and decisively broke with U.S. imperialism. The regime also armed the people, creating large people's militias, armed workers' squads and self-defence detachments which have both defended the revolution against its rightist and ultra-left opponents and served in the struggle against Ethiopia's various secessionist movements, all in all, a rather impressive record.

In the face of the rapid transformation of Ethiopian society, a multi-dimensional struggle broke out. On the one hand, the old feudalist forces and nascent bourgeoisie resisted the socialist measures of the Dergue. Their organization, the Ethiopian Democratic Union (sympathetic to the U.S. and to capitalist development of the country) went into armed struggle against the regime. On the other, a number of ultra-leftist groups composed mainly of students and ex-students, the most prominent of which was the Ethiopian People's Revolutionary Party (E.P.R.P.), also took up arms against the government. The major point of difference between groups like the E.P.R.P. and the dominant leftist faction of the Dergue was whether the military should continue to provide the leadership of the revolution and run the Ethiopian state. In the climate of rapid change and sharp ideological struggle, the E.P.R.P. initiated a systematic campaign of terror and assassination against the leadership of the Urban Dwellers Associations and other supporters of the Dergue. In response, the Dergue launched its own 'Red Terror' against the E.P.R.P. and others committed to the armed overthrow of the regime. This organized terror proved to be very successful in containing the assassination campaign.

In 1977 the increasingly leftist Dergue broke with the U.S. which, until then, had been the exclusive arms supplier for the Ethiopian military. The U.S. suspended deliveries of arms to the Ethiopian government because of its leftist course, while the Ethiopians closed down the U.S.'s military installation in the country.

In addition to precipitating sharp domestic struggles, both between the regime and the old ruling classes and within the revolutionary forces themselves, the 1974 Revolution also stimulated a wide range of separatist movements among the dozens of distinctive ethnic minorities within Ethiopia. Because of the weakening of the central government due to the strains of radical social transformation and a multifront civil war, many of these separatist movements were able to make significant gains, often with the support and arms of the various conservative powers in the region who were interested in preventing the formation of a unified and strong leftist Ethiopia. The two most important such movements were composed of Eritreans in the North and Somalis in the Ogaden in the east.

The eastern third of Ethiopia is sparsely inhabited by Somali-speaking people who, with the active military support of the Somali government, in 1977 attempted to secede from Ethiopia. Seeing Ethiopia weakened by internal strife, the Somali army marched into the Ogaden region to lay the foundations for its annexation to Somalia. (It may be relevant to note that petroleum reserves had recently been discovered in the Ogaden region.) The Somali intervention in the Ogaden region was universally condemned by the states of Black Africa as a violation of the agreed upon covenant not to attempt to redraw political boundaries along ethnic lines by force. This principle is regarded as sacrosanct throughout Black Africa because all its countries are ethnically diverse and all have borders that cut across ethnic groups.

A successful Somali annexation of the regions of Ethiopia which were ethnically Somali might well have been a precedent for similar actions throughout the African continent. Kenya, a country which also has a significant Somali minority, was particularly upset by the Somali invasion of Ethiopia and gave its complete support to the Ethiopian government, in spite of their differences in economic and social policies. Faced with the inability to generate effective international support for their invasion, the Somali armed forces were forced to retreat behind their own boundaries in March 1978.

The other major secessionist attempt was actually a continuation of the 15 year old war for national independence in Eritrea. Eritrea, traditionally the richest Ethiopian province, contained more than half the country's factories (a legacy of the Italian colonial occupation of this region), as well as an important copper mine. It also embraces the entire sea coast of Ethiopia. The resources and relative richness of this region thus make it economically comparable to the former Biafra in Nigeria.

The secessionist movement in Eritrea is divided into three different groups, the Eritrean Liberation Front (E.L.F.), the Eritrean Popular Liberation Front (E.P.L.F.) and the Eritrean Liberation Front-People's Liberation Army (E.L.F.-P.L.A.). As non-Marxist groups the first and last have been getting considerable material support from conservative regimes in the region, mainly the Sudan and Saudi Arabia. The E.P.L.F., the most successful of the three (with substantial support among the Eritrean masses) and committed to Marxism-Leninism, was until 1975 supported, ideologically and militarily, by Cuba and the U.S.S.R. in its struggle against the feudal Haile Selassie regime. However, because of its insistence on carrying on a military struggle against the new progressive Ethiopian regime, this support was cut off. As far as can be determined, in 1976 and 1977, the group was mainly dependent on its own resources for military supplies. However, the unity agreement achieved between the E.L.F. and the E.P.L.F. in early 1978 meant that the E.P.L.F. forces began acquiring military supplies indirectly from the reactionary Arab regimes, as well as through the P.L.O. (It might also be noted that the Dergue may have secured spare parts for its American supplied equipment, which the U.S. would no longer provide, from the Israelis who have an abundance of such supplies plus their own reasons for wanting to see the defeat of the Eritrean secession.)

The Ethiopian government offered the E.P.L.F. (an organization with which it felt ideologically compatible) regional autonomy within a socialist Ethiopian federation. But the E.P.L.F. throughout 1978 rebuffed all attempts to negotiate an end to the secession and instead favoured patching over its differences with the E.L.F. and E.L.F.-P.L.A. in order to win total national independence under a coalition with these non-Marxist forces.

Almost all progressive regimes in the Arab World and Black Africa, as well as all the socialist countries (except Albania and China) have supported the Ethiopian regime in its struggle to maintain territorial integrity against the various secessionist movements. On the other hand, the most reactionary of the Arab states and Iran have been the most active supporters of the dismemberment of Ethiopia, a position supported by the U.S., West Germany and France (along with China). Thus we saw in 1977 the strange phenomenon of the U.S., Saudi Arabia, Egypt, the Sudan, West Germany, France and Iran all apparently sympathizing with 'national liberation movements' since it was these secessionist movements whose victory would mean the destruction of the socialist revolution in Ethiopia. China supported this position.

In 1976, as the character of the Ethiopian Revolution became clear, the two most militant and revolutionary Arab states, Libya and the Democratic People's Republic of Yemen, both of which had been giving active military support to the independence movement in Eritrea, ceased their support and switched instead to the Ethiopian government and its plan for a socialist federation to end the secession. South Yemen in 1977 even sent troops to fight on the side of the Ethiopians.

In January 1978 the Shah of Iran threatened to intervene in the conflict between Somalia and Ethiopia on the side of the Somalis, if Ethiopian troops were to cross into Somaliland. (In response to this threat, the Organization of African Unity warned Iran against seeking to extend her influence into Africa.) Egypt and the Sudan likewise promised to send troops to Somalia if the Ethiopians crossed the border. The Sudan (with Egypt's backing) has also actively been aiding the rebellion in Eritrea with sanctuary and supplies, as well as trying to bring the three Eritrean factions together.

Before the 1977 attack by Somalia on Ethiopia, the Soviet Union (and Cuba) had been important supporters of the revolutionary processes developing in Somalia. Somalia, like Ethiopia, had nationalized most land and businesses and had broken with Western imperialism. Sensitive to the question of the Ogaden as well as Somalia's dispute with France over Djibouti, the Soviets proposed that a federation be created in the Horn of Africa which would link up all the progressive regimes in the region: the Democratic People's Republic of Yemen, Somalia, newly independent Djibouti, and Ethiopia (with Eritrea being an autonomous region). Such a proposal would, the Soviets hoped, resolve the conflicts between Ethiopia and Somalia as well as the Eritrean question, while creating a strong socialist state which would be able to support radical movements both in the Arabian peninsula and East Africa. Colonel Mengistu and the South Yemenis supported the Soviet proposal, but neither the Somalis nor the Eritreans would have any part of it.

When the Somalis in spite of Soviet advice and urging invaded Ethiopia, the Soviet Union, which had equipped the Somali armed forces, decided to withhold further military support for Somalia since it was the aggressor, and instead to provide military equipment to the Ethiopian defenders (who had just been cut off from U.S. arms). The Soviets continued to hope that the Somali government would abandon its aggressive posture and reconcile itself with the new progressive regime in Ethiopia. Cuba also came to send, first doctors and advisers, and then some combat troops, to strengthen the Ethiopian forces in the Ogaden and help drive the invaders out. Both the Soviets and Cubans, together with the South Yemenis, have also been lending material support to the Ethiopian effort to prevent the secession of Eritrea.

The Soviet Union began to get involved in supporting the Ethiopian regime in 1976, as the increasingly leftist government began to ask for assistance from the U.S.S.R. and the East European socialist countries. Weapons began arriving in February 1977. In June 1976 a two-year cultural agreement was signed with the Soviet Union, providing for co-operation in education, culture, the arts and sciences. Seven hundred scholarships for Ethiopian students were provided by the U.S.S.R. and the East European countries and various trade agreements began to be worked out as well. In October 1977, in the face of the Somali conquest of most of the Ogaden and the imminent danger of the collapse of the Mengistu regime, the Soviet Union and Cuba both pledged support for the Ethiopian revolution in its war against Somalia. Between October 1977 and February 1978 the U.S. government estimated that the Soviets sent approximately one billion dollars worth of military equipment to Ethiopia. Libya agreed to pay for much of the Soviet arms. The massive arms support of the Soviet Union, together with the assistance of Cuban military advisers (and perhaps combat troops) resulted in the repulse of the Somali invasion and the reintegration of the Ogaden into Ethiopia.

It could be argued that the attempt by Somalia to annex Eastern Ethiopia, and especially the independence movement in Eritrea, are in some ways similar in character to the Biafran war for independence in the late 1960s. In both cases the wealthiest part of the country (Biafra was both the area of greatest oil reserves and the most developed part of Nigeria) attempted secession. In both cases a successful secession would have meant two (or three) relatively weak countries (rather than one strong one), which could have been easily dominated by imperialism. Almost all Marxists and progressive Third World forces understood the implications of a successful secession and supported Nigeria against Biafra, while Biafra's support came mainly from the most advanced capitalist countries interested in exploiting her wealth.

Likewise, the Ogaden and Eritrean secessionist movements reflect much the same constellation of supporters and opponents (the major exception being China's opposition to Biafran secession, and apparent support of the Ogaden and Eritrean secessions). It must be noted, however, that the domestic character of both the Somali regime and the E.P.L.F. in Eritrea is more progressive than was the Biafran government (which made no claim to being socialist). Nevertheless, it is quite clear that the international, as opposed to the domestic political, parallels between the two cases are very close indeed.

The right of self-determination, up to and including national independence for an ethnic group, has never been an absolute principle of Marxism-Leninism. Marxists have traditionally judged each particular independence movement in terms of the effect it would have on advancing the general socialist and anti-imperialist movement. Thus China opposed both the Biafran and Bangladesh independence movements as weakening anti-imperialist countries. And the Soviet Union intervened to incorporate the bourgeois regimes in the Transcaucasus in the early 1920s and in the Baltic countries in 1940. The Chinese Constitution itself does not (unlike the Soviet Constitution) grant the right of self-determination to its minority regions and the Chinese Communist Party has always opposed its own secessionist movements (e.g. Tibet in 1959) as attempts to weaken the Chinese Revolution. Likewise, virtually all factions of the Indian Communist Party have consistently opposed the break-up of India into its constituent nations (of which there could be hundreds).

Contrary to the suggestions of the conservative Arab regimes, as well as of the pro-Chinese forces around the world, there was nothing in the involvement of the Soviet Union in Ethiopia to reflect social imperialism. The cost to the Soviets of doing all they could in October 1977 to prevent the Somali invasion, including stopping arms supplies to that country which had been a close friend of the Soviet Union for years, was considerable. Its personnel were expelled from Somalia and its naval support station closed down. The Soviets made every effort to resolve the conflicts among the countries of the Horn of Africa in a reasonable way. Their proposed federation would clearly be the best solution for the advance of the revolutionary movement in that part of the world. Their generous support of first the Somalis and then the Ethiopians brought very little by way of economic or military advantages for the Soviet Union (other than the security gained whenever conservative pro-U.S. regimes are weakened or progressive and revolutionary regimes gain strength). A careful evaluation of the developments in the Horn of Africa since 1974 must conclude that the Soviet Union's role there is fully compatible with the thesis that the U.S.S.R. acted on the basis of proletarian internationalism, i.e. in support of revolutionary movements.

Conclusion

This chapter has examined Soviet economic and political relations with the non-socialist countries of the Third World. We have been able to find no evidence that the Soviet Union exploits the countries of Africa, Asia, and Latin America through unequal trade, economic assistance, or any analog of Western style foreign investments. Soviet trade and assistance is more generous than that of the West and is, unlike the latter's, designed to encourage industrialization and independence. The absence of anything like Soviet ownership rights in local productive property means that, unlike such countries as the United States, France and Britain, the Soviet state has no stake in preserving the local class structure which guarantees existing property relations. In summary, the Soviet Union cannot be considered to be a social imperialist in relation to the non-socialist Third World since the fundamental characteristic of imperialism (economic exploitation) is absent in the relationship between the U.S.S.R. and the countries of Africa, Asia and Latin America.

In addition, this chapter has examined the political role of the Soviet Union in the non-socialist countries of the Third World by looking at Soviet military assistance and the actions of the Soviet Union in the creation of Bangladesh, the Cambodian and Angolan civil wars, and in the Horn of Africa. Here we have seen that the Soviets consistently played a progressive role in support of the various national liberation and left movements without attempting to gain special advantages for themselves or unduly directing the course of events. In other words the Soviet Union cannot be considered even hegemonic in its relations with the Third World.

We are driven to the unexpected conclusion that there is a significant difference in the political (but not the economic) relations between the U.S.S.R. and the Third World and that country and Eastern Europe. Whereas she is not hegemonic towards the Third World, in socialist Eastern Europe she is hegemonic, i.e. she does politically dominate the region, and within broad limits does attempt to provide it with political direction.

Of course, there are limits to Soviet support for progressive and national liberation movements. Neither the Soviets in the 1940s, the Cubans in the 1960s, Chinese in the 1950s, Albanians, the Libyans, the Fourth International nor anyone else interested in supporting anti-imperialist and progressive forces, has ever supported every such organization. Everyone must have criteria by which to select which forces are authentic and have a real chance of achieving their goals. For example, the lack of Albanian, Chinese or Fourth International support for the Red Army Faction in West Germany in the 1970s cannot reasonably be considered hegemonism. Nor can the failure of Albania and China to support both the Eritreans and the Dergue as well as both the Somalis and the Dergue in the struggle in the Horn. (All claim to be revolutionary forces.) Obviously, insisting that, in order not to be hegemonic, one must give equal support to all claimants to a progressive role would often involve giving support to both sides in a struggle. Even the most ardent opponents of Soviet social imperialism could not insist that the U.S.S.R. give equal support to all sides in a civil war. They would rather arbitrarily insist that the side not supported by the Soviets was the more progressive one, while at the same time claiming that their support for the anti-Soviet side was not hegemonism. Mere demonstration that the Soviets, Albanians or whoever give support to one group and not to another cannot in itself be reasonably considered proof of hegemonism. To demonstrate the latter it must be shown that a power such as the Soviet Union tends to support only those states and movements which agree with its politics or which it can dominate in order to direct the course of events according to its wishes.

What those who suggest that the U.S.S.R. is hegemonic really mean is not that the Soviet Union applies criteria to its giving support, but rather that: (1) the Soviets in their view support the wrong side or at least act to divide progressive forces; (2) they give their support in order to dominate events in their own interests, and (3) the net result of Soviet involvement is to hold back the development of progressive forces in the world.

Our examination of Soviet involvement in the Third World in recent years shows that these three implicit criteria of hegemonism cannot be substantiated. (1) The Soviets have consistently tended to support the more progressive forces in the Third World which have a reasonable chance of success and by no means only Soviet oriented communist parties or liberation movements and regimes that they can dominate. They support a wide range of movements and regimes and in some cases, such as in Zimbabwe, competing organizations (in such cases Soviet policy is to unify the competing groups). (2) The Soviets do not appear to intervene in their own narrow self-interest although they are of course concerned to weaken U.S. imperialism. They consistently attempt to assist the development of strong progressive and anti-imperialist countries in the Third World. Thus they encouraged a reconciliation between Pakistan and the Bangladesh independence movement within a progressive framework, and have strongly argued for a federation of all progressive states in the Horn of Africa. (3) As the examples of Vietnam, Cuba and Angola, as well as the struggles in Southern Africa and the Arab World clearly demonstrate, Soviet military and economic support has been decisive in advancing liberation movements. In no realistic sense can any informed person argue otherwise. In summary, the Soviet Union cannot be considered to be a hegemonic force in the Third World.

References

1. For discussions of the role of U.S. foreign assistance, see Harry Magdoff, *The Age of Imperialism*, (New York: Monthly Review Press, 1969); Teresa Hayter, *Aid as Imperialism*, (Baltimore: Pelican, 1971); and Steve Weissman, *The Trojan Horse*, (San Francisco: Ramparts Press, 1974).
2. U.S. Department of State, *Communist States and Developing Countries: Aid and Trade in 1974*, Table 2; and U.S. Department of Commerce, Bureau of the Census, *Statistical Abstract of the United States* (1976), Table 1401, (and various previous volumes).
3. U.S. Department of State, *op. cit.*, Table 2.
4. *Ibid.*, pp.5-6; Leo Tansky, 'Soviet Foreign Aid: Scope, Direction and Trends', in Morris Bornstein and Daniel Fusfeld (eds.), *The Soviet Economy*, (Homewood, Illinois: Richard Irwin Inc., 1974), p.457.
5. U.S. Department of State, *op. cit.*, p.6; and Tansky, *op. cit.*, pp.460-2.
6. Sherman, *The Soviet Economy*, (Boston: Little Brown, 1969),p.210; Marshall Goldman, *Soviet Foreign Aid*, (New York: Praeger, 1967), Chapter 11; Elizabeth Kridl Valkenier, 'Soviet Economic Relations with Developing Nations', in Roger E. Kanet (ed.), *The Soviet Union and the Developing Nations*, (Baltimore: Johns Hopkins University Press, 1974).
7. See *Ibid.* Also see discussion of joint enterprises in latter part of this chapter.
8. Tansky, *op. cit.*, p.456; Sherman, *op. cit.*, p.208; and U.S. Department

of state, *op. cit.*, p.6.
9. Goldman, *op. cit.*, pp. 191-2.
10. Orah Cooper, 'Soviet Economic Aid to the Third World', in U.S. Congress: Joint Economic Committee, *Soviet Economy in a New Perspective,* 94th Congress, 2nd session, (1976), p.191.
11. R.P. Sinha, 'Soviet Aid and Trade with the Developing World', *Soviet Studies,* 26:2, (April 1974), p.279.
12. Valkenier, *op. cit.*, and Cooper, *op. cit.*, pp.192-5.
13. *Ibid.*, pp.193-5.
14. Franklyn Holzman, *Foreign Trade Under Central Planning,* (Cambridge, Mass.: Harvard University Press, 1974), pp.27 and 372.
15. US. Department of State, *op. cit.*, pp.6,7.
16. U.S. Department of State, *Special Report: Communist States and Developing Countries Aid and Trade 1965-1974,* (Washington, D.C. U.S. Government Printing Office, 1975), Table 2.
17. Asha Datar, *India's Economic Relations with the U.S.S.R. and Eastern Europe 1953 to 1969,* (Cambridge: Cambridge University Press, 1972), p.43; and R.P. Sinha, *op. cit.*, p.281.
18. Datar, *op. cit.*, pp. 52, 54..
19. Robert Donaldson, *Soviet Policy towards India: Ideology and Strategy,* (Cambridge, Mass: Harvard University Press, 1974), p.214.
20. Datar, *op. cit.*, p.182; Sinha, *op. cit.*, p.278.
21. Datar, *op. cit.*, Appendix I; Marshall Goldman, *op. cit.*, pp.102-103.
22. *Ibid.*
23. Datar, *op. cit.*, pp.69-75.
24. *Ibid.*, Donaldson, *op. cit.*, p.119; and Goldman, *op. cit.*, Chapter 4.
25. Datar, *op. cit.*, pp.24-32; Sinha, *op. cit.*, p.279.
26. U.S. Department of Commerce, *Survey of Current Business,* Oct. 1975, p.53.
27. Cooper, 'Soviet Economic Aid to the Third World' in *Soviet Economy in a New Perspective* , *op. cit.*, p.193; and Valkenier, *op. cit.*, pp.222-4.
28. Valkenier, *op. cit.*, p.223.
29. *Ibid.*, p.222.
30. U.S. Department of Commerce, *Statistical Abstract of the U.S.*, (1975), p.801.
31. United Nations, *Yearbook of International Trade Statistics* (1975) and various previous volumes.
32. *Ibid.*
33. Communist Party of India (M-L), *Soviet Social Imperialism in India,* (Vancouver, B.C.: Indian People's Association in North America, 1976).
34. *Ibid.*
35. U.S. Department of State, *op. cit.*, Table 7.
36. *Ibid.*, Table 9.
37. U.S. Arms Control and Disarmament Agency, *World Military Expenditures and Arms Transfers,* (1965-1974).
38. John Waterburg, 'The Soviet Union and North Africa', in Ivo J. Lederer (ed.), *The Soviet Union and the Middle East,* (Stanford: Stanford University Press, 1974); and Ur R'anan, *The U.S.S.R. Arms The Third World,* (Cambridge, Mass: M.I.T. Press, 1969).
39. See for example the interview with Robert Mugabe of ZANU in the (U.S.)Guardian, 13 September 1978, p.15.

40. The principal sources for the discussion of Soviet involvement in the Bangladesh issue are Vijay Sen Budhray, 'Moscow and the Birth of Bangladesh', *Asian Survey*, (May 1973), pp.482-95 ; Richard Nyrop *et al.*, *Area Handbook for Bangladesh* , (Washington, D.C.: U.S. Government Printing Office, 1975) and Rounaq Jahan, 'Bangladesh', in Richard Starr, (ed.), *Yearbook on International Communist Affairs*, (Stanford, California: Hoover Institute Press, 1976).
41. Jahan, *op. cit.*, pp.239-40.
42. Budhray, *op. cit.*, pp.490-4.
43. Jahan, *op. cit.*, p.240; and Nyrop, *op. cit.*, p.262.
44. The principal sources of information on the Soviet Union's relations with the Lon Nol regime are: *The Economist*, (27 October 1973), p.64; and *Facts on File* (various issues 1975).
45. *The Economist*, (27 October 1973), p.64.
46. The discussion of Soviet involvement in Angola is based primarily on Immanual Wallerstein, 'Luanda is Madrid', *The Nation*, 3-10 January 1976), 222:1; Stephen Larrabee, 'Moscow, Angola and the Dialectics of Detente', *The World Today*, (May 1976); Michael T. Kaufman, 'Suddenly, Angola', *New York Times Magazine*, (4 January 1976); John Marcum, 'Lessons of Angola', *Foreign Affairs*, 54:3, (April 1976); John Stockwell, *In Search of Enemies*, (London: Andre Deutsch, 1978).
47. Quoted in Wallerstein, *op. cit.*, p.16.
48. The discussion of the developments in the Horn of Africa and the role of the U.S.S.R. there is based on the following sources: *Facts on File* (various issues from Jan.1977 to Feb.1978); *Africa Yearbook and Who's Who*, 1976, (London: Africa Journal Limited, 1977); *Africa: Contemporary Record*, (1976-1977), (London: Rex Collings, 1977); *Africa Research Bulletin*, (various issues from Jan. 1977 to Feb. 1978); and *The Guardian*, (US), (various issues from January to April 1978).

9. Soviet Relations with the Socialist Third World

In this chapter Soviet relations with the socialist countries of the Third World are examined by looking in detail at the economic and political relations between the U.S.S.R. and both China and Cuba since their respective socialist transformations. Soviet trade and economic assistance are examined for evidence of social imperialism. Soviet political relations with both countries are also studied in order to determine whether they can rightly be categorized as hegemonic.

China

Between 1950 and 1957 the Soviet Union loaned China approximately $1.8 billion dollars. The bulk of these Soviet credits were for the importation of machinery and equipment for China's industrial development. The credits were to be repaid at one per cent interest over a 10 year period (beginning four years after the loan was granted). Repayments were to be in the form of Chinese exports of raw materials and consumer goods to the Soviet Union.[1] The Soviet Union's industrial aid included many whole plants. It was concentrated on constructing, under Soviet direction, 156 key industrial projects, almost all in heavy industry (63 in machine building, 27 in coal, 14 in non-ferrous metals, 5 in chemicals, 7 in iron and steel and 24 power stations). By 1959 the Soviets had completed the installation of 130 entire plants.[2] This Soviet equipment and technical advice played a key role in Chinese industrial development in the pre-1958 period.[3] It has been estimated that, of the increase in China's productivity in 1953-57, 92 per cent in the iron industry was attributable to Soviet assistance, 83 per cent in steel, 100 per cent in trucks, 45 per cent in power production, 29 per cent in fertilizer, 51 per cent in crude oil, and 50 per cent in metallurgical equipment.[4]

In 1954 the Soviets agreed to sell the Chinese their share of the Chinese-Soviet joint stock companies in the raw materials and transportation sectors (as they were doing at the same time in all the socialist countries). The Soviets also agreed to remove their troops from Port Arthur (where they had been stationed since the end of World War II) and to turn over without charge all installations to the Chinese.[5]

Between 1950 and 1960, 11,000 Soviet experts worked in China assisting development. By 1960 the Soviets had supplied the country with about 10,000 sets of industrial specifications, 4,000 blueprints for the manufacture of machines and equipment, and 4,000 sets of technical specifications. A number of Chinese experts were also trained in the Soviet Union (by 1960 a total of 38,000). With the exception of the specifications and blueprints which were given to the Chinese, all the technical assistance, including salaries for the Soviet technicians in China, was to be paid for by the Chinese.

Soviet industrial assistance to China during the early 1950s represented a significant burden for the Soviets who were still reconstructing their own country after the devastating effects of World War II. In the period when the biggest Soviet loans were made, 1950-52, China was the only country to receive any Soviet credits.

Although the Soviets' terms for assistance were generous (a one per cent interest rate to be paid in goods rather than hard currency), the assistance was entirely in the form of loans. And when they turned over the joint stock companies to the Chinese, the Soviets insisted on total repayment (which they had not done in the cases of Eastern Europe and Mongolia).[6]

Soviet military assistance during the 1950s, much of it in support of Chinese actions during the Korean War, amounted to an additional $1.5 billion. This money too (including the amount for the Korean War effort) had to be repaid to the Soviet Union, and at a higher rate of interest than the one per cent for economic assistance.[7] This requirement that the Chinese repay the Soviets for military assistance rendered during the Korean War, when the Chinese had made such heavy sacrifices in blood, caused considerable resentment, and would certainly seem to be an unjust imposition.

During the Great Leap Forward, 1958-59, friction developed between the Soviet technical advisers who remained sceptical about the whole endeavour, preferring slower and more organized growth, and the Chinese who were promoting rapid industrialization based on grass roots enthusiasm. From 1958 the Soviet advisers were basically ignored. In 1960, after two years of futile argument, the Soviet Union withdrew all of its technical experts from China along with most of the blueprints and specifications for the still uncompleted projects they had been working on.

By the time the technicians were withdrawn, considerable antagonism had developed between the Soviet Union and China on a number of other issues. The Chinese had always resented the fact that the Soviets did not give them active support during the Civil War after 1945; indeed the Soviets advised alliance with and subordination to Chiang Kai-shek. After 1955 they had also become increasingly unwilling to grant more economic assistance to China. Further, they had demanded concessions such as Chinese renunciation of all claims to Mongolia and the establishment of Soviet-Chinese joint stock companies.

In the period 1957-63, public antagonism between the two developed regarding the possibility of peaceful co-existence with the West. The two sides disagreed to what extent support for the world revolutionary movement was to be restrained in the interests of avoiding world war between the U.S.S.R. and the NATO powers. The Chinese and the Soviets both supported the principle of peaceful co-existence (a concept initially developed by Lenin for the Soviet Union). Indeed the following principles were incorporated into virtually every treaty made by the People's Republic of China after 1954: mutual respect for each other's territorial integrity and sovereignty, non-aggression, non-interference in each other's internal affairs, equality and mutual benefit, and peaceful co-existence.[8]

The difference between the Soviets and Chinese on the question of co-existence with the capitalist countries was a matter of degree. The Chinese felt the Soviets were unnecessarily withholding military support for Third World struggles, especially the Algerian, the Congolese, the Cubans and the Vietnamese, in order to appease the United States and avoid the risk of war. It was during this period that the Soviets increasingly emphasized the imminent danger of nuclear hostilities and the importance of ending the Cold War and achieving peaceful co-existence with the U.S.A. The question of nuclear war was central in the Sino-Soviet dispute. The Soviets had originally promised that they would provide China with the atomic bomb, but in 1957 they reneged on their agreement claiming that nuclear proliferation represented a danger to world peace. This of course implied that the Chinese might use the Soviet provided weapons to start a war that the Soviets would be drawn into.[9] Although the Chinese felt that they needed to have the Bomb to protect themselves from possible intervention by the U.S., and American backed regimes such as Taiwan, the Chinese did recognize the great danger of nuclear warfare. For example in 1963 they proposed to the world that:

> All countries in the world, both nuclear and non-nuclear solemnly declare that they will prohibit and destroy nuclear weapons completely, thoroughly, totally and resolutely. Concretely speaking, they will not use nuclear weapons, nor export, nor manufacture, nor test, nor stockpile them, and they will destroy all the existing establishments for the research, testing and manufacture of nuclear weapons in the world . . .
> The Chinese Government and people are deeply concerned that nuclear weapons can be prohibited, nuclear war can be prevented and world peace preserved. We call upon the countries in the Socialist camp and all the peace loving countries and people of the world to unite and fight unswervingly to the end for the complete, thorough, total and resolute prohibition and destruction of nuclear weapons and for the defence of world peace.[10]

The Chinese have consistently gone on to argue however that, if nuclear war does break out, in spite of efforts to stop it, then the surviving people of the world will surely make a revolution and what is left of the world will become socialist. Thus nuclear war is not a thing to be avoided at all costs.

The dispute between the Chinese and the Soviets did not involve disagreement over whether peaceful co-existence with capitalist regimes was desirable; the Chinese insisted that it was. Rather the dispute related to the risks to be taken in sending military assistance and offering diplomatic support to liberation movements such as those in the Congo, Algeria, Vietnam and Cuba. Likewise, they did not disagree about whether progressive non-socialist regimes should be supported and encouraged to move to the left. The difference between them was merely over which countries showed the most promise and how actively the process of encouraging such non-revolutionary progressive processes should be pursued. In the last half of the 1950s, the Chinese were guided by the spirit of the Bandung Conference which tried to build unity among all the newly independent countries of Asia and Africa, no matter how reactionary, in order to struggle more effectively against imperialism. During this period, the Chinese insisted on not supporting intervention or interference in the internal affairs of established Third World governments. See, in this regard, Chou En-Lai's speech at the Bandung Conference in April 1955.[11]

In the first half of the 1960s, the Chinese changed direction and tried to create a coalition of progressive Third World countries, including Cambodia and Indonesia, to constitute a militant anti-imperialist force. This third force was to be based on both socialist and non-socialist countries. China's major partner in this endeavour, Sukarno's Indonesia, had the biggest Communist Party of any non-socialist country in the world. The Indonesian Communist Party's programme looked to a peaceful transition to power and a gradual transition to socialism. It was not until July 1967, two years after the Party was smashed, that the Chinese stopped supporting these principles and backed the reconstructed Indonesian Communist Party's new insistence on armed struggle as the only way to power. [12]

The Chinese in the 1960s insisted on more active support for both revolutionary forces (Algeria, Cuba up to 1966, and Vietnam) and non-revolutionary anti-imperialist forces (Cambodia, Burma and Indonesia until 1965) than the Soviets were willing to extend. They challenged the Soviets' more cautious interpretation of peaceful co-existence, by eventually arguing that only world revolution can stop world war since the logic of imperialism results in inter-imperialist war, and in any case if nuclear war were to break out it would give rise to revolution.

In the late 1950s the Soviets and Chinese also disagreed on the questions of Taiwan and the Chinese border with India. During the 1957-58 confrontation between China and Taiwan plus the U.S. over the islands of Quemoy and Matsu, the Soviets counselled a de-escalation of hostility while the Chinese tried to pull them into more active support of their cause. Again in 1959-60, after the Chinese had suppressed the feudal led insurrection in Tibet and incorporated the province fully, a confrontation between India and China developed over their common border. The Soviets, in spite of Chinese pleas for support, remained neutral, counselling a peaceful settlement although Soviet maps supported the Chinese definition of the border. In the subsequent 1962 border war between India and China, the Soviets continued to remain neutral, but actually supplied India with planes. Needless to say, the lack of Soviet support during these confrontations with Taiwan and India greatly angered the Chinese. [13]

The growing antagonism and, after 1960, increasingly public Chinese disagreements with Soviet policies and actions led the Soviet Union to put pressure on the Chinese to modify their positions. The Soviets, insisting on being the leading force in the world communist movement, did not at all like the challenge to their leadership. By the early 1960s the Chinese were openly accusing the Soviets of revisionism (i.e. of having betrayed the basic principles of Marxism-Leninism), and as a result were *de facto* claiming to be the new centre of the world revolutionary movement. Soviet displeasure with the increasingly independent course the Chinese were taking was the major cause of the withdrawal of Soviet technicians and blueprints in 1960, the cessation of other forms of Soviet assistance, and the drastic cut (by two-thirds) in Soviet exports to China. In 1961 Albania was likewise cut off by the Soviets because of its support for the Chinese positions. This made it clear to other socialist countries and parties that the U.S.S.R. was insistent on the isolation of China. These measures were clear cases of Soviet hegemonism. [14]

Although in many ways Soviet assistance to China in the 1950s was less generous than her assistance to Eastern Europe, especially in that China alone had to pay the Soviets for their share of the joint stock companies and pay for Korean War military assistance, it would not be correct to conclude that the Soviet Union had an imperialist relationship with China in the 1950s. China benefited considerably from the technical assistance provided and, as was clearly shown by the post-1957 Chinese actions, she was able to act thoroughly independently of Soviet desires. The relationship between the two until 1958 while clearly not a manifestation of social imperialism could fairly be called one of Soviet hegemonism. As long as the Chinese followed the development policies preferred by the Soviets and generally supported Soviet foreign policies, the Soviets gave them considerable support. But when they began to pursue independent development policies, such as the Great Leap Forward, and began developing an independent and more militant foreign policy, the Soviets cut back on assistance and exports in order to put pressure on the Chinese to tow the line. When the Chinese refused to accept Soviet leadership in economic and foreign policy questions and tried rather aggressively to convince other communist parties that the Chinese position was correct and that the Soviets were tending towards revisionism, the latter responded by taking drastic sanctions against China, trying to isolate her in the world communist movement. This clearly reflected Soviet hegemonistic policies.

Cuba

Before 1960 approximately 70 per cent of all Cuban trade was with the U.S.A. Cuba was as integrated into the American economy as most of the U.S. states. When the U.S.A. imposed a total prohibition on exports to and imports from

Cuba in an attempt to overthrow her new revolutionary regime, the Soviet Union immediately stepped in to prevent the collapse of the Cuban economy, thus allowing the Revolution to consolidate itself.

The Soviet Union has remained Cuba's principal trading partner ever since. In the period 1972-74, 36.6 per cent of all Cuban exports and 52.1 per cent of all her imports were with the Soviet Union. The percentage of total Cuban imports from the U.S.S.R. has been more or less constant since the mid 1960s. But the percentage of total exports going to the U.S.S.R. has declined significantly (from 45.8 per cent in 1964-67 to 36.6 per cent in 1972-74).[15] The Cubans have been increasingly able to find alternative markets for their exports while remaining heavily reliant on the U.S.S.R. to provide them (at a subsidized rate) with the goods necessary for their development.

The Soviets have been consistently exporting far more to the Cubans than the Cubans have to them. In 1960-63 the ratio of Cuban imports from the U.S.S.R. to her exports to that country was 1.58; in 1964-67, 1.57; in 1968-71, 2.03; and in 1972-74, 1.67. Clearly the Soviets have been heavily subsidizing Cuba by providing a large share of her vital imports without a return.

One way the Soviets have provided a major subsidy to the Cubans has been by consistently buying Cuban sugar at more than the world price. In 1965-70 they paid 261 per cent of the world market price for Cuban sugar, which amounted to an average annual Soviet subsidy of $173 million a year. In 1960-70 as a whole, they paid $1,168 million to the Cubans over and above the prevailing world market prices for Cuban sugar (see Table 9.1). The Soviet price for Cuban sugar from 1965 to 1973 was 6.11 U.S. cents a pound. Until 1972 this was considerably above the world price. In 1972 the world sugar price went above the Soviet price (to 7.3¢) for only the second time and the Soviet price was then renegotiated upward to about 11 cents a pound, once again significantly above the world price level.[16] The Soviets have consistently renegotiated the sugar price upwards whenever the free market price has come to exceed the agreed upon price between the two countries. A further renegotiation occurred in 1974 when the world price sky rocketed temporarily to 29.7¢. Thus, even in the period of exceptionally high world sugar prices (1974-76), the Soviets paid 25 per cent more than the world market price for their sugar imports from Cuba.[17] The predetermined and stable price (except for upward adjustments) for Cuban sugar paid by the Soviet Union and other COMECON countries has allowed the Cubans to plan production and projects paid for by their sugar exports. The Soviet guarantee of sugar prices and its subsidy have enabled socialist Cuba to avoid the inherent discrimination and economic dislocations normally suffered by Third World agricultural exporters in capitalist world markets.

The Soviets also subsidize and offer a guaranteed market for the Cubans' second major export, nickel. They have consistently bought Cuban nickel at twice the world price, providing another important source of the island's income. Soviet guaranteed purchases of sugar and nickel have been especially important to Cuba because of the international boycott initiated by the U.S. government and transnational corporations. Pressure from the United States

Table 9.1
Soviet Sugar Imports from Cuba, 1960-1970

Year	Volume (in millions of metric tons)	Value (in millions of rubles)	Price Paid (in cents per pound)	Average Yearly Price on World Market (in cents per pound)	Cost to U.S.S.R. of Sugar Subsidy (in millions of $U.S.)
1960	1.467	93.4	3.21	3.15	1.94
1961	3.345	270.4	4.00	2.70	95.87
1962	2.233	183.5	4.13	2.78	66.46
1963	0.996	123.2	6.22	8.29	− 45.45*
1964	1.859	222.6	6.00	5.72	11.48
1965	2.330	273.3	6.00	2.03	203.93
1966	1.841	225.7	6.11	1.76	176.55
1967	2.479	302.3	6.11	1.99	225.17
1968	1.749	212.7	6.11	1.12	192.41
1969	1.332	161.9	6.11	3.38	80.17
1970	3.000	364.3	6.11	3.69	159.72

Source: Leon Goure and Julian Weinkle, 'Soviet-Cuban Relations: The Growing Integration', in Jaime Suchlicki, *Cuba, Castro and Revolution*, p.170.

* In this year the Soviet Union unexpectedly gained.

goes so far as to prohibit the import of other countries' steel, etc. if it contains Cuban nickel. Without Soviet purchases, it is doubtful whether the Cuban Revolution could have survived the impossible economic situation it was put in by the U.S.[18]

The Soviets also provide most of Cuba's imports of petroleum, minerals, fertilizer, steel, machinery, trucks, tractors and other agricultural machines, as well as other raw materials and many basic foodstuffs such as grains. A large number of Cuban factories have been built with Soviet assistance.[19] In 1971 there were about 3,000 Soviet technicians and military advisers in Cuba. In 1973 about 1,500 Cubans were undergoing advanced technical training in the U.S.S.R. (85 per cent of them engineers and technicians).[20] The Soviets from the beginning committed themselves to all-round development of the Cuban economy.[21] In 1973 they again demonstrated their commitment to the development of Cuba by granting about $300 million worth of technical aid to mechanize the sugar harvest, and to modernize and expand nickel, electricity, oil refineries, textile and metallurgical operations (this credit to be repaid from 1976 to the year 2000).[22] To a large extent because of Soviet aid in its multitudinous forms, Cuban industry has grown at a respectable rate. Heavy industry increased 2.9 times from 1958 to 1975. In the period 1970-75 the rate of industrial growth was 11 per cent per annum.[23]

The first Cuban-Soviet trade agreement, signed in 1961, stipulated that the Cubans would pay for Soviet imports 80 per cent in Cuban goods and 20 per cent in convertible currency. As it became clear that the Cubans would not easily be able to pay, the Soviets increasingly gave the Cubans credits for their purchases. These credits have virtually amounted to grants because of the repeated deferment of repayments and their interest-free nature. In 1973 all outstanding repayments on Cuba's debt to the Soviet Union were postponed until 1986. These repayments were then to be spread out over a 25 year period, repaid without interest and in Cuban products. In addition an agreement was signed granting Cuba generous export credits for the 1973-75 period to be repaid on the same terms.[24] It is difficult to imagine more generous terms, short of outright grants. Since past Cuban debt repayments have been put off when Cuba has had difficulty repaying, it can be assumed that the repayments, when and if they start in 1986, will not be a major burden for her.

The Soviets have also provided military assistance to the Cubans. Up to 1971 they received about $1.5 billion to modernize and build up their armed forces. Although most of this military assistance was formally granted on credit, for all practical purposes the aid has been a gift.[25] It is clear that this assistance to Cuba has cost the U.S.S.R. a lot. There has never been a more generous programme of economic and military assistance to a Third World country (with the possible exception of U.S. aid to its puppet regimes in South Korea and South Vietnam).

Soviet generosity to Cuba has transcended the often serious political differences they have had with each other, especially in the pre-1969 period. However, the Soviets have from time to time put pressure on the Cubans, as is their habit with socialist countries with which they disagree. This has taken the form of reductions in economic assistance when Cuba has been too actively opposed to Soviet policies, and corresponding increases in assistance when the two parties concur. For example, at the height of the quarrel between Moscow and Havana in 1967-68 when the Cubans were giving active support to revolutionary movements in Latin America and attacking the reformism of the continent's communist parties, irregularities and delays appeared in Soviet deliveries of fuel and other crucial goods to Cuba. There were delays in the signing of new trade agreements and the Soviets even began to press for payment of interest on new credits.[26] At the end of 1968, after the quarrel had been resolved, these rather minor economic sanctions were removed and Soviet assistance became more generous than ever. In the early 1970s the two countries became closer politically than ever before. Cuba at long last accepted Soviet economic advice about the need to emphasize material incentives, careful economic planning and not too head-long industrialization, while at the same time reducing somewhat her support for *adventurist* guerrilla movements and her attacks on Latin American communist parties.

The peak of Cuban-Soviet disagreement had occurred in 1967-68. In January 1966 the Tricontinental Congress of world revolutionary forces, including both the Chinese and the Soviets, was held in Havana. Both these powers had hopes of emerging from the conference as the leading force in the struggles of Third World revolutionaries. But an alliance of North Korea, North Vietnam, the National Liberation Front of South Vietnam and Cuba emerged to isolate both the Soviets and Chinese. Both were excluded from the Executive Secretariat of the Tricontinental organization (the only communist countries represented on this body were Cuba as secretary-general, North Korea and the National Liberation Front of South Vietnam). However, they were both given seats on the Committee of Assistance and Aid to the National Liberation Movements and of Struggle against Neocolonialism. This meant they were being encouraged to provide money and military assistance to liberation struggles while being denied a directing role. Neither the Chinese nor Soviets were happy with the outcome. January 1966, the very month of the Tricontinental Congress, marked the sharp outbreak of antagonism between Cuba and China. This followed a sudden halt in Chinese rice ship-ments to the island. The same period also marked the beginning of a deterior-ation in relations between Cuba and the Soviets. The Tricontinental Congress indicated the emergence of Cuba as a third independent Communist centre, more actively committed to armed revolutionary struggle in the Third World than either the Soviets or the Chinese.[27] In the summer of 1967, Castro stated in an interview with *The New York Times* that 'true Marxism-Leninism is not communism as it is practised in Russia, Eastern Europe or China.'[28]

In the period that followed (1966-68), the Cubans vociferously advocated Soviet intervention on the side of North Vietnam. They published Regis Debray's *Revolution in the Revolution* which was sharply critical of both the Chinese and Soviet theories of revolution and considerably more activist

than either. Cuba also sent Che Guevara and others to start a revolution in
Bolivia, and gave active support to many guerrilla struggles throughout Latin
America and Africa. They escalated their attacks on the traditional Latin
American communist parties for being reformist, submissive, conciliatory,
and enemies of revolutionary armed struggle.[29]

The struggle between the Cubans and the Soviets in 1966-68 was mani-
fested domestically by a purge of pro-Soviets from the Cuban Communist
Party. Anibal Escalante, a top leader of the pre-1959 Cuban Communist
Party and about 40 other leading pro-Moscow Communists were expelled in
January 1968 from the Party, and many tried and sentenced as traitors.
Members of this 'micro-faction' were accused of spreading pro-Soviet and
anti-Castro propaganda, passing secrets to the Soviets and pressuring the
Cuban leadership into adopting a pro-Moscow line.[30]

The fact that the Cubans didn't hesitate to take independent action in
support of Third World revolution — even though they were in an extremely
vulnerable position vis-a-vis the U.S., reliant economically on the Soviet Union
and had been cut off by China — demonstrates that they are nobody's pawns.
And the fact, in turn,that the Soviets exerted only minor economic pressure ·
on them during this period, in spite of rather grievous insults and provocat-
ions, furthermore suggests that the Soviets are not a typical hegemonic power
insistent on submissive behaviour as the reward for their benevolence.

The subsequent reconciliation between the U.S.S.R. and Cuba which
occurred in late 1968 was motivated more by the Cubans' actual experiences
than by any pressure put on them by the Soviets. The failures of the Cuban
economy were summed up as being a product of adventurist economic
policies and attempts to skip stages on the road towards full communism.
These failures convinced the Cubans that the Soviets were correct in their
economic advice to rely on more material incentives, more careful planning,
an only gradual transition to communism and a more careful and balanced
industrialization policy. The failure of Che Guevara in Bolivia and the inability
of any guerrilla movements in Latin America to come close to success, likewise demonstrated the errors of the rather adventurist Cuban line in international affairs, and suggested that perhaps the more traditional Soviet and
Latin American C.P. approach to revolution was not totally bankrupt after
all. To persist in disastrous domestic and international policies in the face of
obvious failures would have been suicidal. And if followed long enough, it
would have meant the discrediting of Cuba as an international revolutionary
force and probably the eventual collapse of its socialist regime. By late 1968
it was becoming clear to the Cubans that Soviet policies were not as wrong
as they had thought, while Soviet benevolence in continuing to support Cuba
in spite of the hostility between the two countries, came to be regarded as
evidence that the Soviet Union was a true friend.

The Soviet intervention in Czechoslovakia in the middle of 1968 was also
an important influence on the Cuban leadership's decision to reverse its
course. The Cubans wanted the Soviets to promise the same kind of help to
them as they had provided the Left in Czechoslovakia, in the event of an

attempt at counter-revolution in Cuba. They also wanted the Soviets to intervene against the reformist forces in the Latin American communist parties.
Fidel Castro argued in August 1968:

> The essential thing is whether the Socialist bloc could permit the develop-
> ment of a political situation which might lead to the breakdown of a
> Socialist country . . . From our viewpoint, it is not permissible and the
> Socialist bloc has the right to prevent it in one way or another . . .
> I ask, in the light of the facts and in the light of the bitter reality which
> led the Warsaw Pact countries to send their forces to crush a counter-
> revolution in Czechoslovakia and to support a minority there . . . against
> a majority with rightist positions; I ask if they will cease supporting also
> in Latin America those rightist, reformist, submissive, and conciliatory
> leaders, enemies of revolutionary armed struggle who oppose the people's
> liberation struggle.[31]

It is interesting to recall that the relations between China and Cuba deterior-
ated sharply in January 1966 after the Chinese cut off vital imports of rice and
insisted that all future trade with Cuba would have to be balanced. The
Chinese refused to subsidize the Cuban economy in any way because of Cuba's
friendship with the U.S.S.R., even though the Cubans maintained their independence from both China and the Soviet Union. The Chinese economic
sanctions followed caustic Chinese barbs against her.[32] This move by China
in 1966 (which foreshadowed China's treatment of Albania and Vietnam in
1978) was comparable to similar Soviet actions against other socialist
countries whose foreign policies displeased the Soviet Union (Yugoslavia in
1948, China in 1960, Albania in 1961, North Korea in 1962, and Romania
in the late 1960s. It shows that there is no qualitative difference between
Chinese and Soviet treatment of weaker socialist countries.

The reconciliation between Cuba and the Soviet Union after 1968 and the
especially warm relations which have existed since 1973 by no means imply
that Cuba has a satellite status in relation to the Soviet Union. Nor do they
point to a reduction in Cuban commitment to aiding revolutionary struggles
in the Third World. All the evidence indicates that the Cubans are legitimately thankful for the extremely benevolent Soviet assistance and advice
since 1960 and they tend genuinely to agree on most international issues
nowadays, while still giving crucial support to Third World struggles. Here
the most outstanding example is Cuban assistance to the revolutionary
struggle of the M.P.L.A. in Angola (perhaps the best illustration of proletarian internationalism since the raising of the International Brigades during
the Spanish Civil War of the 1930s). Cuban assistance to the Angolan Revolution was comparable to Soviet assistance to the Spanish Republic (when it
was threatened by Italian and German fascist intervention in the 1930s) and
Chinese assistance to the Democratic People's Republic of Korea (when it
was threatened by U.S. intervention in the 1950s). Cuba gave heroic support
to the Angolan people's struggle against the C.I.A. and South African

intervention in Angola, although it put her in great jeopardy on account of her vulnerability to the U.S. This indicates once again that Cuba puts the interests of the Third World revolutionary struggle above her own short-run state interests to a greater extent than either the Soviets or especially the Chinese.

Cuba is now on better terms with the traditional Latin American communist parties than it has ever been. And while support has been extended to other roads for social change, particularly progressive nationalist military regimes in Peru and Panama and the electoral road in Chile (1970-73), Cuba continues to train revolutionaries and give support to guerrilla actions such as those in Uruguay, Argentina and Nicaragua. Cuban backing for guerrilla groups is, however, no longer granted to virtually any group seeking it, no matter how small or impossible the task, but has tended to be limited to just the more serious major groups who produce results and have some chance of success. The Cubans by no means unconditionally back the traditional Latin communist parties whom the Soviets still favour over other major leftist forces in Latin America.[33]

The attitude of the Cubans toward the Soviets, which by all indications is based upon a genuinely independent judgment (whether or not it is valid) can be summed up by the following quote from Fidel Castro's speech to the First Congress of the Cuban Communist Party in 1975:

> There will be many changes in the future, the day will even come when capitalism disappears in the United States, but our feeling of friendship for the people that helped us in those decisive and critical years, when we faced starvation and extermination, will be everlasting. This adds to our gratitude to the people that blazed the trail of the socialist revolution and that, at the cost of millions of lives, freed the world from the scourge of fascism. Our confidence in Lenin's Homeland is unbounded, because in the course of more than half a century the Soviet revolution has proved its adherence to the principles and consistent line of behaviour in its international policy. It has shown this not only in Cuba but also in Viet Nam, in the Middle East, in the Portuguese colonies fighting for their independence, in Chile, Cyprus, Yemen, Angola and every other part of the world where the national liberation movement confronts colonialism and imperialism, as it once did in an exemplary manner with the heroic Spanish people. This incontestable truth has not been invalidated by a single exception, and in the long run any slanderous attempt to deny history's objective facts will be useless. The U.S.S.R. has also made a decisive contribution to world peace, without which, in this epoch of growing scarcity of raw materials and fuel, the imperialist powers would have launched upon a new and voracious partition of the world. The mere existence of the powerful Soviet State makes this alternative impossible. Its detractors, who try to deny this, are like dogs barking at the moon.[34]

Conclusions

There is no evidence of social imperialism in Soviet economic relations with the socialist countries of the Third World such as China and Cuba. Soviet economic relations with China in the 1950s, while considerably less benevolent than its relations with Cuba in the 1960s and 1970s, and with Eastern Europe after 1956, nevertheless played an important positive role in the development of China without securing any economic advantages for the Soviet Union in return. The massive and extremely generous economic support of Cuba by the Soviets since 1960 is probably the leading case to disprove the thesis of social imperialism.

But, while there is no evidence that the Soviet Union is social imperialist in her dealings with the Third World socialist countries, there is a lot of evidence to show that it has tried to be hegemonic, during the 1950s and early 1960s. The sanctions taken against China for her independent course, as well as the failure to be as generous with her as with the other much smaller socialist countries, indicates Soviet hegemonism in the pre-1960 period. Lesser sanctions taken against the Democratic People's Republic of Korea in 1962-64 for becoming too close to China, and the minor sanctions taken against Cuba in the 1966-68 period for its independent and extremely militant course, also reflect hegemonism. While Soviet relations with China in the 1950s would appear to be as clear a manifestation of Soviet hegemonism as exists, its behaviour towards North Korea and Cuba have clearly been rather minor aspects of overall Soviet relations with these two countries. The Cubans in particular established themselves as an independent revolutionary force subservient to no one, while the Soviets have consistently provided essential economic support to the revolutionary regime.

It would seem that the case of China is a special one, having to do with: (1) its serious potential for becoming an alternative world centre for the communist movement; and (2) with the tendency for its independent development to occur earlier than any other communist movement or state, except the Yugoslavs who were dealt with in a manner much more drastic than the Chinese. Soviet treatment of the Chinese cannot be considered the archetypal case of Soviet relations with Third World socialist countries.

While in the 1950s the Soviets clearly tried to preserve their hegemony over the world communist movement (including over the governing communist parties of the Third World) by the 1960s they came, as a result of considerable pressure, to abdicate more and more from this role, becoming increasingly tolerant towards alternative perspectives in the world communist movement. The minor sanctions applied against North Korea and Cuba in the mid 1960s, compared to the serious sanctions taken against China earlier and the even more drastic sanctions taken against Yugoslavia in the 1940s, clearly indicate a considerable reduction in Soviet hegemonism. Their admittedly unhappy tolerance of the major Eurocommunist parties in the 1970s, together with their continuing conciliatory gestures towards China, indicate a still further decline in Soviet hegemonism during that time. In summary, while there are still some minor elements of hegemonism in Soviet relations with Third World socialist countries, these relations are in fact essentially governed by what the Soviets call proletarian internationalism.

195

Summarizing our findings about Soviet relations with the countries of Eastern Europe and the socialist and non-socialist countries of the Third World, we can only conclude that there are both important similarities and differences in them. Most importantly, in none of the three sets of countries is there any substantial evidence to show that the Soviet Union is social imperialist. In none of the three does the Soviet Union engage in exploitation through trade, economic assistance or foreign investments. Nor does she, in any of them, dominate their economies in order to make them into raw material suppliers or economic dependencies of the U.S.S.R. In all cases, Soviet involvement facilitates the autonomous economic development and industrialization of these countries. She is not social imperialist.

In some areas, nevertheless, namely Eastern Europe, the Soviet Union is still hegemonic. And in others, namely the socialist countries of the Third World, hegemonism has been, albeit decreasingly, a major component of Soviet relations. While it was perhaps the dominant aspect of such relations in the 1950s, it is clearly only a secondary component in the 1970s. As for the non-socialist countries of the Third World, on the other hand, no substantial evidence can be found that the Soviet Union is, or attempts to be, hegemonic, although she clearly and correctly intervenes in support of progressive regimes and national liberation struggles.

This long exploration of the relationship between the Soviet Union and other socialist countries, as well as with the non-capitalist Third World, forces us to conclude that the Soviet Union cannot be called a social imperialist superpower. The Chinese are wrong.

There are no mechanisms analogous to overproduction operating in the Soviet economy which force the pursuit of overseas investment outlets, or trade surpluses in order to facilitate the accumulation of capital. Soviet foreign relations generally benefit liberation and other progressive forces against conservative and reactionary ones. Soviet overseas involvements do not advance the economic interests of the Soviet Union at the expense of the peoples of other socialist countries or of the Third World. The Soviet Union does not seek or obtain expansionist oriented military bases overseas. And Soviet policies do not generally hinder the advance of the world socialist movement, although they have spread considerable dissension, and in places demoralization, among communists and progressives.

Soviet hegemonism, benevolent as it might often be, is still however a force in the world communist movement and especially among the socialist COMECON countries of Eastern Europe and Mongolia. The Soviets still tend to maintain that they have the best understanding of the correct road to socialism and communism, although they have grown more tolerant towards opposition in the Western communist parties and in the East European countries, than ever before. Soviet hegemonism is gradually being eroded as each communist party and socialist regime increasingly comes to decide its own policies. These policies, of course, often tend to converge in particular regions — for example towards Euro-Communism or revisionism in the major parties in the advanced capitalist countries, Maoism in much of South-east

Asia and pro-Sovietism in most of Eastern Europe and the smaller communist parties outside of Western Europe.

References

1. Howard Sherman, *The Soviet Economy*, (Boston: Little, Brown and Co. 1969) p.200; Robert Owen Freedman, *Economic Warfare in the Communist Bloc*, (New York: Praeger, 1970), Chapter 4, p.107.
2. Sherman, *op. cit.*, p.199; and Roy Grow, 'Soviet Economic Penetration of China, 1945-1960', in Steven Rosen and James Kurth, *Testing Theories of Economic Imperialism*, (Lexington, Mass: D.C. Heath and Co. 1974).
3. *Ibid.*
4. *Ibid.*
5. Freedman, *op. cit.*, p.111.
6. Grow, *op. cit.*
7. Grow, *op. cit.*, and Freedman, *op. cit.*, p.106ff.
8. Alan Lawrance, *China's Foreign Relations Since 1959*, (London: Routledge and Kegan Paul, 1975).
9. Freedman, *op. cit.*, p.118.
10. *Peking Review*, 2 August 1963, cited in Lawrance, *op. cit.*, pp.85-6.
11. This speech was reprinted in the *New York Times*, 25 April 1955, quoted in Lawrance, *op. cit.*, pp.165-8.
12. Freedman, *op. cit.*, Chapter 4; and Lawrance, *op. cit.*, Chapter 2.
13. Lawrance, *op. cit.*, Part IV.
14. Freedman, *op. cit.*, Chapter 3, especially p.79.
15. United Nations, *Yearbook of International Trade Statistics*, (1975) and various previous volumes.
16. Leon Goure and Julian Weinkle, 'Soviet-Cuban Relations: The Growing Integration', in Jaime Suchlicki, (ed.), *Cuba, Castro and Revolution* (Coral Gables: University of Miami, 1972); Carmelo Mesa-Lago, *Cuba in the 1970s*, (Albuquerque: University of New Mexico Press, 1974), pp.13-20; Fidel Castro, 'The U.S.S.R.-Cuba Economic Agreements', *New World Review*, 41:2, (1973) p.60.
17. International Sugar Organization, *Sugar Yearbook*, (London: 1976) and the Food and Agriculture Organization, *Trade Yearbook*, 1976.
18. Castro, *op. cit.*, p.60.
19. Mesa-Lago, *op. cit.*, p.11; and Goure and Weinkle, *op. cit.*, p.167.
20. Mesa-Lago, *op. cit.*, p.18.
21. Goure and Weinkle, *op. cit.*, p.160ff.
22. Mesa-Lago, *op. cit.*, p.20.
23. Fidel Castro, *Speech to the First Congress of the Communist Party of Cuba*, (Moscow: Progress Publishers, 1976).
24. Goure and Weinkle, *op. cit.*, p.160; Mesa-Lago, *op. cit.*, pp.20-1; Castro, 'The U.S.S.R.-Cuba Economic Agreements', *op. cit.*, pp.55-60.
25. Mesa-Lago, *op. cit.*, p.18.
26. Goure and Weinkle, *op. cit.*, p.168.

27. D. Bruce Jackson, *Castro, the Kremlin and Communism in Latin America*, (Baltimore: John Hopkins Press, 1969), esp. Ch. 6; Foy Kohler, 'Cuba and the Soviet Problem in Latin America', in Suchlicki, (ed.), *op. cit.*
28. *Ibid.*, p.131.
29. *Ibid.*, pp.130-2; M. Michael Kline, 'Castro's Challenge to Latin American Communism', in Suchlicki (ed.), *Cuba, Castro and the Revolution* (Coral Gables, Florida: University of Miami Press, 1973).
30. Kohler, *op. cit.*, p.132; Kline, *op. cit.*, p.211.
31. *Ibid.*, p.214.
32. D. Bruce Jackson, *Castro, the Kremlin and Communism in Latin America*, (Baltimore: Johns Hopkins Press, 1969), pp.32-3; Goldman, *Soviet Foreign Aid*, (New York: Praeger, 1967).
33. Kline, *op. cit.*, pp.218-20.
34. Fidel Castro, *Speech to the First Congress of the Communist Party of Cuba, op. cit.*, p.64.

10. The Soviet Union: Retrospect and Prospect

In this final chapter, I will attempt to sum up the evidence from the earlier chapters about the class nature of the Soviet Union. I shall examine briefly the historical development of Soviet society (specifically the Stalin years), look at the development of Soviet hegemonism and speculate about the possible future of the Soviet Union. In conclusion, I will look at the political implications of this study for the world socialist movement.

The Class Nature of the U.S.S.R.

Our long road through the available empirical data has led us to the inexorable conclusion that the Soviet Union is a socialist society, albeit a somewhat distorted one. Markets do not have a logic of their own in the Soviet Union and so the laws of the labour market do not prevail. The Soviet economy, including labour allocation, is governed by a central plan and not by the pursuit of profit, as are all market capitalist formations. No exploiting class controls the means of production nor dominates the state and party.

To show that an exploiting class exists, it must be demonstrated that the people who are in leading roles operating the means of production exercise control over the production process in ways that benefit themselves at the expense of the actual producers. It must be specifically shown that they appropriate the economic surplus of the producers for their own ends. This is not the case to any appreciable degree in the Soviet Union. Although the salaries and fringe benefits of the managerial and government power elite are significantly greater than those of the average productive worker (by a factor of four or five), this is very small compared to either the differential between ruling class families and the productive classes in the Western capitalist countries *or* in comparison to the size of the economic surplus which is disposed of in the U.S.S.R. The high and growing level of free goods and services, the rapidly rising standard of living, and above all the rapidly diminishing economic inequality and the increasing depth and breadth of political debate and participation are strong indicators that the power elite are not benefiting at the expense of the productive masses. Moreover the former prerogatives and privileges of these people are steadily diminishing.

199

Nothing like a social class of owners and controllers of industry, such as exists in the capitalist countries, is present in the Soviet Union. Although the professional intelligentsia are able to give their children a chance some three times greater than that of the manual working class, to make it into the intelligentsia (even then half the recruits to this stratum come from the working class), there is no inheritance of top managerial or government positions. In fact about 75 per cent of top positions continue to be filled by people from backgrounds outside the intelligentsia. While the occupants of leading managerial and governmental positions do have significant privileges in comparison to factory workers, in relative terms these are far less than in the West. They are also fully compatible with the official Soviet view that they are necessary as incentives to motivate workers and students to take on the responsibilities of leading roles (an argument not unlike that of the functionalists in the West). These facts do not amount to evidence for the emergence of a new ruling class which exploits the workers.

The picture which has emerged from this study is that Soviet society can best be seen as composed of the following social strata: (1) the peasantry who are the poorest and least influential group; (2) the manual working class, who, economically and politically, are considerably better off relative to peasants, white collar employees, managers and the professional intelligentsia, than are their counterparts in Western capitalist countries; (3) enterprise managers and Party and state officials, most of whom have humble backgrounds, and relatively (compared to the West) few privileges vis-a-vis the industrial working class; (4) the lower level white collar employees, who have little influence or privileges; and (5) the professional intelligentsia who are definitely the most privileged group in Soviet society as well as the most socially cohesive. It is important to note that, unlike the case in capitalist societies, occupants of the most powerful economic and political positions are not the same as those who have the most privilege. In sum, the picture emerges of a petty bourgeoisie, who the Soviets themselves call highly educated workers (and who much of the New Left would have referred to as 'new working class'), led by technical experts and scientists who play an important, but not politically leading, role in the Soviet Union; an industrial working class, which is relatively privileged and powerful; and a group of managers and officials who do not form a distinct social class, let alone a ruling class.

There appears to be a high level of political support for the Soviet system by the producing classes, as well as a high level of political participation. The working class plays a central and growing role in both basic society-wide decision making and in day-to-day operation of the enterprises where they work and the communities in which they live. There appear to be considerable obstacles to the power elite making decisions which run against the basic interests of the masses or which reverse the trend of the last 20 years towards greater equality and popular democracy. It is most likely that greater actual power resides with the producing classes than with a small power elite of managers and officials.

In sum, the Soviet Union must be categorized as an authentically socialist country, albeit one in which party and state officials play the central role both in initiating decision making and in day-to-day operation of the economy. There appears to be a distortion in the Soviet Union's state socialism towards concentration of power and to a lesser degree privileges, in the hands of experts – engineers, economists, scientists, professionals, technicians and specialists in general. Compared to a decentralized socialism, such as the Chinese (*circa* 1966-76), these latter strata in the U.S.S.R. appear to be playing a disproportionate role vis-a-vis common working people. For the most part, however, it seems that their superior decision making role is not so much used for their own personal benefit, as to guide Soviet society according to their almost technocratic ideology of efficiency and scientific expertise. The state socialism of the Soviets has a strong technocratic, rather than bureaucratic or charismatic bias, enabling it to be categorized as a *technocratic state socialism.*

Stalin

It is peculiar that many Marxists who maintain a consistently materialist position when analysing the development of capitalist or pre-capitalist societies (always looking for class forces and class struggles to explain historical developments) resort to explaining developments in the Soviet Union from the 1920s to the 1950s largely in terms of individual personalities – 'Great Men', personal motivations, power hunger, and so on. This is true of both apologists for Stalin and their arch opponents the Trotskyists. The reason for using these latter (and un-Marxist) categories, when analysing the transitional years of Soviet history, lies in the intense political commitments, loyalties and bitternesses experienced by various Marxist parties and factions during these years. They consequently feel the need either to legitimate among the masses (who are not always fully conscious Marxists) what was happening in the Soviet Union by attributing super-human characteristics to Stalin, or conversely to attempt to win widespread support for movements antagonistic to the Soviet Union, among people who make no pretence of accepting the materialist conception of history. The bitterness of the struggles between the mainstream communist parties of the world and their social democratic and Trotskyist opponents outlasted the death of Stalin and continues to colour analyses of Soviet history. The personal experiences of the post-1953 Soviet leadership, bitter about the treatment they had received during the Stalin years, resulted in Khrushchev's denunciation of the cult of personality in 1956. This analysis by the post-1953 leadership (which subsequently became entangled in the Sino-Soviet split, with the Chinese essentially defending Stalin) has reinforced the tendency to ignore historical materialist categories in the analysis of Soviet history. [1]

Almost three decades have passed since the death of Stalin. Sufficient time, surely, for the world Marxist movement to gain enough distance from

the events of which he was at the centre, to evaluate objectively the meaning
of the policies and events which occurred in the years when he was the
leading figure in the world communist movement. Just as an objective
analysis of the role of other revolutionary figures — Cromwell or Robespierre
— had to wait a respectable number of years after their deaths, so too must
a scientific analysis of the meaning of Stalin.

Although emotions should by now have died down to the point where an
objective analysis is possible, the consequences of a scientific understanding
of the Stalin period remain considerable for the future of the world communist movement. What if the analyses of Western anti-Marxist, or Trotskyist,
or social democratic organizations are correct? What if Stalin really was one
of the two most brutal despots of the twentieth century — responsible for
the destruction of workers' power in the U.S.S.R. and the creation of a new
bureaucratic class; responsible for the putting to death of millions for
resisting his whims; and responsible for dealing with both domestic issues and
foreign communist parties to the detriment of the development of socialism
in the Soviet Union and the advance of the Communist movement overseas?
If all this is so, very serious questions are necessarily raised about the liber-
ating promise of Marxism. If the mainstream of the world Marxist movement
followed Stalin's leadership for 30 years in spite of these gross injustices and
abuses, are Marxists, now or in the future, ever to be trusted to come to
correct analyses and inspire the workers' movement towards communism?
If the revolutionary situation in the U.S.S.R. could so evolve in the 1920s
that it turned into its opposite, what is to stop this from happening after
revolutions in other countries? Perhaps it is better that we do not support a
revolutionary process at all. Indeed if the claims, now accepted by virtually
all leftists not closely associated with Albania or China (both of which
continue to celebrate Stalin) are true, the Marxist Left faces terrible
embarrassment.

While it is undoubtedly true that Stalin sometimes demonstrated personal
characteristics of rudeness, arrogance and distrust, that he sought to increase
his own power (which became considerable), and that he was quite often
vindictive, mistaken and caught up in the collective paranoia of this period
in which the Soviet state was the most threatened, these factors can only be
incidental to the material forces which were at work in the Soviet Union from
the 1920s to the 1950s and which acted to produce the policies followed, as
well as the results obtained. The policies in the period of Stalin's leadership,
as well as the mechanisms for decision making and mass involvement, were
dictated in their broad outlines by the situation and were not the product of
Stalin's personal motives or psychological state. On the contrary, the personalities and motives of Stalin and the other leaders were socially formed
according to the requirements of the situation, and the leadership itself was
socially selected on the basis of the effects of these two elements. Just as
Marx did a class analysis of Napoleon III, we must do a class analysis of the
Stalin period in order to uncover which class forces were operating through
Stalin's leadership and what the effects were of the policies of the Stalin

years on the class structure and development of socialism.

The 1930s and 1940s, when the country was under severe international and domestic pressures, were the heroic period of Soviet history. Decision making undoubtedly became highly centralized at the expense of both Soviet and Party democracy. Economic inequality also increased. But, at the same time, the last vestiges of private capitalism were eliminated, the country was industrialized (with all that this meant for rising levels of consumption), and the working class expanded until it became a majority of the population. The people, also, were educated in basic Marxist principles. And the institutional framework was consolidated, something which was to be the basis for greatly expanding popular participation after the mid 1950s. In the period of Stalin's leadership the Soviet Union successfully repulsed the Nazi invasion and destroyed fascist rule in central Europe (90 per cent of all German World War II casualties were caused by the Soviets). The U.S.S.R. was the only country able to resist the Nazi *blitzkrieg*. This success must in good part be attributed to the popular support and unity of Soviet leadership (they had no Quislings or Petains, the purges of the late 1930s, excessive as they were, had seen to that), and the ability of the Stalin leadership to inspire confidence in the Soviet people.

This period also saw the coming to power of communist parties in a dozen other countries and their becoming major political forces in Western Europe, as well as in many Third World countries. On balance, the net gains for international and Soviet Communism during this period were considerable.

In order to account for these achievements in the period of Stalin's leadership, three lines are commonly taken. The first argues Stalin was a genius who more or less single-handedly fought against all odds to win these great victories. This is the position of most Maoist groups. The second maintains that the communist parties of the world, especially the Soviet Union's, were so strong, their ties with the masses so firm, and the working class and peasant movement so overwhelming that, in spite of Stalin's arbitrariness and venality, these great victories were accomplished. This is the position of the U.S.S.R.'s current leadership and of most non-Maoist communist parties. The third line of argument alleges these accomplishments were bought at a cost which made their achievement not worth the effort. The suffering of the peasants during forced collectivization was not justified by the result of rapid industrialization; the Chinese Revolution was distorted by Stalin's influence; the Western communist parties became bureaucratized and betrayed their revolutionary roles; millions died needlessly in the war against Hitler because of Stalin's bungling etc. This position is commonly held by Trotskyists and Social Democrats.

All three of these positions raise serious problems and all must be rejected. Materialism cannot accept the Great Man or genius theories of history. Honest Marxists must recognize as great achievements the Chinese Revolution, the new socialist regimes in Eastern Europe, the growth of the Western communist parties, the destruction of Hitler, the industrialization of the U.S.S.R. and so on. To assume that these achievements could have been accomplished in spite of venal and arbitrary leadership makes no sense. Leadership is produced by the situation in which it occurs. Classes and institutions develop the leadership they need in order to accomplish what they want to achieve. Stalin's leadership, then, must be credited with being one which realized the great advances of the Soviet Union in the 1920s to 1950s period. And the nature of that leadership, including its harsh characteristics, must in turn be accounted for by the material forces at work in the U.S.S.R. and the world at the time.

If the Soviet Union was to survive and Communist leadership be preserved, the stumbling around of the first ten years after the Revolution had to be ended. The country had to industrialize rapidly, firstly to adequately feed, clothe and house its population and thereby prevent growing disaffection, and secondly to build a military machine that could successfully defend the country against any repeat of the invasion by the leading capitalist powers that had occurred during the Civil War of 1918-21. Since the working class who had made the Revolution was only made up of a small percentage of a still basically peasant country, the regime's active social basis was not all that large. This was unlike the situation in China where most of the 20 year struggle was carried on by the peasantry. Thus the process of rapid industrialization, dictated by the desperateness of the situation, had of necessity to be largely a top down process. In fact, in the countryside, the collectivization of agriculture occurred with considerable class struggle between the poor landless peasants and the rich employer farmers (the Kulaks). The upheaval caused by collectivization and the sharp struggle waged by both sides around it, together with the rapid growth of cities, created a potentially explosive situation. Peasant rebellions, spontaneous rioting of new urban migrants, divisive factionalism in the Soviets and the Party, and the rapidly worsening international situation, could easily have paralysed the country and ensured defeat at the hands of foreign invaders. It might even have provoked a new civil war which the Bolsheviks could have lost.

Careful studies of the factional battles in the C.P.S.U. in the 1920s show that Stalin emerged as leader because he obtained the genuine support of most of the Party's leadership, as well as the confidence of its rank and file. Virtually the entire Party supported the move to isolate and oust Trotsky from the leadership because of a widespread feeling that he aspired to be a Soviet Napoleon. Trotsky had only joined the C.P.S.U. in the summer of 1917, a few months before the Revolution and after 15 years of factional battles and hostility with Lenin and the Bolsheviks. He was distrusted by virtually all because he had not shared the Bolsheviks' harsh experiences of underground life in the pre-revolutionary period, and because of his long history of independent radicalism and his oratorical abilities and position as head of the Red Army. The general feeling among nearly all the Bolshevik leaders was that he did not have a sufficiently realistic sense of what had to be done in a period of retreat for both the Revolution in the U.S.S.R. and for the world revolutionary movement as a whole. They also felt that his incessant factional activity in the Party spread disunity and undermined morale at a time when they were vitally necessary for survival. Stalin, unlike Trotsky and Zinoviev, did have a realistic sense of what could be done in the unfavourable conditions of the 1920s and how to inspire people to do it. His slogan of Socialism in One Country gave Party members hope that they could succeed, even in the face of the defeat of revolutionary forces in Europe and China. In contrast, the Trotsky-Zinoviev position that a socialist transformation in the U.S.S.R. had to wait until a revolution in Europe, was seen as defeatist and demoralizing. Stalin came to symbolize commitment to building the future.

The subsequent conflict between Bukharin and the group around Stalin in 1927 centred on whether rapid industrialization and collectivization of the peasantry should be undertaken. Bukharin argued the New Economic Policy had to be continued indefinitely, allowing the Kulaks to carry on enriching themselves, and that only a slow process of industrialization must be undertaken. The Stalin group, on the other hand, felt that the U.S.S.R. could not afford go-slow economic development policies. In 1928 Stalin made a speech which predicted that the country only had about 10 years to industrialize before the likelihood of being invaded again, and that only rapid industrialization would create a military machine capable of saving socialism. Again, most of the Party genuinely rallied behind the Stalin leadership which was committing the Party to the heroic effort of modernization of agriculture, industry and the military.

To explain the struggles among the Trotsky, Bukharin and Stalin groups as being essentially personal intrigues on the part of Stalin to gain absolute power is poppycock. Very real issues were at stake. Historical hindsight allows an objective evaluation which puts the policies of the group around Stalin in a most favourable light. It was the objective situation dictating certain policies that was responsible for the victory of the Stalin group. And the group allowed its position to evolve under pressure of the Soviet masses and Party members who needed a leadership which would articulate their enthusiasm to move ahead, even against the greatest odds. Stalin provided that leadership and inspiration and it is for this reason that he became and remained the key leader.

Soon after the triumph of the Stalin group in the C.P.S.U., a cult of personality began to develop around the person of Stalin. In 1929 the U.S.S.R. publicly celebrated his birthday. Soon cities and mountains were being renamed after him, his picture became omnipresent, statues were erected to him in every town. All this happened before a serious case could be made of despotic leadership on his part. Was the cult of Stalin (which came to supplement the cult of Lenin created after the latter's death in 1924) a result of the man's own vanity? Again, materialists must look to material factors for an explanation of both the Lenin and the Stalin cults.

The personality cult around Stalin (and that around Lenin) served the function of winning the support of the peasantry and the new working class. In *lieu* of the peasants' fundamental involvement in making the socialist revolution, the Bolshevik regime had to be personalized for it to win their loyalty. Even in China and Cuba, where there was authentic massive peasant support, the charisma of Mao and Fidel have played important roles. It would seem that any revolutionary regime has to have a period of personalization in which the charisma of its leading figure is necessary in order to create legitimacy. Such a personality cult has no necessary relation to the actual degree of decision making power of the principal leader, as the role of Mao Tse-tung immediately before the Cultural Revolution showed. The personality cult, instead, serves a key social function when circumstances don't allow for the much slower development of the class-conscious understanding and struggle needed to win people to a socialism without individual heroes. Such early post-revolutionary regimes, notably Cuba and the Stalin period in the U.S.S.R., might then best be called 'charismatic state socialism'. 'Socialism' because the productive classes in the last analysis really do have power; 'state' because the initiative and day-to-day operational control resides with state and party officials; and 'charismatic' because the public personality of the leading figure plays such a key role in the legitimacy of the regime.

The successful accomplishment of mobilizing a people to achieve a difficult end (such as protracted people's war, or the rapid and radical economic and social transformation of a society) requires a considerable unity of leadership as well as suppression of opposition, in order to generate the solidarity and enthusiasm necessary for the task. Whether the costs of such unity and suppression are judged legitimate depends solely on how important the goals are considered. All societies are periodically faced with the need to generate solidarity and hence to repress opposition. The United States, for example, has periodically gone through such times. During the War of Independence, British Loyalists in liberated areas were not only forbidden to express publicly their opinions, but were actively persecuted. During the late 1790s, supporters of the French Revolution and opponents of the framers of the U.S. Federal Constitution were denied freedom of the press and were arrested. During the Civil War, the Bill of Rights was suspended for Confederate sympathizers in the North, and after that War, civil liberties were denied to the leaders of the Confederacy. (Robert E. Lee did not have his citizenship rights restored until the 1970s!) During World Wars I and II, neutralists and groups sympathetic to the Germans (e.g. the I.W.W. and the Socialist Party in 1917) were suppressed. And of course, during the 1950s the American Communist Party was repressed, its leaders jailed and its right to participate in elections revoked. Any leadership that is serious about its goals, especially in a crisis situation which requires total mobilization, will do all in its power to create solidarity and popular enthusiasm by repressing those forces fostering disunity and demoralization.

The process of socialist transformation is as important as any previous progressive transformation (such as the U.S. War of Independence and Civil War). It requires at least the same degree of popular enthusiasm and solidarity as did these earlier events. To allow opponents of socialism, or even socialists who have radically different strategies, to organize actively against the leadership will sap morale and enthusiasm to the point that social transformation could well become impossible. It is far easier to preserve a *status quo* than it is to transform social relations radically. Thus far more unity and enthusiasm are necessary in revolutionary situations than in times of stability. Suppression of opposition is far more important in such periods. This 'law of transformation' is independent of mode of production and simply reflects a common-sense understanding of the need for legitimation and of the factors which produce enthusiasm.

Becoming aware of the draining effects of inter-party rivalry and intra-party factionalism, the Lenin leadership (supported enthusiastically by Trotsky) first suppressed the other left parties (the Mensheviks, Anarchists and Left Social Revolutionaries) as they became obstructionist, and then in 1921 banned organized factions in the Communist Party itself. This did not mean that the Party discouraged an active internal democratic life. It only meant that Party members now became committed to supporting actively official Party policies once adopted. Commitment to the Party as a whole was placed before commitment to one's faction. These measures also did not mean that the one party state created by the suppression of the other parties was non-democratic. The Party, by its overwhelmingly working-class base in the 1920s, continued to express that class's interests. Under Lenin's leadership the C.P.S.U. had devised a mechanism which combined centralization (with its solidarity and enthusiasm generating, and hence transforming, ability) with democracy.

Such was the political situation that the Stalin leadership found in existence when it succeeded Lenin. The need to generate enthusiasm and solidarity intensified with the rapid collectivization and industrialization of the 1930s, and became even more necessary with the growing threat of foreign invasion in the late 1930s. These pressures led decision making to become more and more centralized.

This danger of foreign invasion during the late 1930s should not be underestimated. Japan, Italy and Germany formed an alliance in 1937 – the Anti-Comintern Pact (also known as the Axis) – explicitly directed against the Soviet Union and world communism. Japan had been rapidly expanding on the Soviets' eastern borders since its conquest of Manchuria in the early 1930s. Germany had been re-arming and expanding since 1935. In 1938 the British and French agreed to let Germany annex Czechoslovakia which lay between the Soviet Union and Germany, rather than joining with the Soviet Union to fight to protect Czechoslovakia (as the Soviets offered to do if either Britain or France would support her). And, of course, in 1941 Germany invaded the U.S.S.R. and within a few months was in the suburbs of Leningrad and Moscow. It was only when over 20 million Soviets were killed, that the German invader was finally defeated.

It is almost certain that the intelligence services of Japan and Germany were present in the Soviet Union in the 1930s and acting very much as the North American C.I.A. did in Eastern Europe in the late 1940s, and how other branches of the U.S. intelligence operate (e.g. the F.B.I.'s Cointerpro to infiltrate and subvert the American left). In the late 1940s in Eastern Europe the C.I.A. did all it could to get the Soviets and local communist parties to believe that some of their best leaders and cadres were working with the C.I.A. This was designed to encourage divisiveness and demoralization and to eliminate some of the most effective communist leaders. For a few years this policy succeeded as witnessed by the purge trials of 1949 and 1950. The C.I.A. planted stories and — given the atmosphere of paranoia induced by the real threat of World War in this period — the purges mushroomed into treason trials of loyal leading communist figures.[2]

It is very likely that, in the even greater period of tension induced by imminent foreign invasion in the late 1930s, a similar planting of fabricated stories by Japanese and German intelligence agents, to the effect that various honest cadres and leading figures were working for them, produced very similar results to what happened ten years later as a result of C.I.A. intervention. The extreme pressure which the Communist Party was under in 1937-38 predisposed its cadres to believe the worst. As a result, tens of thousands of sincere members, especially top leaders in the Party and top government and military officials, were executed and many thousands more were demoted and imprisoned. While the vast majority of people persecuted in these years were innocent of any wrong doing and were loyal to the Communist Party, many of them had serious doubts about the correctness of the Soviet leadership's policies and thus potentially could have become rallying points for opposition. Secondly, those purged were mostly C.P. leaders or senior state or military officials, (substantial evidence in itself that there was nothing like a ruling class in the U.S.S.R. at this time). The unifying effect of the purges was illustrated when the Nazis invaded. Though the military efficiency of the Soviet Army had been reduced by the purge of its general staff in 1938, there was no split in the Soviet leadership during the war. All Soviet leaders and virtually all Soviet military officers expressed the greatest resolve to defeat the Nazis. The Soviet Union was unique in Europe in this regard. As I have already stated, there were no Petains or Quislings in the U.S.S.R. The unified Soviet leadership was able to mobilize and inspire the Soviet people to defeat the Nazis. Although harsh and sometimes unjust methods were used and innocent people killed, this unity, greatly strengthened by the purges, played an important part in the Nazi defeat. It should be noted that the massive purges and trials of Communists for treason which swept the Soviet Union in 1937 and 1938 were ended by 1939, never to be repeated. This was an implicit admission that such witch hunts were divisive and in good part promoted by foreign agents.

Between 1934 (the year of the assassination of Kirov, one of the top Communist leaders) and the last of the three great Moscow treason trials in 1938, Stalin became incredibly powerful. He began sometimes to make important decisions without consulting the Central Committee or Politburo. The centralization of decision making had reached extreme lengths. However this should not be confused with the question of which class was in power in the U.S.S.R. in the post-1934 period. That question must be understood in terms of what class forces produced the situation within which decisions were made, and what were the viable historical options, and what effects decisions had on classes. If such an analysis is made, we see that, in spite of the abuses of his position and collective paranoia of 1937-38, Stalin continued broadly to express the interests of the Soviet working people (as opposed to both the older capitalist or landlord classes *and* to the new rising strata of state bureaucrats and the professional intelligentsia). He must therefore be considered, in the last analysis, to be their instrument. The objective results of his period of stewardship amounted to a considerable advance along the winding road to socialism, not only for the U.S.S.R. but also for the world as a whole.

The fact that the 1937-38 purges were primarily directed against the leaders of the Soviet Union reflected the constant pressures acting on Soviet leaders, including even the highest Party officials, to maximize production and popular mobilization and to create the conditions for a successful military defence and socialist transformation. Which class or stratum in Soviet society could be considered to benefit and which incipient classes or strata to suffer from such pressures? Clearly not the bureaucratic stratum. Indeed it is not surprising that Stalin's own proteges began to publically denounce him in 1956, for he was not their representative and did not defend their prerogatives. We must conclude that either Stalin was above class forces or that he was essentially the tribune of the working people, albeit sometimes a harsh one. The latter analysis fits best into a historical materialist analysis of the facts, i.e. the U.S.S.R. was in fact a socialist society in the 1930s and 1940s.

The fact that there were abuses of power as well as collective paranoia must not be attributed to Stalin's personality. They are byproducts (negative to be sure) of the need to create both great unity and a cult of personality to enhance legitimacy. The process of socialist transformation is not the best of all possible worlds; in fact it is simply the necessary stage to create such a world – communism. As a result, some people unjustly suffer and there are negative consequences of otherwise positive developments. Abuses of the personality cult and the danger of arbitrary decision making were the most serious of these negative consequences. It is rare that a crisis becomes as intense and prolonged as that experienced by the Soviet Union from 1928 to 1950 (a period of rapid social change and bitter class and international warfare). It is therefore unlikely that the need for such a high degree of unity required in the first of the world's socialist revolutions, will ever recur. Its attendant abuses are therefore also unlikely to appear in future socialist transformations.

As we have established, the basic course of Soviet history from the 1920s through to the 1950s was dictated by the international and domestic situation of the Soviet Union and the imperative of preserving Bolshevik rule. It had little or nothing to do with the personality of Stalin. With the exception of the scope, viciousness and paranoid nature of the 1937-38 purges, most of the basic decisions made by the Soviet leadership in this period turn out, with historical hindsight, to have been the best possible choices, given the very real

constraints of the situation and the limited number of viable options. Of
course, it would have been better, in the most perfect of all worlds, to have
relied on the masses, instead of on top leadership. But such policies, given
the degree of peasant resistance to the regime, would have been suicidal in
the 1930s. The system of material incentives was the only viable way to
motivate quickly the new working class and the peasantry to the heroic
efforts necessary for industrialization. The international situation of the
1930s did not allow the luxury of a Great Leap Forward or a Cultural Revolution. (It was the protection provided by the existence of the Soviet Union
that ensured the Chinese the space to perform these world historic experi-
ments in the next generation.)

The post-1953 leadership of the Soviet Union often likes to contrast
itself with the Stalin period by claiming responsibility for the growing
democratization of the state and Party since 1953, the greater freedom of
public debate, expanded social services, greater equalization of incomes,
expanded workers' participation in industry, etc. In fact, however, these
measures, just as much as the measures in the opposite direction in the 1930s,
were a product of the logic of Soviet society and the international situation.
They have no more to do with the good intentions and personalities of these
leaders than the earlier policies had to do with Stalin's. There is no reason to
believe that the course of post-1953 Soviet history would have been appreci-
ably different if Stalin had lived another 25 years. At best, because Stalin
was tempered in the desperate period of the 1930s, his considerable personal
influence might have slowed down some of the democratizing measures of
the 1950s and 1960s and likewise slowed the tendency for the experts to
consolidate their positions. But it would probably not have blocked the
income equalization measures, since the goal of motivating workers to up-
grade their skills and increase their devotion to job performance had been
achieved.

The principal contrast between the period of Stalin's leadership and the
post-1953 period lies in the difference between the policies pursued by the
Soviet state and Party and the viable historical options to speed the development towards Communism. During the 1930s and 1940s it is difficult to
conceive of alternative policies which would have more effectively speeded
such a development. The immediate pursuit of this goal had to be postponed
in the interests of saving the country and preserving the rule of the Bolsheviks.
But since the destruction of fascism, the consolidation of popular support,
and becoming a leading industrial and military power, there has been considerable room in which to pursue more directly the goal of communism and to
expand the direct day-to-day involvement of the masses in running their own
lives (as the Chinese did during the Cultural Revolution). Compared to what
would now seem to be historically possible (as borne witness to by the
Chinese, who are, it must be remembered, at a much lower level of industrial
development), the Soviets appear to be progressing somewhat slowly. This
may be due to the conservative attitudes of well-intentioned leaders who grew
to political maturity during the heroic years of strategic retreat from the goal

of communism. It may also be due to the interests of those in relatively privileged and powerful positions who want to preserve their prerogatives.

This disparity between the heroic period of the 1930s and 1940s and the most recent period of Soviet history reflects the fundamental difference between the charismatic state socialism of the earlier period and the techno-cratic state socialism of the latter. Leadership in the first period was held by a small number of revolutionaries, formed before and during the Bolshevik Revolution, who relied heavily on popular appeals to mobilize the masses. This leadership used material incentives and recruitment into the C.P.S.U. to ensure the rapidly expanding strata of experts' service to the socialist state. The demise of Stalin, which coincided with the end of the heroic period, saw a struggle between the declining forces of charismatic state socialism (led by top Party officials) and the ascendant forces of technocratic state socialism (based on the technical experts). Khrushchev's leadership thus marked a transition period, not between socialism and capitalism, but between these two forms of socialism. It was marked both by a continuation of the style of direct popular appeal and by sudden changes in policy, characteristic of charismatic leadership. But this period also saw a consolidation of the position of the scientists, engineers, economists, technicians, etc., whose struggle with Khrushchev ultimately resulted in his dismissal. The victory of this intelli-gentsia stratum led to the Brezhnev period (post-1965) in which routine gradual progress, a low level of popular mobilization and efficiency and science dominated.

The Origins of Soviet Hegemonism

Soviet hegemonism, the attempt by the Soviet Union to dominate both the world communist movement and the other socialist countries, is by no means a phenomenon of the last generation. Its roots go back to the very founding of the Third International in 1919. Soviet hegemonism was far more pro-nounced in the period from 1928 to 1958 than it has been since. In fact, since the mid 1950s, it has continually declined to the point where most communist parties operate quite independently of Soviet desires and most socialist countries with considerable autonomy from, where not actual hostility to, the C.P.S.U.[3]

It was the great prestige of the Russian Revolution, the Bolshevik Party and V.I. Lenin himself that from the beginning gave such authority to the positions of the Russian Communist Party. The Russians had the only party in the world that was able to make a revolution. As such it was looked up to by virtually all revolutionaries as a source of wisdom and guidance. This early tendency to have great respect for the ideas of Lenin and the Russian Communist Party on questions of theory, strategy, tactics and organization was legitimately based in the successes of the C.P.S.U. The world communist movement down to the mid-1950s continued to have strong reasons to respect the authority of the Soviet Union, not only because it represented the only socialist revolution in the world, but because in the post-1943 period it was the inspiration, if not the leader, of the rapid expansion of Marxist-Leninist regimes in Europe and Asia. Soviet hegemony, then, was not a thing imposed on unwilling subjects or manipulated by a sinister Moscow, but something enthusiastically and spontaneously generated throughout the world by communists who needed an inspiration for their endeavours.

From the founding of the Soviet system in 1917 through to at least the 1950s, one of the prime tasks of communists worldwide was the defence of the Soviet Revolution. They did all in their power both to undermine the efforts of the capitalist powers to destroy the Soviet regime, and to lend what support they could to the Soviet attempt to consolidate socialism in the U.S.S.R. This goal was sometimes taken to mean the acceleration of a given revolutionary situation (e.g. in the 1928-35 period), and at other times the building of broad popular fronts to isolate anti-communist forces (e.g., the 1935-39 and 1941-47 periods). Far from being a tool of the Soviet leaders to influence the policies of other countries in favour of Soviet interests, the principle of defending the Soviet Union made considerable sense as part of a world revolutionary strategy for all communist parties. The living example of a socialist revolution in the Soviet Union was a tremendous inspiration to the revolutionary and working class movements throughout the world. It was much easier for communist parties to win recruits because they could point to an actual example of socialism that provided a real alternative to capitalism. The existence of the Soviet Union was powerful propaganda both for the socialist vision (even when the popular conception of what life in the U.S.S.R. was like was exaggerated) and for revolutionary strategies and organizational principles of the local communist parties. Had the Soviet Union been overrun in 1919 or 1941, the world revolutionary movement would have suffered a grievous loss. The defeat of any other revolutionary movement could not possibly be compared in seriousness to the smashing of the Soviet Revolution, as a setback for the world revolutionary movement as a whole. All this is quite aside from whether the Soviet leadership ever did in fact manipulate the world communist movement to slow down a viable revolutionary process so that their country's own narrow interests would be advanced. Although this might possibly have happened from time to time, it was not the essence of the policy of the defence of the U.S.S.R. This policy clearly functioned to the advantage of the world communist movement which gained far more from the Soviet Union simply because it existed, than might have been lost in a few specific cases because of missed opportunities. In fact, for the most part, the actual policies advocated by the Soviet leadership corresponded to the needs of the world revolutionary movement independently of the need to preserve the Soviet Revolution as a living example.

From 1919 to 1923, the Comintern under Soviet inspiration pursued policies of preparing for and leading insurrections throughout the world. Given the massive dislocations following World War I, this was a very reasonable policy which came close to success in a number of cases (e.g. Germany and Hungary). It ultimately failed because of the inexperience of the local communist movements, as well as the overwhelming power of world capitalism. The 1923-28 period of united fronts between the various socialist parties corresponded correctly with a time of economic and social stability, in which revolutionary adventures were doomed to fail and the primary task was to build working-class solidarity in preparation for a future crisis in which it would once again be viable to try and seize power.

In 1928, at the Sixth Congress of the Comintern, the line of the world communist movement under the leadership of the Soviets moved radically to the left. The 1928 Comintern analysis saw a return to a period of economic depression and of inter-imperialist rivalry and wars. This in turn would provoke social upheavals and revolutionary situations. Consequently, the world communist movement was redirected to prepare itself once again to lead insurrections and to accelerate the revolutionary process. This involved combatting the social democratic parties' non-revolutionary leadership of the working class since these parties would, unless discredited, cause revolutionary opportunities to be missed.

The correctness of 1928 Comintern analysis was borne out by the outbreak the very next year of the most serious economic crisis capitalism has ever experienced. This led to the Japanese, Italian and German military expansion into China, Ethiopia, Spain and Czechoslovakia in the mid-1930s, and finally to the outbreak of all-out inter-imperialist war in 1939. Communists had every reason to expect that such a situation would be a hot-house for the growth of revolutionary forces. Indeed, in Spain, France, China and elsewhere, the communist movement grew considerably during the 1930s because of the Great Depression; and of course grew much more rapidly in the wake of World War II, in virtually all the countries affected by that war. Nevertheless, the 1928 Comintern strategy proved to be seriously faulty regarding how to deal with reformist socialists and other non-revolutionary progressive forces whom it called social fascists. It also grossly underestimated the growth of radical rightist movements such as the fascists. These came to have great popular appeal, to the point of being able (in conjuction with the capitalist class) to smash the communist movement in many countries.

Whether or not this period in Comintern policies was justified, it would be difficult to interpret it as simply the Soviets cynically manipulating the world communist movement for their own narrow defensive ends. If defending the U.S.S.R. was the only concern, it could have been done much more efficiently by adopting reformist policies which did not antagonize the Western powers. Instead the Comintern returned in 1928 to insurrectionary politics despite the fact that this could only be expected to renew fears among Western capitalists that the continued existence of the Soviet Union, which was supporting domestic fifth columns pledged to overthrow them at the first opportunity, was such a danger that it had to be destroyed. Indeed, the new Comintern policy might well have provoked them to invade the Soviet Union once again as they had done in 1919 in support of the whites during the Civil War. The 1928 policies were clearly premised on the idea that revolution in the West should be supported, regardless of what the

Western capitalists thought about the Soviet Union as a result.

At the 7th World Congress of the Comintern in 1935 the world communist movement, still under the leadership of the Soviets but with considerable independent input based on the experience of both the Chinese and various European parties, did a fundamental self-criticism of what had proved to be the ultra-left errors of its Third Period (1928) line. These policies had clearly been ineffectual in stopping the growth of fascism or in producing a workers' revolution in any country. This Congress developed the new policy of the Popular Front, a coalition of all progressive working class and middle class forces — communist, socialist and liberal — who were opposed to fascism and who favoured a defence of democratic rights (the rights of trade unions, minimum wages, paid holidays, civil liberties, unemployment insurance, old age pensions, full employment policies etc.). By leading a massive popular movement which was not revolutionary in its goals, the Comintern thought that the rapid world-wide growth of fascism could be stopped and the role of communist parties enhanced to the point where they would eventually gain enough popular support to lead a revolutionary process.

The policies of the Popular Front produced considerable gains for the communist movement. The French Communist Party, as a result of the Popular Front victory in the 1936 elections, gained considerably as did the French working class as a whole. The Spanish Communist Party also grew very rapidly in the course of the Spanish Civil War (1936-39), to a great extent because of the Popular Front policies it followed. But the greatest success of all occurred in China. After the adoption of the 7th Comintern Congress analysis which dictated seeking an alliance of the four anti-imperialist classes, and following policies of rent reduction rather than confiscation of the land of rich peasants and the small landlords, the Chinese Communist Party abandoned its pre-1935 left-adventurist policies of rural Soviets and attacks on the national bourgeoisie and rich peasants, and began to grow very rapidly. It eventually came to power in good part because of 15 years of Popular Front strategies. The People's Republic of China in 1949 was initially modelled on the People's Democracies of Eastern Europe created a year or two before — all built on Popular Front ideas of the alliances of various classes and a gradual transition to a socialist economy.

The Comintern/Soviet policy which most fits the thesis that narrow Soviet self-interest set international Communist policy to the detriment of the world revolutionary movement was probably the 1939-41 policy of considering Nazi Germany and the major Western capitalist powers as equal enemies of world revolution. During this period the world communist movement reverted to the policies of the Third Period (1928-35), abandoning the Popular Front (except in China). It was terribly disillusioning for many Communists to have to abandon the anti-fascist Popular Front strategy which had won them so much sympathy in favour of a policy that did not consider Fascism as any special danger. During this period world communism was subordinated to the interests of the Soviet Union to the detriment of the short-term growth of the movement. This policy proved especially detrimental in those countries which had been, or were about to be, overrun by the Fascists. There is no doubt that this return to Third Period politics was dictated by the Soviet leadership without any genuine discussion and democratic decision making in the world communist movement. It can be argued, however, that, detrimental as the policy was in many cases, it was the correct or necessary line for the world communist movement to follow. This is so if one accepts, first, how important it was to preserve the Soviet Union as a socialist state, and second, the importance therefore of postponing a Nazi invasion for two years while the U.S.S.R. strengthened its defences.

Prior to the Munich agreement between Hitler, France and Britain in 1938, the Soviet Union since 1934 had done everything possible to build an anti-German alliance with Britain and France to stop Hitler. It signed a mutual defence treaty with France. It also promised to intervene in Czechoslovakia against the Germans, if either France or Britain were to do likewise. And the U.S.S.R. joined the League of Nations at the same time as Japan and Germany left it. Despite all this, the Western powers rejected the Soviets' attempts to stop the Nazis in 1938. Instead they decided to give in to Hitler's imperialist intentions towards Czechoslovakia, hoping that by agreeing to a German easternward expansion in the face of strong Soviet opposition, they would succeed in keeping themselves out of war with Germany. They probably also hoped that this would create the conditions for a Soviet-German conflict which would greatly weaken both anti-Western powers. In the face of this betrayal by the French and British, the Soviets were led to play the same game as the Western powers, i.e. sign a non-aggression pact with the Nazis that would turn Hitler westwards, setting up the conditions for a war between Germany on the one side, and France and Britain on the other. The Soviets had every reason to expect such a war to be as prolonged and devastating as World War I and to so weaken both sets of powers as to provoke working-class revolution in all these countries. At the very least, such a war would be expected to so weaken and distract Germany as to put off, perhaps indefinitely, a German attack on the Soviet Union.

The Soviet Union, like the entire world, was surprised by the quick collapse of France in the face of the Nazi *blitzkrieg.* Instead of a protracted and exhausting war and a consequent growth of revolutionary movements, Germany's quick victory in the West resulted in greatly strengthening her war machine's material base which was then used against the Soviet Union in 1941. Nevertheless, the two year respite that the non-aggression pact gave the Soviets allowed the latter to double the size of their armed forces and modernize their equipment. It is very likely that, if the Nazis had attacked the Soviet Union at the beginning of the war, they would have been able to overrun the country (they came very close to doing so even in 1941-42). They might have then used the Soviet Union's economy as a base, permanently to consolidate their hold on all Europe and to conquer all of the Middle East, India and North Africa. As it turned out, the Nazis arrogant assumption that the Soviet Union would collapse in a few months with minimal German casualties (an expectation based on their racist theory of the inferiority of

Slavs) proved to be fatal to them. Rather than a quick conquest of the Soviet Union, they became bogged down in a murderous conflict which led to their defeat. By the end, about 20 million Soviets had been killed by the Nazis and 90 per cent of all German war casualties were on the Eastern Front. World War II in Europe turned out to be primarily a war between the Soviets and the Germans with all other theatres being virtual side-shows. (American casualties amounted to only one per cent of Soviet casualties.) It was the Soviet Union that fought World War II and destroyed Hitler. The Red flag was hoisted in Berlin and the world communist movement everywhere grew by leaps and bounds as a result. Looking back on it, it may well be that the long-term result of the 1939-41 Comintern policies, in spite of the short-term setbacks in most countries that it represented for the communist movement, was greatly to accelerate the growth of the movement in all countries, owing to the breathing space it gave the Soviets to build the base necessary to defeat Hitler. In any event the developments of 1944-48 certainly made Soviet policies look good to the common working people of Western Europe, and led to a huge rise in support for many of the Western communist parties.

Popular Front policies were considerably modified in 1947 as a result of the Western capitalist powers' growing hostility to the communist movement and the Soviet Union. The communist parties were thrown out of the governments in Italy and France and the Cold War against the Soviet Union was begun. This led the communist movement to return to rather more militant tactics than those pursued since 1941. Once again, this new tendency was not so much dictated by the Soviet Union's narrow self-interest, as by the rapidly changing world situation.

The rapid growth of communist forces, especially throughout Europe, China and Vietnam, was a result of the continuing Popular Front policies of the immediate post World War II period. This was also the case in China where the Communist Party made every effort, short of capitulation to the Kuomintang, to unite anti-imperialist forces. These advances led to the West's counter-attack (in the form of the Cold War etc.) on the communist movement and the Soviet Union. In fact had the communist movement not grown so rapidly in Europe and Asia, the Western powers would not have seen the Soviet Union as such a threat. A good case could be made that the rapidly expanding world communist movement forced the Soviet Union defensively to confront the U.S.A., when narrow self-interest would have dictated abandoning communist parties everywhere except those in Germany, Czechoslovakia, Hungary and Poland (the line of any future attack from the West on the Soviet Union).

It must be admitted that the Soviets continued to advise the Chinese Party to seek a coalition with the Kuomintang in which the Communists would be the subordinate partner. They also did not provide material support to the Chinese Communists apart from turning over a considerable armoury of captured Japanese weapons to them in Manchuria. And they advised the communist parties in Italy and France not to attempt armed insurrection. Nevertheless, in the immediate post-War period, the role of the Soviets in the world was a progressive one, which helped the growth of communist parties and progressive regimes even at the cost of growing U.S. hostility towards the U.S.S.R., as in Greece, Korea and Vietnam.

Another major accomplishment of the Comintern and the Soviet leadership was the shifting of the world revolutionary movement's emphasis to the countries of Asia, Africa and Latin America. After the revolutionary wave in Europe receded in 1923, the attention of the world communist movement shifted towards China, India, the Middle East and other parts of the colonized world. The liberation of Third World countries was given priority for the first time. In the mid-1920s it was said that the road to Berlin and Paris lay through Peking and Delhi. Theories of national liberation were developed as the communist movement spread from Europe to the Third World; these theories supported and inspired anti-imperialist movements everywhere. The surge of communist activity, to a great extent inspired by the existence of the Soviet Union and its hostility to the imperialist countries, was given further impetus during and immediately after World War II when communist-led movements came to power in China, North Korea and North Vietnam. Communists became major forces in the national liberation and anti-imperialist movements of many countries. Once again, as the revolutionary wave in Europe receded in the late 1940s, the major thrust of world communism shifted to the Third World. The Soviet inspired communist movements, unlike the social democratic parties of the old Second International and the Trotskyist movement (both of which continued to focus on Europe and the other advanced capitalist countries) broke new ground in their emphasis on, and leadership of, anti-imperialist and revolutionary struggles in Asia, Africa and Latin America.

In the light of what thus appeared to most communists to be the wisdom of Comintern/Soviet leadership in the world communist movement from 1917 through to the late 1940s, it is no surprise that deference to Soviet leadership was forthcoming. It was not until the 1950s and 1960s – in the face of the stagnation of the world communist movement, disagreements between the U.S.S.R. and the socialist regimes in Eastern Europe and China, and the arguments about revolutionary strategy that developed within the world movement – that Soviet hegemony broke down. In fact, Soviet hegemony outlived spontaneous consensus about the wisdom of Soviet leadership by only a few years. Once local communist movements began to have doubts (stemming from the diverse nature of their own experience) about Soviet policies for making revolution and consolidating socialist regimes, a multi-centred world communist movement soon became a reality. Soviet hegemony was in good part a product of the state of seige to which the international communist movement was subjected from 1928 through to 1949. This was the period in which there was only one socialist regime, and hence only one leadership that could speak on the basis of its successful experience, a leadership furthermore that had to be defended for the sake of the health of the world movement.

The Third International under Lenin introduced the idea of international discipline, i.e. the idea that the various communist parties of the world were sections of the Third International and subject to its discipline just as much as regional and local party organizations within a nation were subject to national party discipline. Since monopoly capitalist corporations and the leading imperialist states operated on a world level, and there was one international capitalist market, it was considered desirable for the world movement to behave in a unified fashion. For this would confront international capital as a single unified force. It was also considered wise for the experience of each party to benefit all the other parties which would then not have to learn separately the lessons already learned (most commonly these lessons were drawn from the Soviet Party, the only one to have made a successful revolution).

Having the international communist movement operate as a single force in all countries had both negative and positive results. On the one hand, international discipline sometimes meant that policies inappropriate to local conditions were forced on a local Party (e.g. some of the insurrections directed by the Comintern in Central Europe and China in the 1920s). On the other hand, the greater revolutionary experience of the Comintern at times forced reluctant local parties to take measures that benefited the growth of the world movement (e.g. the universal establishment of Leninist organizational principles in the 1920s, or the ending of left-wing adventurist tendencies in the early 1920s). To a world socialist movement which, in 1914,had seen the major social democratic parties of Europe support their respective governments in a war amongst one another, while the Bolsheviks had called for the subversion of the war efforts of each country by the international working class, the idea of one co-ordinated world revolutionary policy under the leadership of the proven revolutionaries of the Soviet Union made considerable sense. It was further validated by the great triumphs of international communism in the 1940s.

Two very important consequences of international discipline under the leadership of the Soviet party were the containment of factionalism and sectarianism, and a relative insulation from revisionism or reformist-opportunist degeneration of isolated parties acting under national pressures (as the parties of the Second International had been subject to). In country after country, Comintern prestige and intervention succeeded in eliminating or containing the factionalism that had traditionally plagued the left wing and sapped the energy of the revolutionary movement. This greatly facilitated the development of a unified and energetic revolutionary left. For example in the U.S., disparate groups, originating in the I.W.W., the left wing of the Socialist Party and independent nationality based socialist currents, formed three different and mutually antagonistic communist parties. But these were welded together by Comintern intervention into a single party. The continuing factionalism within that unified party was then eventually eliminated by further Comintern intervention.

Similar processes occurred throughout the world to force the various factions to come to terms with one another. Although mistakes were undoubtedly made by the Comintern, in siding with one or another local leadership group, the net result of its intervention was unquestionably beneficial in creating unity. One can see the difference that absence of an international arbitrator with universally acknowledged prestige makes, in the disarray and mutual hostility of the revolutionary leftist groups of the 1970s. Again, it should be stressed that what allowed the Soviet led Comintern successfully to intervene to create unity in the local parties was its prestige, which was pretty much universally acknowledged by all factions.

Allegiance to the Soviet led Comintern also had the effect, by holding out the living example of socialist revolution in the Soviet Union, of hindering any opportunist policies from developing under the inducement of the short-term advantages of reform. While the old socialist parties had only a vague conception of socialism, a conception that was easily malleable to suit political exigencies (it was easy for the ideas of Bernstein to become current in a party desirous of winning an election when there was no clear alternative to capitalism generally recognized by the working class), the new Bolshevik parties had a clear vision and inspiration in the Soviet Union. As a model (even with its imperfections and romanticized character), it provided a very real alternative to Bernstein-type revisions of the socialist alternative. Even when the communist movement was following essentially reformist policies, as it was in 1935-39 and 1941-47, the living example of the U.S.S.R., and (especially in the latter period) its active support of the armed struggle against fascism and colonialism which was occurring in much of Europe and Asia, tended to keep the local communist parties true to their revolutionary intentions.

The origins of Soviet hegemonism must be sought, then, not in the self-interested manipulations of Soviet leadership, but rather in its historically useful functions for the world communist movement. The world movement had every reason to look to Lenin and his successors for both inspiration and concrete leadership, and accepting such leadership more often than not made considerable sense. In much of the world, it eventually proved itself by the rapid growth of communism. Leaving aside the mistaken Soviet pressures on the Chinese Communist Party in the immediate post World War II period, it was not until the 1950s that a reasonable case could be made that unquestioned Soviet leadership in the world movement was becoming in balance a negative force. With the defeat of Nazi Germany, the Soviet development of the atom bomb, and the rapid spread of socialism (especially in China), the existence of the Soviet Union was no longer tenuous. Furthermore, as a result of the events of the 1940s, communist parties became dominant among revolutionary working-class and intellectual forces in many countries, at the expense of social democracy and syndicalism. There were now a number of socialist regimes which had more or less by their own efforts made a revolution — in China, Vietnam, Yugoslavia, Albania and eventually Cuba. Thus revolutionary socialists could now look to these countries too as authorities, both on how to come to power and how the revolutionary process ought to proceed after the seizure of power. In such a world, unquestioned Soviet leadership was bound to collapse. This was especially so since the Soviets sometimes tended to put considerations of detente or co-existence with the U.S. ahead of promoting revolution or anti-imperialist policies in a given area. A factor which, initially, had been on balance a strong force for the growth of socialism, had by the 1960s more often than not become a hindrance to the revolutionary process. The most progressive course for the world movement after the 1950s was one of polycentrism, with the different parties following more independent courses than they had had to pursue in earlier periods. Soviet resistance to no longer being the sole and leading centre of the world movement caused considerable resentment in many circles — especially in China, the major Western communist parties, and in much of Eastern Europe. It resulted in some unnecessary splits and serious ongoing mutual antagonisms in the world communist movement.

It is not surprising that the leaders of the Soviet Communist Party resisted the trend to polycentrism forced on it by the other socialist regimes and large communist parties. They had all grown up taking for granted the idea that the oldest and most experienced Communist Party was always the wisest, and should be deferred to. From their viewpoint it was Soviet wisdom and Soviet sacrifices that brought socialism to Eastern Europe and inspired the great growth of communism in the West, as well as the Asian revolutions. It is natural that they regarded the Yugoslav, then the Chinese and Albanian and finally the various Western parties, as upstarts and insufficiently appreciative of Soviet contributions and experience. There is no need to assume that some kind of self-interested bureaucratic or state capitalist class or stratum was in control of Soviet foreign policy in order to explain the behaviour of the Soviet leadership. As we have seen, they had no special economic interest in dominating other countries and thus no inherent reason to contain the world revolutionary process for the sake of a narrow Soviet self-interest. Especially given the relative reasonableness and moderation with which the Soviets generally dealt with the successive challenges to their hegemony (especially after 1961), the analysis given here is fully adequate to account for the Soviet tendencies toward hegemonism.

The Future of the Soviet Union

A purely linear projection of the trends of the last 20 years predicts a steady Soviet advance towards communism. If the trends in income equalization and expansion of free goods and services continue, something very like a communist mode of distribution should exist in the Soviet Union by the first half of the twenty-first century. A linear projection of the trends in the distribution between managers and manual workers, of day-to-day decision making power in enterprises, also suggests a transition to real workers' self-management within a comparable period. Therefore, it is quite possible that a communal decentralized socialism will replace the current state socialism.

However, it is problematic whether the trends of the last 20 years will continue in linear fashion. There could well be limits to all these processes imposed by the interests of the power elite of managers and officials and the professional intelligentsia in preserving their privileges. Although there has been significant decentralization and egalitarianization, the high level of the productive forces and of support for the principles of socialism in the Soviet Union suggests that more could be done in these areas. That more rapid progress is not being made, may be because of a conservative rearguard action by the power elite, and especially the professional intelligentsia. Opposition from these strata could well be expected to grow in the future, putting an end to further equalization and democratization. In such an event, a cultural revolution of the Chinese type would become a distinct possibility. The continuing (if sometimes erratic) progress towards communism which the Soviet regime has been making since the 1930s, and the high level of popular acceptance of the communist goal, have created a high expectation that continuing progress will be made toward democratization and equalization. Halting this trend would fly in the face of the officially expressed and widely accepted ideology. This could well promote massive resistance to the power elite and professional intelligentsia. A process even more disruptive, and a struggle even more sharp, than the one in China in the late 1960s, could then well ensue. A fullscale violent revolution, however, is unlikely since no minority ruling class exists which would have its very existence threatened by the masses. On the other hand, the threat of such an outbreak might force the power elite and professional intelligentsia into continually making concessions to the manual working class. Each concession would strengthen the latter's role and weaken the position of the other two groups. There thus seems a real possibility in the Soviet Union of peaceful transition from a state socialism, biassed in favour of technical experts, to a decentralized socialism and finally to full communism.

A transition to capitalism, of either the state or market types, therefore seems an increasingly remote possibility. There used to be a distinct possibility that the extreme measures the Soviets were forced to resort to in the 1930s and 1940s could have resulted in a permanent concentration of decision making powers and privileges in the hands of a relatively small number, and that this eventually would have resulted in state capitalism. There was a real danger that the practices of the 1930s and 1940s would lead to the crystallization of a social class which would take control of the means of production and disposition of the economic surplus. This danger, although it has not altogether disappeared, would now seem less and less likely as mass involvement and egalitarianization grows. As for a transition to market capitalism, as is in progress in Yugoslavia, this was a possibility in the 1960s when markets and the pursuit of profits were given a larger role. However, the subsequent reversal of the trends of 1965-71 and the ascendancy of cybernetic central planning in their place, would seem to have greatly reduced the probability of such a transition.

The two most likely futures for the Soviet Union thus seem to be a peaceful transition, through decentralized socialism to communism *or* an attempt to further consolidate technocratic state socialism and to block all further progress towards communism. But this second alternative might well precipitate a cultural revolution which would establish a decentralized communal socialism that would in turn eventually lead on to a transition to full communism. A materialist perspective which sees classes and class struggle emerging from differences in the relationship to the means of production, even under socialism, would seem to predict the latter as the most probable outcome.

Implications for the World Struggle

The Chinese Communist Party is mistaken. The Soviet Union is neither the major, nor equal, nor even ascendant threat to the people of the world and the revolutionary process in the Third World and the advanced capitalist countries. It is not a state capitalism of the fascist type (such as existed in the 1930s and 1940s in Germany). It is not an expansionist imperialist power. The Soviet Union is rather an authentically (but somewhat distorted) socialist country which is actively pursuing both domestic and international policies which are for the most part progressive. On balance it is a friend of progressive and revolutionary forces around the world.

Although communists and progressives can learn from the Soviet Union and gain from an alliance with it, it must not necessarily be taken as the model for post-revolutionary societies in other countries. The distortions produced by its uniqueness in being the first socialist country and having had to start from a low level of productive forces, means that, although it must be respected, it should not always be imitated. Although the Soviets do side with the more progressive and revolutionary forces in the world, they have a tendency towards hegemonism (i.e. of trying to impose their conception of the revolutionary and post-revolutionary process on others). Since they have a long history of defending their national interest and avoiding war with the United States, mechanical acceptance of Soviet (or for that matter Chinese) leadership could mean missing a revolutionary opportunity the Soviets (or the Chinese) might prefer not to see. Post-revolutionary regimes, most notably China's, have also suffered from the Soviet insistence that they, as the first and richest socialist country, best know how to consolidate socialism and build communism. Thus, although the Soviet Union is generally a friend and ally, it must not automatically be deferred to. Each communist party and progressive movement must find its own bearings, lead its own revolution and advance along its own road to communism, illuminated, but not led, by the examples of those that have gone before.

The young revolutionary movements of the Western capitalist countries which grew out of the New Left movement of the late 1960s have paralysed themselves by mechanically following the Chinese into the dead end of escalating polemics against the Soviet Union. 'Maoist' groups in these countries have degenerated into the most vulgar dogmatism in competing with one another for the mantle of 'Maoist' orthodoxy. By 'Maoist', I mean here those who follow the positions (past or present) of the Chinese Communist Party in all things, rather than establishing their own lines on the basis of independent and scientific analysis of concrete conditions. Their most acid venom is reserved, not for capitalism, nor even for the 'revisionist' communist parties, but for one another. They have a considerable predisposition to read each other out of the ranks of 'honest revolutionaries' at the drop of a hat, pinning the label of 'revisionist' on them. Although a few of them at one point showed a little promise, they have cancelled each other out, remained isolated from the masses, and shown no objective differences from the myriad of tiny Trotskyist groups spawned over the last 40 years.

The bankruptcy of 'Maoism' in the West is now apparent to all who care to open their eyes. Nowhere, either in the Western capitalist countries or in the Third World, outside of Albania and a few countries of South East Asia, has a Communist Party or progressive movement with deep roots in the working class and peasantry come to support the Chinese position on the Soviet Union. The experience of the split in the Second International after World War I has not been repeated. Most authentic revolutionaries in the Third World — such as the Vietnamese, Koreans, Cubans, liberation movements and other progressives in Black Africa and the Middle East — reject the Chinese analysis. So do most class conscious workers in Western capitalist countries. 'Maoism' with few exceptions, remains pretty much based in the intelligentsia and those who have voluntarily left it to colonize the working class.

World communism made the mistake of mechanically following the lead of a single country once before. The tailing of the Soviets and the uncritical acceptance of their advice in the 1940s and 1950s led to some serious mistakes. As a result of their experience with Soviet leadership, the Chinese reached the correct conclusion that all communist parties are equal and that there should no longer be a centre to the world communist movement. We must digest the Chinese experience and their conclusion on polycentrism. We must not fall into the trap of replacing mechanical acceptance of Soviet leadership with mechanical acceptance of the Chinese. In this we should be inspired by the examples of the Vietnamese and Koreans, the two communist parties which more than any other in the last 25 years have proved themselves in the struggle against imperialism.

We have much to learn, and plenty to gain, from coalition with both the Soviet Union and the People's Republic of China. But the growing Communist Movement around the world will have to do its own analysis, work out its own strategy and vision, and rely primarily on its own working class and organization. In the vitriolic polemics between the Chinese and Soviets, it is all too easy to lose one's bearings under the fire of being accused of being a revisionist, opportunist, dogmatist, centrist, Kautskyite, ultra-leftist, Trotskyist, etc., by one or another sectarian tendency which feels that to be orthodox is more important than building a revolutionary movement. But we must brave the fire and follow where scientific analysis and the concrete needs of revolutionary class struggle lead. We must support and involve ourselves in all progressive and revolutionary struggles, domestic and international, regardless of how the Chinese or Soviets feel about them.

References

1. The discussion of Stalin is based on the following sources: Communist Party of the Soviet Union, *History of the Communist Party of the Soviet Union* (Moscow: Foreign Languages Publishing House, 1961); Isaac Deutscher, *Stalin: A Political Biography* (New York: Oxford University Press, 1949); Bruce Franklin's introduction to *The Essential Stalin* (Garden City, N.Y.: Doubleday, 1972); Anna Louise Strong, *The Stalin Era* (New York: Mainstream, 1957); Robert Tucker, *Stalin as a Revolutionary* (New York: Norton, 1973); and Adam Ulam, *Stalin: The Man and His Era* (New York: Viking, 1973).
2. For an excellent discussion of the C.I.A.'s disruptive role in Eastern Europe in the immediate post-war period, see Steven Steward, *Operation Splinter Factor* (New York: Lippincott, 1974).
3. The discussion of the origins of Soviet hegemonism is based on the following sources: Julius Braunthal, *History of the International,* Vol.II (New York: 1967); Fernando Claudin, *The Communist Movement; From Comintern to Cominform* (New York: Monthly Review Press, 1975); William Z. Foster, *History of the Three Internationals* (New York: International Publishers, 1955); Alvin Rubinstein (ed.), *The Foreign Policy of the Soviet Union* (New York: Random House, 1972).

Bibliography

Soviet Domestic Political Economy and Social Structure

Arutiunian, Iu, V. 'Culture and the Social Psychology of the Soviet Rural Population' in M. Yanowitch and W. Fisher (eds.), *Social Stratification and Mobility in the U.S.S.R.* (White Plains, N.Y.: International Arts and Sciences Press, 1973).

Arutiunian, Iu. V. 'The Distribution of Decision Making among the Rural Population of the U.S.S.R.' in Yanowitch and Fisher, *op. cit.*

Azrael, Jeremy. *Managerial Power and Soviet Politics* (Cambridge, Mass.: Harvard University Press, 1966).

Barry, Donald, and Berman, Harold. 'The Jurists' in H. Gordon Skilling and Franklyn Griffiths (eds.), *Interest Groups in Soviet Politics* (Princeton, N.J.: Princeton University Press, 1971).

Bettelheim, Charles. *Cultural Revolution and Industrial Organization in China* (New York: Monthly Review, 1974).

Bornstein, Morris. 'Soviet Price Theory and Policy' in Bornstein, Morris and Fusfeld, Daniel (eds.), *The Soviet Economy: A Book of Readings* (4th ed., Homewood, Illinois: Richard Irwin, Inc., 1974).

Brodersen, D. *The Soviet Worker: Labor and Government in Soviet Society* (New York: Random House, 1966).

Brown, Emily Clark. 'Continuity and Change in the Soviet Labor Market' in Bornstein and Fusfeld, *op. cit.*

Burnham, James. *The Managerial Revolution* (Bloomington, Indiana: Indiana University Press, 1966).

Cliff, T. *State Capitalism in Russia* (London: Pluto Press, 1974).

Communist Party of the Soviet Union. *History of the Communist Party of the Soviet Union* (Moscow: Foreign Languages Publishing House, 1961).

Conquest, Robert. *Industrial Workers in the U.S.S.R.* (New York: Praeger, 1967).

Deutscher, Isaac. *Stalin: A Political Biography* (New York: Oxford University Press, 1949).

Deutscher, Isaac. *The Unfinished Revolution: Russia 1917-1967* (New York: Oxford, 1967).

Dobson, Rich. 'Mobility and Stratification in the U.S.S.R.' in *American Sociological Review*, No.3. (1977).

Fainsod, M. *How Russia is Ruled* (Cambridge: Harvard University Press, 1963).

Feshbach, Murray. 'Manpower Management', *Problems of Communism*, (November – December 1974).

Foreign Languages Publishing House. *Down with the New Czars* (Peking, 1969).

Foreign Languages Publishing House. *How the Soviet Revisionists Carry Out All Round Restoration of Capitalism in the U.S.S.R.* (Peking, 1968).

Franklin, Bruce. Introduction to *The Essential Stalin* (Garden City, N.Y.: Doubleday, 1972).

Garry, George. 'Finance and Banking in the U.S.S.R.' in Bornstein and Fusfeld, *op. cit.*

Gordon, L.S. and Klopov, E.U. 'Some Problems of the Social Structure of the Soviet Working Class' in Yanowitch and Fisher, *op. cit.*

Gorlin, Alice. 'Socialist Corporations: The Wave of the Future in the U.S.S.R.' in Bornstein and Fusfeld, *op. cit.*

Granick, David. *The Red Executive* (Garden City, N.Y.: Doubleday, 1961).

Gregory, Paul, and Stuart, Robert. *Soviet Economic Structure and Performance* (New York: Harper & Row, 1974).

Griffiths, Franklyn. 'A Tendency Analysis of Soviet Policy Making' in Skilling and Griffiths, *op. cit.*

Grossman, Gregory. 'The Soviet Economy at Middle Age' in *Problems of Communism*, Vol. 25 (Nov.–Dec. 1974).

Hardt, John, and Frankel, Theodore. 'The Industrial Manager' in Bornstein and Fusfeld, *op. cit.*

Hill, Ronald. 'The C.P.S.U. in a Soviet Election Campaign' in *Soviet Studies*, XXVII, No. 4 (October 1976).

Hill, Ronald. *Soviet Political Elites* (London: Martin Robertson, 1977).

Hill, Ronald. 'Patterns of Deputy Selection to Local Soviets' in *Soviet Studies*, Vol. 25, No.2 (October 1973).

Hopkins, Mark. *Mass Media in the Soviet Union* (New York: Pegasus, 1970).

Hough, Jerry. 'The Brezhnev Era: The Man and the System' in *Problems of Communism* Nov.–Dec. 1974).

Hough, Jerry. 'Political Participation in the Soviet Union' in *Soviet Studies*, 28:1 (January 1976).

Hough, Jerry. 'The Soviet System, Petrification or Pluralism' in *Problems of Communism* (March–April 1975).

Judy, R. 'The Economists' in Skilling and Griffiths, *op. cit.*

Kelley, D. 'Environmental Policy-Making in the U.S.S.R.' in *Soviet Studies*, XXVIII, No. 4 (October 1976).

Kolkowicz, Roman. 'The Military' in Skilling and Griffiths, *op. cit.*

Kosygin, A.N. 'Report to the C.P.S.U. Central Committee' in Nove, Alec, and Nuti, D.M. (eds.), *Socialist Economics* (Baltimore: Penguin, 1972).

Lane, David. *The End of Inequality: Stratification Under State Socialism* (Baltimore: Penguin, 1971).

Lane, David. *The Socialist Industrial State* (London: George Allen and Unwin, 1976).

Lieberman, E.G. 'The Plan, Profit and Bonuses' in Nove, Alec, and Nuti D.M., (eds.), *op. cit.*

Liss, L.F. 'The Social Conditioning of Occupational Choice' in Yanowitch and Fisher, *op. cit.*

Little, D. Richard. 'Soviet Parliamentary Committees after Khrushchev' in

Soviet Studies, 24:1 (July 1972).

Mandel, Ernest. *Marxist Economic Theory* (New York: Monthly Review, 1968).

Marcuse, Herbert. *Soviet Marxism* (New York: Columbia University Press, 1958).

Matthews, Mervyn. *Class and Society in Soviet Russia* (New York: Walker and Co., 1972).

Matthews, Mervyn. *Privilege in the Soviet Union* (London: George Allen & Unwin, 1978).

Minagua, Shugo. 'The Function of the Supreme Soviet Organs and Problems of Their Institutional Development' in *Soviet Studies,* 27:1 (January 1975).

Mokronosov, G.V. 'On the Criteria of Intraclass Differences in Socialist Society' in Yanowitch and Fisher, *op. cit.*

Moore, B. *Soviet Politics: The Dilemma of Power* (Cambridge, Mass.: Harvard University Press, 1950).

Nicolaus, Martin. *Restoration of Capitalism in the U.S.S.R.* (Chicago: Liberator Press, 1975).

Nove, Alec. 'Is There a Ruling Class in the U.S.S.R.?' in *Soviet Studies,* 27:4 (October 1975).

Osborn, Robert. *'Soviet Social Policies: Welfare, Equality and Community'* (Homewood, III.: The Dorsey Press, 1970).

Parkin, Frank. *Class Inequality and Political Order: Social Stratification in Capitalist and Communist Societies* (New York: Praeger, 1971).

Perfilyev, M. *Soviet Democracy and Bourgeois Sovietology* (Moscow, Progress, n.d.).

Progress Publishers. *The Soviet Form of Popular Government* (Moscow: Progress Publishers, 1972).

Progress Publishers. *The Soviet Union Today* (Moscow: Progress Publishers, 1975).

The Revolutionary Union. *How Capitalism has been Restored in the Soviet Union and What this means for the World Struggle* (Chicago: The Revolutionary Union, 1974).

Rigby, T.H. *Communist Party Membership in the U.S.S.R.: 1917-1967* (Princeton, N.J.: Princeton University Press, 1968).

Rigby, T.H. 'Communist Party Membership under Brezhnev' in *Soviet Studies,* XXVIII (July 1976).

Rigby, T.H. 'The Soviet Politburo A Comparative Profile 1951-1971' in *Soviet Studies,* 24:1 (July 1972).

Rutkevich, M.N., and Filippev, F.R. 'The Social Sources of Recruitment of the Intelligentsia' in Yanowitch and Fisher, *op. cit.*

Schachtman, Max. *The Bureaucratic Revolution* (New York: The Donald Press, 1962).

Schroeder, Gertrude. 'Recent Developments in Soviet Planning and Incentives' in Bornstein and Fusfeld, *op. cit.*

Schroeder, Gertrude. 'Consumption in the U.S.S.R.' in Bornstein and Fusfeld, *op. cit.*

Shahnazarov, G. *Socialist Democracy* (Moscow: Progress Publishers, 1974).

Sherman, Howard. *The Soviet Economy* (Boston: Little Brown and Co., 1969).

Shkaraton, O.I. 'Social Groups in the Working Class of a Developed Socialist Society', in Yanowitch and Fisher, *op. cit.*

Shkaraton, O.I. 'Social Ties and Social Mobility' in Yanowitch and Fisher, *op. cit.*

Shkaraton, O.I. 'Sources of Social Differentiation of the Working Class in Soviet Society' in Yanowitch and Fisher, *op. cit.*

Simmons, Ernest. 'The Writers' in Skilling and Griffiths, *op. cit.*

Skilling, H. Gordon. 'Group Conflict in Soviet Politics' in Skilling and Griffiths, *op. cit.*

Skilling, H. Gordon. 'Groups in Soviet Politics: Some Hypotheses' in Skilling and Griffiths, *op. cit.*

Steward, Steven. *Operation Splinter Factor* (New York: Lippincott, 1974).

Strong, Anna Louise. *The Stalin Era* (New York: Mainstream, 1957).

Sweezy, Paul, and Bettelheim, Charles. *On the Transition to Socialism* (New York: Monthly Review, 1971).

Szymanski, Albert. Review of two books: Revolutionary Union, *How Capitalism has been Restored in the Soviet Union and What this means for the World Struggle;* and Nicolaus, Martin. *Restoration of Capitalism in the U.S.S.R.* in *Science and Society* (Fall, 1977).

Timiashevskaia, M.U. 'Some Social Consequences of a City Building Experiment' in Yanowitch and Fisher, *op. cit.*

Titma, M.Mh. 'The Influence of Social Origins on the Occupational Values of Graduating Secondary School Students' in Yanowitch and Fisher, *op. cit.*

Torovtsev, Victor. *People's Control in Socialist Society* (Moscow: Progress Publishers, 1973).

Trotsky, Leon. *The Revolution Betrayed* (New York: Pioneer Publishers, 1945).

Tucker, Robert. *Stalin as a Revolutionary* (New York: Norton, 1973).

Ulam, Adam. *Stalin: The Man and his Era* (New York: Viking, 1973).

Voinovich, Vladimir. 'Oh, for a Room of My Own' in *New York Times Magazine* (June 20 1976).

White, Steven. 'Contradiction and Change in State Socialism' in *Soviet Studies,* 26:1 (January 1974).

Wilczynski, J. *The Economics of Socialism* (Chicago: Aldine Publishing Co., 1970).

Wiles, Peter. *Distribution of Income: East and West* (New York: American Elseview Publishing Co., 1974).

Yanowitch, Murray. *Social and Economic Inequality in the Soviet Union* (White Plains, N.Y.: M.E. Sharpe, 1977).

Yenan Books (ed.). *Social Imperialism: The Soviet Union Today* (Berkeley: 1977).

Yenan Books (ed.). *Social Imperialism: Reprints from Peking Review* (Berkeley: n.d.).

Soviet Foreign Relations

Aptheker, Herbert. *The Truth about Hungary* (New York: Mainstream Publishers, 1957).

Bass, Robert, and Marbury, Elizabeth (eds.). *The Soviet-Yugoslav Controversy, 1948-58* (New York: Prospect Books, 1959).

Brainard, Lawrence H. 'Soviet Foreign Trade Planning' in U.S. Congress (Joint Economic Committee, 94th Congress, 2nd sess. 1976) *The Soviet Economy in a New Perspective.*

Braunthal, Julius. *History of the International*, Vol.II. (London: Nelson, 1967).

Budhray, Vijay Sen. 'Moscow and the Birth of Bangladesh' in *Asian Survey* (May 1973).

Business International Corporation. *Investing, Licensing and Trading Conditions Abroad* (Europe: June 1976).

Business International Corporation. *Doing Business with the U.S.S.R.* (Geneva: 1971).

Castro, Fidel. Speech to the *First Congress of the Communist Party of Cuba* (Moscow: Progress Publishers, 1976).

Castro, Fidel. 'The U.S.S.R.-Cuba Economic Agreement: A Model of Fraternal Relations' in *New World Review*, 41:2 (2nd quarter 1973).

Center for Strategic and International Studies. *Soviet Sea Power* (Washington: Georgetown University, 1969).

Claudin, Fernando. *The Communist Movement: From Comintern to Cominform* (New York: Monthly Review Press, 1975).

Coffey, Joseph. *Deterrence in the 1970s* (Denver: University of Denver, 1971).

Communist Party of India (M-L). *Soviet Social Imperialism in India* (Vancouver, B.C.: Indian People's Association in North America, 1976).

Cooper, Orah. 'Soviet Economic Aid to the Third World' in U.S. Congress, Joint Economic Committee, *Soviet Economy in a New Perspective, op. cit.*

Current Digest of the Soviet Press. 'Fuel and Raw Materials for CMEA Lands', 28:23 (July 7 1976).

Datar, Asha. *India's Economic Relations with the U.S.S.R. and Eastern Europe, 1953-1969* (Cambridge, England: Cambridge University Press,1972).

Dedijer, Vladimir. *The Battle Stalin Lost* (New York: Viking 1970).

Donaldson, Robert. *Soviet Policy towards India: Ideology and Strategy* (Cambridge, Mass.: Harvard University Press, 1974).

Fallenbuchl, Z.M. 'Comecon Integration' in Bornstein, Morris, and Fusfeld, Daniel, (eds.). *The Soviet Economy* (Homewood, Illinois: Richard Irwin, Inc., 1974).

Foster, William Z. *History of the Three Internationals* (New York: International Publishers, 1955).

Freedman, Robert Owen. *Economic Warfare in the Communist Bloc* (New York: Praeger 1970).

Gilbert, Guy. 'Socialism and Dependency' in *Latin American Perspectives*, 1:1 (Spring 1974).

Golan, Galia. *The Czechoslovak Reform Movement* (Cambridge, England: The Cambridge University Press, 1971).

Goldman, Marshall. *Soviet Foreign Aid* (New York: Praeger, 1967).

Goure, Leon, Kohler, Foy, and Harvey, Mose. *The Role of Nuclear Forces in Current Soviet Strategy* (Center for Advanced International Studies,

University of Miami, 1974).

Goure, Leon, and Weinkle, Julian. 'Soviet-Cuban Relations: The Growing Integration' in Jaime Suchlicki (ed.). *Cuba, Castro and Revolution* (Coral Gables, Florida: University of Miami Press, 1973).

Gregory, Paul, and Stuart, Robert. *Soviet Economic Structure and Performance* (New York: Harper and Row, 1974).

Grow, Roy F. 'Soviet Economic Penetration of China, 1945-1960' in Rosen, Steven, and Kurth, James, (eds.). *Testing Economic Theories of Imperialism* (Lexington, Mass.: D.C. Heath and Co., 1974).

Holzman, Franklyn. *Foreign Trade under Central Planning* (Cambridge, Mass.: Harvard University Press, 1974).

Jackson, D. Bruce. *Castro, The Kremlin and Communism in Latin America* (Baltimore: Johns Hopkins Press, 1969).

Jahan, Rounaq. 'Bangladesh' in Richard Starr (ed.). *Yearbook on International Communist Affairs* (Stanford, California: Hoover Institute Press, 1976).

Jones, David. *Soviet Armed Forces Review*, Annual 1 (Academic International Press, 1977).

Kaufman, Michael T. 'Suddenly Angola' in *New York Times Magazine* (Jan.4 1976).

Kecskemeti, Paul. *The Unexpected Revolution* (Stanford: Stanford University Press, 1961).

Kinter, William, and Scott, Harriet, (eds.). *The Nuclear Revolution in Soviet Military Affairs* (Norman: University of Oklahoma Press, 1968).

Kline, M. Michael. 'Castro's Challenge to Latin American Communism' in Jaime Suchlicki (ed.). *op. cit.*

Kohler, Foy. 'Cuba and the Soviet Problem in Latin America' in Jaime Suchlicki (ed.). *op. cit.*

Kramer, John. 'The Energy Gap in Eastern Europe' in *Survey*, 21:1-2 (Winter-Spring 1975).

Kulski, W.N. *The Soviet Union in World Affairs* Syracuse: Syracuse University Press, 1973).

Larrabee, Stephen. 'Moscow, Angola and the Dialectics of Detente' in *The World Today* (May 1976).

Lawrence, Alan. *China's Foreign Relations Since 1949* (London: Routledge and Kegan Paul, 1975).

Marcum, John. 'Lessons of Angola' in *Foreign Affairs*, 54:3 (April 1976).

Marer, Paul. 'The Political Economy of Soviet Relations with Eastern Europe' in Rosen, Steven, J, and Kurth, James. R (eds.). *op. cit.*

Marer, Paul. *Soviet and East European Foreign Trade 1946-1969* (Bloomington: Indiana University Press, 1972).

Mesa-Lago, Carmelo. *Cuba in the 1970's* (Albuquerque: University of New Mexico Press, 1974).

Mickiewicz, Ellen. *The Handbook of Soviet Social Science Data* (New York: The Free Press, 1973).

Nyrop, Richard *et al. Area Handbook for Bangladesh* (Washington, D.C.: U.S. Government Printing Office, 1975).

Parkin, Frank. *Class Inequality and Political Order* (New York: Praeger, 1971).

Pravda, Alex. 'Some Aspects of the Czechoslovak Economic Reform and the Working Class in 1968' in *Soviet Studies*, 25:1 (July 1973).

Ra'anan, Ur. *The U.S.S.R. Arms the Third World* (Cambridge, Mass.:

M.I.T. Press, 1969).

Revolutionary Union. *How Capitalism has been restored in the Soviet Union and what this means for the World Struggle* (Chicago, 1974).

Rubenstein, Alvin (ed.). *The Foreign Policy of the Soviet Union* (New York: Random House, 1972).

Sherman, Howard. *The Soviet Economy* (Boston: Little, Brown and Co., 1969).

Sinha, R.P. 'Soviet Aid and Trade with the Developing World' in *Soviet Studies*, 26:2 (April 1974).

Stevens, Christopher. *The Soviet Union and Black Africa* (New York: Holmes and Meier, 1976).

Stockwell, John. *In Search of Enemies* (London: Andre Deutsch, 1978).

Tansky, Leo. *Soviet Foreign Aid, Scope, Direction and Trends* in Bornstein, Morris and Fusfeld, Daniel, (eds.). *op. cit.*

Triska, Jan, and Finley, David. *Soviet Foreign Policy* (New York: Macmillan and Co. 1968).

U.S. Arms Control and Disarmament Agency. *World Military Expenditures and Arms Transfers 1965-1974* (Washington, D.C.: U.S. Government Printing Office, 1975).

U.S. Department of State, Special Report. *Communist States and Developing Countries Aid and Trade in 1974* (Washington, D.C.: U.S. Government Printing Office, 1976).

U.S. Department of the Interior. *Mineral Yearbook for 1973* Vol. III. Area Reports: International (Washington, D.C.: U.S. Government Printing Office, 1976).

Valkenier, Elizabeth Kridl. 'Soviet Economic Relations with Developing Nations' in Roger Kanet (ed.). *The Soviet Union and the Developing Nations* (Baltimore: Johns Hopkins University Press, 1974).

Wallerstein, Immanuel. 'Luanda is Madrid' in *The Nation*, 222:1 (Jan.3-10 1976).

Waterburg, John. 'The Soviet Union and North Africa' in Ivo Jededer (ed.), *The Soviet Union and the Middle East* (Stanford, Calif.: Stanford University Press, 1974).

Wilczynski, J. *The Economics of Socialism* (Chicago: Aldine Publishing Co., 1970).

Zimmer, Paul. *Revolution in Hungary* (New York: Columbia University Press, 1962).

Index